★ ★ ★ ★ ★ ★ ★ ★ ★ ★ ★ ★ ★ ★ ★

# THE CASE FOR IMPEACHMENT

★ ★ ★ ★ ★ ★ ★ ★ ★ ★ ★ ★ ★ ★ ★

✳ ✳ ✳ ✳ ✳ ✳ ✳ ✳ ✳ ✳ ✳ ✳ ✳ ✳ ✳

# THE CASE FOR IMPEACHMENT

✳ ✳ ✳ ✳ ✳ ✳ ✳ ✳ ✳ ✳ ✳ ✳ ✳ ✳ ✳

The Legal Argument for Removing
President George W. Bush from Office

*Dave Lindorff*
*and*
*Barbara Olshansky*

THOMAS DUNNE BOOKS
St. Martin's Press ❧ New York

THOMAS DUNNE BOOKS.
An imprint of St. Martin's Press.

www.stmartins.com

Library of Congress Cataloging-in-Publication Data

Lindorff, Dave (David P.)
    The case for impeachment : the legal argument for removing Presi-
dent George W. Bush from office / David Lindorff and Barbara Olshansky.
        p. cm.
    ISBN-13: 978-0-312-36016-0
    ISBN-10: 0-312-36016-9
    1. Bush, George W. (George Walker), 1946– —Impeachment. 2.
Impeachments—United States. 3. Presidents—Legal status, laws,
etc.—United States. 4. Misconduct in the office—United States. 5.
United States—Politics and government—2001–

KF5075 L56 2006
342.73'062—dc22

                                                    2006040296

First Edition: May 2006

10   9   8   7   6   5   4   3   2   1

A republic, if you can keep it.

— BENJAMIN FRANKLIN

# CONTENTS

# PREFACE

*"He should be impeached!"*

How often have we heard those words expressed—at anti-war demonstrations, at work, on the bus, at a party? Not just over these past few years but through the Clinton years as well.

The Republicans during President Clinton's second term actually took the impeachment process to a trial in the Senate—as far as presidential impeachment has ever gotten—and they did this on the basis of Clinton's having had a couple of adulterous liaisons and lied about them.

This time around the calls for impeachment are targeting a Republican president whose high crimes and misdemeanors are of a much more serious nature: lying to Congress and the American people to trick the nation into a war, undermining the basic rights of citizenship that have always seemed as natural as breathing, indeed shredding the very fabric of government as it was woven by the Founding Fathers.

On the merits, the articles of impeachment detailed in this book should be an open-and-shut case (we have deliberately limited ourselves to those issues where the crimes are clear and almost self-evident). The evidence of George W. Bush's constitutional transgressions, violations of federal and international law, abuse of power, and criminal negligence as chief executive—all laid out in this volume—are so blatant one might think conviction would be a foregone conclusion. And yet, five years into his "high crimes and misdemeanors" spree, President Bush, far from being impeached, has yet to even face a bill of impeachment in the House.

Many Americans cannot understand this. They hear, for example, that the president admits to having deliberately violated the 1978 Foreign Intelligence Surveillance Act, which requires the National Security Agency to seek warrants from a special court before secretly monitoring the telecommunications of any American citizen, and they simply assume he should be impeached and tossed out of office.

If impeachment were just another criminal justice procedure, perhaps he would already be gone. A prosecutor like Patrick Fitzgerald, the special counsel who indicted Vice President Cheney's chief of staff I. Lewis "Scooter" Libby in 2005, would surely have no trouble drawing up a FISA violation indictment—or convincing a Washington jury to convict. But, for good reason, presidents cannot be indicted, and impeachment is not a criminal procedure. Presidents are impeached not for violations of law, but for political crimes—for offenses against the people of this country and the principles underlying our democratic system of government. And presidents impeached by the House of Representatives are tried not by an impartial jury but by a "jury" of politically aligned U.S. Senators, fully two-thirds of whom must vote to convict to oust a president from office.

We are under no illusion that House Republicans will pass a bill of impeachment, or even, probably, that the current Congress will see a bill of impeachment filed by a House Democrat. The Republican majority is committed to protecting the president from impeachment, even though some of its own members have condemned his actions as unconstitutional and damaging to the country. Meanwhile, the Democratic leadership seems so timid (and often complicit in some of the president's worst crimes, such as the war, domestic spying, and undermining civil liberties), that little action can be expected from that quarter, either. We do believe, however, that the American public is way ahead of the Congress. *We the People* have become increasingly angry at Bush's imperious, unconstitutional, and inhumane behavior. As of the Ides of March, 2006, a scant one third of us still backed Bush, while other polls showed a majority of us thinking he should be removed from office for his NSA spying authorization and his lying about the need to invade Iraq.

The authors believe that just as the president's many impeachable "high crimes and misdemeanors" are political in nature, so, too, they demand a political response. What is required is that *We the People* rise up this year, throw off years of lethargy and cynicism, and elect to Congress in November 2006 representatives who are committed to standing up for the Constitution, for the tradition of three coequal branches of government, for the civil liberties that hundreds of thousands of Americans have died defending, and for justice, fairness, and humanity. *We the People* have not lost our voice . . . yet. Even the election of a baker's dozen new representatives committed to impeachment would enormously strengthen the shriveled spines of incumbent Democratic colleagues and of those few principled Republican members of the House who have spoken out against presidential transgressions.

If a Democratic majority is elected to the House in November 2006, we are confident a bill of impeachment will be introduced early in the next Congress, and that it will begin the process of impeachment in the Judiciary Committee.

At that point, we are also confident that the administration's myriad crimes will begin to come out in all their hoary detail, and that the demand for President Bush's removal from office will grow.

The nation is clearly at a fork in the road. A president who never should have even taken office in the first place has brazenly usurped power over the course of five years in ways the Founding Fathers long feared and sought passionately to guard against. He and his handlers have accomplished this creeping coup by spreading fear, by creating and then hiding behind a perpetual war on terror, and by intimidating the political opposition with jingoistic charges of treason or lack of patriotism.

*We the People* can continue to tremble at the president's words of fear. We can look to him for a false sense of protection. We can give him another three years to aggrandize presidential power. And we can then hand the damaged goods of American government to a successor who, whether Democrat or Republican, will likely be glad to have all that power.

Or we can choose the other road and take back our country, our government, and our rights. We don't need pitchforks and guns; we can use the Constitution and its remedy of impeachment.

The authors are aware that impeachment is a drawn-out process, and that the end is uncertain at best. Let's face it: there is little or no likelihood that the president would be removed from office, even if a new Democratic-led House were to impeach him, given the requirement of a two-thirds Senate vote to convict. But democracy is not about presidents or congresses or political parties; it is about people acting in their own interest. If *We the People* stand up in November, and if our elected representatives do their duty in the next Congress and initiate the impeachment process, we are confident this president's crime spree will be over, and that the next president will be much more respectful of the Constitution . . . and of all of us.

*—Dave Lindorff and Barbara Olshansky*
*March 15, 2006*

# ONE

## *Why Impeachment?*

**The President, vice President and all civil Officers of the United States, shall be removed from Office on Impeachment for, and Conviction of, Treason, Bribery, or other high Crimes and Misdemeanors.**
    —*Constitution of the United States, Article II, Section 4*

**IT'S TIME.**

On April 29, 2004, a nervous President George W. Bush went before the bipartisan 9/11 Commission to answer questions about how his administration had responded to the attack. The commission had already taken testimony from a long string of witnesses in the military, intelligence, justice, and other agencies of government. All had been questioned under oath about their knowledge of the events leading up to the attacks on the World Trade Center and Pentagon, including the government's response—or lack of response—to early warnings. All of that testimony had been widely reported, even televised. Only a handful of people know what happened after President Bush entered that room, though, because he (who had opposed creation of the commission in the first place) had made some curious demands before agreeing to appear.

He insisted that only a few selected members of the ten-member body could be present, that he not be placed under oath, that he could have Vice President Dick Cheney by his side, and that no recording or notes be made of his testimony. The entire interview was conducted behind closed doors, with the press and public barred.

The only possible explanation for this behavior is that the president did not want the American public to know the truth—or that he had no intention of telling the truth—about his knowledge of the attack on America. Not only had his administration been criminally negligent during the months before the attacks, he, Cheney, and their neo-conservative advisers had shamelessly exploited that American tragedy to accomplish the greatest executive power grab and the worst descent into secret government in the history of the republic. They had used it as an excuse to launch two wars and a full assault on the Bill of Rights, the courts, and the political opposition.

Flash back more than a year to January 29, 2003. Standing before the assembled joint session of the Congress for his State of the Union address, President Bush told a hushed chamber of senators and representatives, and millions of Americans who were watching, that they were facing the imminent threat of a nuclear attack from Iraqi dictator Saddam Hussein. With the Pentagon already engaged in an all-out campaign to ferry troops and materiel to the Persian Gulf region in anticipation of war, and with U.S. fighter/bombers stepping up provocative aerial attacks in Iraq under the guise of maintaining several "no fly" zones in that country, the president said:

> The International Atomic Energy Agency confirmed in the 1990s that Saddam Hussein had an advanced nuclear weapons development program, had a design for a nuclear weapon, and was working on five different methods of enriching uranium for a bomb.
>
> The British government has learned that Saddam Hussein recently sought significant quantities of uranium from Africa.
>
> Our intelligence sources tell us that he has attempted to purchase high-strength aluminum tubes suitable for nuclear weapons production.

Saddam Hussein has not credibly explained these activities. He clearly has much to hide.

Bush went on to drive the terrifying message home, saying:

With nuclear arms or a full arsenal of chemical and biological weapons, Saddam Hussein could resume his ambitions of conquest in the Middle East and create deadly havoc in that region.

And this Congress and the American people must recognize another threat. Evidence from intelligence sources, secret communications, and statements by people now in custody reveal that Saddam Hussein aids and protects terrorists, including members of Al Qaeda. Secretly, and without fingerprints, he could provide one of his hidden weapons to terrorists, or help them develop their own.

Before September the 11th, many in the world believed that Saddam Hussein could be contained. But chemical agents, lethal viruses, and shadowy terrorist networks are not easily contained.

Imagine those nineteen hijackers with other weapons and other plans, this time armed by Saddam Hussein. It would take one vial, one canister, one crate slipped into this country to bring a day of horror like none we have ever known.

We will do everything in our power to make sure that that day never comes.

Some have said we must not act until the threat is imminent. Since when have terrorists and tyrants announced their intentions, politely putting us on notice before they strike?

If this threat is permitted to fully and suddenly emerge, all actions, all words and all recriminations would come too late. Trusting in the sanity and restraint of Saddam Hussein is not a strategy, and it is not an option.

Scary stuff, but it was just not true. According to a series of memos written at that time, two days after this speech was given the president had informed Tony Blair, the British prime minister, that with or without UN approval, he intended to take America to war. In fact, he was considering flying a U2 surveillance aircraft painted in UN colors over Iraq, hoping to provoke an attack to which America could respond in force. Additionally, the president already knew at that point that the documents suggesting that Iraq had tried to buy yellow-cake uranium ore from Niger were forgeries and that no such effort had been made. (Indeed, as we shall explain later, there is reason to suspect that the Bush administration may have been involved in those forgeries.) The president was also aware that there were other far more likely and permissible uses for those aluminum tubes—such as fuselages for small rockets. In fact, scientists had noted that the pre-cut tubes were too short for use in a centrifuge, as was being claimed by Bush. Finally, the president also knew by the time of his address that not only was there no credible evidence of a link between Saddam Hussein and Al Qaeda—an organization which had, in fact, condemned Hussein as a godless apostate—but that Hussein viewed Al Qaeda as a potential threat to his regime.

It is commonplace for politicians and presidents to lie. Some lies though, are more serious than others. Only five years before Bush's State of the Union address, the House of Representatives had voted 228–206 to impeach President Bill Clinton for lying to a grand jury convened by Special Prosecutor Kenneth Starr, who was investigating, among other things, the weighty matter of whether Clinton had had consensual sex with an intern. The House also voted 221–212 to impeach Clinton for obstruction of justice. Nobody died (or even got pregnant) as a result of Clinton's deceit, but the impeachment effort, which purported to focus not on the sex but on the lying, nonetheless led to a bitter political battle and ultimately to a trial in the U.S. Senate, where Clinton was acquitted of the charges.

Meanwhile, Bush's dissembling and fabrications are more than garden-variety whoppers about illicit sex. His lies were designed to make the Congress and the public ready and willing to support a war of aggression against Iraq, a battered and impoverished country of 26 million people, which the president and his advisers knew posed no credible threat to the United States, or even, thanks to years of embargo and sanctions, to its neighbors. They are lies that led directly to a war that by March 2006 had killed over 2,300 American troops and grievously wounded more than 19,000, as well as killing an estimated 100,000

Iraqis, most of them civilians. And they have cost hundreds of billions of dollars.*

Where impeachment is concerned, the issue is not whether an official was under oath or not; rather it is the significance of the lie, and what the liar was attempting to accomplish. Furthermore, there is a precedent for impeaching a president for lying to the public and to Congress, even if he was not under oath. Richard Nixon is the model here. On July 27, 1974, the House Judiciary Committee voted 27–11 for an impeachment article accusing Nixon of

> making false and misleading public statements for the purpose of *deceiving the people of the United States* [author's emphasis] into believing that a thorough and complete investigation has been conducted with respect to allegation of misconduct on the part of personnel of the Executive branch of the United States and personnel of the Committee for the Re-Election of the President, and that there was no involvement of such personnel in such misconduct.[1]

As we will see, this is remarkably similar to President Bush's role in revealing the identity of undercover CIA operative Valerie Plame Wilson. Speaking through his press spokesman, on several occasions Bush has falsely assured reporters and the public that he knew of nobody in the White House who was responsible for disclosing her identity. In fact, there is evidence that well before those assertions, Bush had criticized his closest adviser, Karl Rove, for his involvement in the outing of Plame to the media.[2]

But Bush's lies about Iraq and the Plame affair are only the beginning of the case for his impeachment. Over the course of his one and a half terms, this president and his administration have committed a staggering string of what could clearly qualify as high crimes and misdemeanors. Among them:

---

*According to one study, the full cost of the Iraq war, including lost incomes, lifetime medical costs of wounded veterans, and interest on debt, could top $2 trillion. The long-term medical and emotional damage to U.S. veterans will take years to fully tally.

- The arrest and detention without charge of American citizens, who have been denied their constitutional rights to due process and a speedy and public trial.
- The violation of international treaties that the United States has signed, and which have thus become the law of the land, such as the Geneva Conventions regarding the treatment of soldiers, military detainees, and civilians, and the conventions against torture—protocols that the current U.S. Attorney General, Alberto Gonzales, in his earlier role as White House counsel, advised the president is just a "quaint" artifact of an earlier time.
- Willfully ignoring or violating acts of Congress, through the issuance of hundreds of so-called "signing statements" by the president, in which Bush declared his intention to interpret laws in his own way and to obey only those that he feels like obeying.
- The blatant violation of the Foreign Intelligence Surveillance Act and Fourth Amendment to the Constitution, by secretly authorizing secret warrantless spying on thousands of American citizens by the National Security Agency.
- The foolish and disastrous transfer of the nation's first-line defenders—police, firefighters, and border patrol personnel who were long encouraged to supplement their income by joining their local National Guard units—to Iraq, leaving the nation unprotected against both cross-border infiltration and natural disasters like Hurricane Katrina, which destroyed much of the city of New Orleans.

As the list grows, so have calls for the president's impeachment. In June 2005, Zogby International, a well-respected nonpartisan polling organization, found that 42 percent of Americans thought that Bush should be impeached if it were determined that he had lied about his reasons for invading Iraq. That was an astonishing number, particularly because at the same time an even higher percentage of Americans were telling pollsters they believed the president *had* lied about the reasons we went to war. Compare that to polls taken at the height of the Republican campaign to impeach President Clinton; according to sixteen major polls conducted during the summer and fall of 1998, only 36 percent of the public thought impeachment should be considered, while only 26 percent thought the president should be removed from office.

Since June 2005, support for impeachment of President Bush has steadily increased. A poll conducted in early October 2005, by Ipsos Public Affairs, another nonpartisan polling firm, found support for the impeachment of the president up to 50 percent. A month later Zogby asked the same impeachment question which it had asked four months earlier: of 1,200 Americans polled, 53 percent said they supported impeachment while only 42 percent of Americans opposed impeachment. Even among self-identified Republicans, 29 percent said that if the president lied about the war, he should be impeached. Another Zogby poll, this one conducted in January 2006, found that 52 percent of Americans supported impeaching President Bush if he authorized warrantless domestic spying on Americans by the NSA, an action he openly admits to.

Impeachment isn't a popular election, nor is it simply a legal matter to be tried in a court of law. Impeachment is a political process played out in the Congress. Technically, it is an action taken by the U.S. House of Representatives, which must first consider a bill of impeachment, vote articles of impeachment out of the Judiciary Committee, and then put the question to the full membership. If a majority of the House votes for an article or for multiple articles of impeachment, this becomes the equivalent of an indictment, which must then be "tried" in the U.S. Senate. A two-thirds majority is required to convict and to remove the president from office. There have been two presidential impeachment trials in American history—both of them brought for political rather than legal reasons. In 1868, Democratic President Andrew Johnson was impeached and came within a single vote of being removed from office.

In 1998, President Clinton was confronted by a House that had a Republican majority. His own Democratic Party still held a narrow edge in the Senate, meaning there was no chance he would be convicted and removed from office, but there were plenty of Representatives, the vast majority of them Republicans, ready to vote for impeachment. In contrast, approaching midterm elections in Bush's second term, the Republican Party has a firm grip on power in both the House and the Senate, making even a hearing on impeachment in the House Judiciary Committee almost inconceivable, no matter how serious the president's crimes.

The two situations are almost mirror opposites. In the Clinton case, a popular president's congressional Republican enemies were seeking impeachment, while a majority of Americans did not support it. In the present case, Bush, an unpopular president, has the backing of a majority of both houses of Congress, so more than five years into his presidency only a handful of Democratic legislators had even suggested calling for his ouster. Despite the unpromising political situation in the Congress, a number of grassroots campaigns promoting impeachment have sprung up, and numerous polls suggest widespread support for impeachment. What would be the point of impeaching Bush though, if the Republican Senate would never consider removing the president?

"There is in a sense an impeachment campaign whether we want one or not," says David Swanson, co-founder of the organization After-DowningStreet.org, which, together with Democrats.com, has been one of the main proponents of impeachment. "Half the signs at anti-war marches say: 'Impeach Bush and Cheney.' "

Swanson concedes that impeachment, at least in Bush's sixth year in office, is a long shot, but argues that impeachment efforts are much more than just tilting at windmills. "A campaign for impeachment erodes further any of this administration's remaining credibility," he says. "It focuses people's attention on the *reasons* for an impeachment. Finally, an impeachment campaign during the months leading up to the 2006 off-year congressional elections can help to reshape the Congress in such a way that impeachment becomes possible. Some people may say we should wait until the Democrats are in the majority and then consider impeachment, but we're saying the Democrats won't be the majority unless they give people a reason to make them a majority, and impeachment is clearly a way to do that. It's a movement builder. Besides, if you can't have impeachment now, with all the crimes of this administration, you're basically saying you can only have impeachment for adulterous sex."

Granted, even for some ardent Bush critics, impeachment is a hard sell. Lowell Weicker, the former Republican senator from Connecticut who, as a member of the Senate Watergate Committee, took a leading role in investigating and condemning Richard Nixon, professes no love for Bush. "I am doing everything I can to see that he doesn't have a Congress after November 2006," he says. Weicker, whose criticism of Nixon earned him a spot on that president's notorious "enemies list," argues against impeachment, saying "Bush obviously lied to the country and to Congress about the war, but we have a system of elections in this country. Everyone knew about the lying before the 2004 election, and they didn't do anything about it. The famous Democratic Party didn't stand up about it. Sen. John Kerry didn't stand up, and so Bush got elected. The horse is out of the barn now."

John Dean, Richard Nixon's White House attorney during the Watergate scandal, knows a fair bit about impeachment from personal experience, having served as minority counsel on the House Judiciary Committee before joining the White House staff. He has a very different view. He claims that Bush's war scandal is, as his recent book title puts it, *Worse than Watergate,* and as such deserving of impeachment. However, he also considers impeachment, at least at the time of this writing, to be "inappropriate." A key witness to the collapse of the Nixon presidency, Dean himself pleaded guilty to participation in the cover-up that led to Nixon's having three articles of impeachment voted out of the Judiciary Committee of the House. Now a retired investment banker living in Beverly Hills, he argues that "no responsible member of Congress" would "talk about impeachment unless they have solid evidence of a high crime or impeachable misdemeanor." Furthermore, while he agrees impeachment could become a campaign issue in the 2006 congressional elections, and could even lead to a Democratic takeover of the House, until that occurs he insists there will be little or no action in Congress on impeachment. "Impeachment is the most serious constitutional charge you can make against a federal official," he says, "and only an irresponsible judiciary committee would take up charges that could not be proven in a Senate trial. Only an irresponsible House of Representatives would pass a bill of impeachment that could not succeed in the Senate." For precisely that reason, Dean considers the Clinton impeachment to have been improper and irresponsible.

"It may be true that you couldn't have an impeachment in the House today," counters Democrats.com's Bob Fertik. "But things may not look the same tomorrow—for example, what if we had an indictment of Karl Rove or Dick Cheney—and we know enough already to know that those things are possible. We're taking the position that Bush and Cheney *have* to be impeached because they've committed so many crimes. The one that is farthest along in terms of exposure at this point is the Plame case, but there are a whole bunch of others. If the Republicans block all efforts to investigate these crimes, and if they block efforts to impeach, then it's our job to organize the majority who want to impeach Bush and the even larger majority who believe that the Iraq War is wrong, and to elect a Democratic majority in 2006 that will do the job."

Ralph Nader, a third-party candidate for president in both Bush election campaigns, 2000 and 2004, has drawn up his own proposed bill of impeachment. "It really doesn't matter whether it's politically possible to impeach," says Nader. "If the Constitution has been violated, you have to call for impeachment. Presidents are more and more out of control. They're above the law in so many ways. They have to be held accountable." In an op-ed essay in *The Boston Globe,* he and colleague Kevin Zeese explain why they and their supporters are pressing for impeachment:

> Did the administration mislead us into war by manipulating and misstating intelligence concerning weapons of mass destruction and alleged ties to Al Qaeda, suppressing contrary intelligence, and deliberately exaggerating the danger a contained, weakened Iraq posed to the United States and its neighbors?
>
> If this is answered affirmatively, Bush and Cheney have committed "high crimes and misdemeanors." It is time for Congress to investigate the illegal Iraq war as we move toward the third year of the endless quagmire that many security experts believe jeopardizes U.S. safety by recruiting and training more terrorists. A Resolution of Impeachment would be a first step. Based on the mountains of fabrications, deceptions, and lies, it is time to debate the "I" word.[3]

For the moment, impeachment is not a word one hears uttered out loud in the nation's capital, where politicians prefer to battle more politely over pork programs. Indeed there is evidence that the Democratic Party leadership has been actively working to prevent party members in the House from filing an impeachment bill, as the late Rep. Henry Gonzalez (D-TX) did against the elder President George H. W. Bush over the 1991 Gulf War, fearing that such a radical move might hurt Democrats with independent voters. This may explain why efforts in mid-November and December 2005 to elicit a comment on impeachment from the often outspoken House Judiciary Committee minority chair John Conyers, and from several more radical Democratic House members, including Cynthia McKinney (D-GA) and Dennis Kucinich (D-OH), were rebuffed with terse "no comments" from their staffs.* Nor is impeachment yet much of a topic of stories in the national media, where caution still rules when it comes to challenging the provenly ruthless Bush administration. There is no other rational explanation why a dramatic piece of news like the Zogby data showing a majority of Americans favor impeachment can be blacked out in our normally poll-obsessed media.

Yet the impeachment idea is gaining a life of its own among the broader public, where the president's lying, his extraordinary attempts to expand presidential power, his inept handling of the wars in Iraq and Afghanistan, his administration's corruption and possible crimes, and, in the case of the Katrina disaster in New Orleans, his inaction and incompetence, are leading more and more people, some mainstream Republicans among them, to ponder about how to get rid of him and his whole White House gang without having to wait until 2008. The mood in Congress, particularly among Democrats, is also in flux. In December 2002, just before revelations that Bush had approved a warrantless domestic spying campaign that has been conducted by the National Security Agency, Representative Conyers introduced bills of censure for both Bush and Cheney, as well as a third bill calling for creation of a Watergate-style select committee to investigate constitutional violations by the president and vice president. To some people, this is simply a pre-

---

*It also explains why, when Sen. Russ Feingold (D-WI) introduced a censure motion against the president in early March 2006, he only got the support of two colleagues, Sen. Barbara Boxer (D-CA) and Sen. Tom Harkin (D-IA). Party Chairman Howard Dean denies any such pressure by the DNC.

liminary step that could lead to impeachment proceedings. Seven other Democrats joined Conyers as cosponsors, a number that had risen to thirty-two by the time this book went to press.

"I'm having a hard time keeping up with all the impeachable offenses," laughs attorney Francis Boyle, who, together with former Lyndon Johnson–era attorney general Ramsey Clark, drew up an impeachment bill for consideration by House Democrats on the eve of the Iraq War. Boyle, Nader, Swanson, and others who have been pressing the issue, cite lying to Congress, violating international laws, breaking international treaties, ignoring court orders, eliminating *habeas corpus,* refusing to deal with the global warming crisis, undermining U.S. emergency preparedness by sending off National Guard troops to Iraq and gutting first-responder organizations at home, undermining the United States and global response to the AIDS pandemic, blocking the full investigation of 9/11, as well as election interference, fraud, and manipulation, as some of the issues that could lead to impeachment charges. In fact, Boyle argues that the real challenge isn't finding grounds for impeachment, which he claims are legion, but rather "finding some member of Congress with the courage to introduce an impeachment bill."

Impeachment, meanwhile, is becoming not just a word, but a popular idea. The March 2006 issue of the liberal monthly magazine *Harper's* featured a cover story titled "Impeach Him" by editor Lewis Lapham, and a number of the nation's newspapers by 2006 had published opinion pieces calling for Bush's impeachment. This is something new and fundamentally different from the presidential impeachment efforts of the past. All three previous impeachment attempts were essentially efforts by a president's political enemies in Congress to remove the chief executive from office mid-term. None of those campaigns had broad public support. What we are seeing now is a mounting *public* desire to undo, via impeachment, the results of the last election.

This became clear to Tony Trupiano, a Michigan talk-radio host seeking the 2006 Democratic nomination to run for Congress against two-term Republican Thad McCotter. Trupiano has made a call for impeachment one of his main campaign promises. At campaign events during the fall of 2005, Trupiano reportedly had to halt his speeches after announcing that one of his first actions upon being elected would be to introduce a bill of impeachment for both President Bush and Vice President Cheney. The uproar from the enthusiastic crowds completely drowned out the public address system. "This is not a difficult position to take," says Trupiano. "I think it's clear that the American people, including many Republicans, want accountability. People are realizing that the president and vice president lied about the war, and they're wondering what else they've lied about. There's certainly enough to investigate, and it's my sense that if the Democrats gain control over Congress next November, there will be an impeachment resolution and there will be hearings in the House Judiciary Committee."

Howard Zinn, a prominent scholar of popular movements in American history, noting that few Democratic House incumbents have been willing to echo Trupiano's call for impeachment, says, "This situation is different than previous moves for impeachment, in that it is being driven by popular will, with no response thus far from the political leaders of either party. It is a damning indictment of our political system, and of the way that a regime in power can ignore public opinion. It is also a sad commentary on the cowardice of what is supposed to be the opposition party, the Democrats, that none of those leaders has broached the idea of impeachment, though in our history there has been no case for impeachment more powerful than in the present circumstance. If there is any situation calling for a popular upsurge against the president, and a nationwide campaign for impeachment that would frighten the leaders of both political parties into some sort of response, this is it."

"But it's not a movement yet," cautions Nader. "To have a mass movement, you have to have organization. It's certainly a call for a mass movement, though."

IN A sense then, an effort to impeach Bush may have more in common with the various anti-war movements or the civil rights movement, in that it has begun among the ordinary citizenry, rather than their elected officials. With a bitter campaign for control of Congress underway in 2006, it is surely only a matter of time before impeachment moves from Main Street to Washington, D.C., and before the "I" word makes it into the mainstream media. If it becomes an issue in the contested congressional campaigns, and if the public's frustration with the Bush administration is reflected in the voting, it could conceivably lead to a fourth presidential impeachment drama in the Capitol building before Bush's second term can run its course.

It is not our purpose here to make tactical arguments about which among the president's high crimes and misdemeanors are the most likely to succeed as articles of impeachment, though it seems clear that, for example, a House Judiciary Committee would be much more likely to pass a measure accusing the president of violating a federal statute, or of deceiving Congress and the public, than one accusing him of violating an international law like the Nuremberg Charter. Our purpose here is to try to lay out for examination the vast range of presidential crimes, misdemeanors, abuses of power, and threats to the Constitution and to the republic.

And there are a lot of them. As Bob Graham, the former Democratic senator from Florida who headed the Senate Intelligence Committee during 9/11 and over the following year, writes, after listing eleven serious presidential crimes, abuses of power, and obstructions of justice in his book *Intelligence Matters*:

> Any one of these things would warrant a leader's removal from office. Taken together, they are a searing indictment of a president who, despite lofty words to the contrary, has not been a leader, has not been honest, and has not made America safer.[4]

The American public, and the people's elected representatives, have the responsibility to decide which of his many actions constitute impeachable offenses.

One thing is alarmingly clear: the threats posed to the American constitutional tradition of separation of powers and of checks and balances in government, to the various supposedly inalienable rights enumerated in the Constitution's Bill of Rights, and to the rule of law in a dangerous world, are all in grave danger if the American people do not take a stand in their defense against an administration that is clearly intent on eroding or destroying all these things.

It's time.

★ ★ ★ ★ ★ ★ ★ ★ ★ ★ ★ ★ ★ ★

# TWO

★ ★ ★ ★ ★ ★ ★ ★ ★ ★ ★ ★ ★ ★

## *An Agenda of Deceit and a Case of Overreaching*

**ONE OF** the most important challenges prosecutors face in a trial is giving jurors sufficient reason to believe that the evidence they will hear is true. That's because in many serious crimes the behavior of the accused on some level simply defies belief—ordinary people just don't do these kinds of things; there has to be a history and a motive. So, to make the case, a prosecutor typically will present jurors with a history of the defendant, emphasizing those events that might have predicted the kind of criminal behavior for which he or she is on trial. The prosecutor will try to show that the accused's action is simply the latest in a series of similar events. The prosecutor will also create a story line—a framework into which the behavior of the accused will fit logically.

The crimes and abuses of power of George W. Bush are breathtaking, and undoubtedly will cause some to wonder how anyone in such a position of power, someone entrusted with the solemn responsibility to defend the Constitution and protect the nation, could engage in such unconstitutional and even criminal actions. Those who have no trouble believing Bush and his administration team—among them Vice President Dick Cheney, Secretary of Defense Donald Rumsfeld, Attorney General Alberto Gonzales, and Secretary of State Condoleezza

Rice—could subvert and commit crimes against the Constitution may wish to skip ahead to the chapters laying out the case for impeachment. But for those who want a better understanding of who George W. Bush is, and why his presidency chose to travel down such a dark road, please read on.

**LET'S TURN** back to that peculiar and disturbing 2000 presidential election.

Election Day 2000 had ended inconclusively. There was no doubt that Al Gore, not George Bush, had won the popular vote by more than half a million votes, but the crucial electoral vote, which actually determines who takes the White House, was left in doubt because of a squeaker of an election in the state of Florida. There the process had been thrown into the courts because of disputes over how the ballots should be counted. This was the infamous "hanging chad" election, in which a poorly designed ballot apparently had caused many people to vote for the wrong candidate or simply to neglect to push a tiny piece of paper completely out of the ballot. For weeks there was no decision, as Democrats and Republicans fought over how to count thousands of disputed ballots. In the end, the election was decided in a wholly unsatisfactory way (one that would no doubt have horrified the founding fathers), with the five-member conservative majority of the U.S. Supreme Court—all of them appointees of Republican presidents— ordering a halt to recounting of the Florida votes. It was a transparently political decision that made Bush the winner by a razor-thin 537-vote margin.

It didn't help matters that a subsequent analysis of all the impounded ballots, conducted under Florida's open-records statute, strongly suggested that the state had actually voted for Gore by a significant margin. There was substantial and compelling evidence that the national election had really been won by the Democrat, both in terms of the electoral vote and the popular vote. In addition to the extremely questionable results, investigative journalists like Greg Palast and activists like Bev Harris of Blackbox Voting have exposed a shady

Republican-run operation* that, through an array of methods, ensured that hundreds of thousands of potential Florida voters, mostly Democrats, were illegally and unconstitutionally blocked from voting or had their votes improperly discarded.**

In one sense, all the after-the-fact investigating has been academic. The decision by the U.S. Supreme Court—blatantly political or not—was final. There is no provision in American electoral law to undo a national election once its outcome has been certified. But in another sense the dispute over the 2000 presidential election's outcome, which left a majority of Americans—and perhaps even Bush himself—feeling that the new presidency was illegitimate, set the stage for everything that followed. And what followed has been an astonishing assault on the foundations of America's democratic governance, the Constitution, and basic civil liberties dating back to the Magna Carta. "Essentially," says presidential scholar John White, a professor of political science at Catholic University of America in Washington, D.C., "what we've seen over the course of the president's first term has been a kind of coup d'etat that has been aimed at what Bush and Cheney consider to be restor-

*Several months before Election Day, the Florida Secretary of State, Katherine Harris, who was also Bush's Florida campaign manager (a conflict of interest that, tellingly, was repeated in another controversial presidential election four years later, this time in the contested state of Ohio), ordered county boards of election to purge their files of felons from a list of 57,700 alleged felons which her office had compiled—a list that some counties found to be as much as 95 percent in error. Those improperly purged from the voter rolls were overwhelmingly Democrats.
**Palast found that in counties in Florida where blacks accounted for at least 25 percent of the population, close to 10 percent of ballots were not counted, largely because the "reject" option on voting machines, which causes them to spit out invalid ballots before counting (thus allowing the voter to redo and recast her or his paper ballot), was deactivated. In contrast, the rejection rate for ballots cast in counties where blacks accounted for less than 5 percent of the population (and where the "reject" option was activated), the percentage of rejected ballots cast was between 0.5 and 3 percent.

ing the power of the presidency—something they see as having been in decline since Nixon's Watergate scandal."

The Bush administration's deceptiveness, secretiveness, corruption, and its utter contempt for the Bill of Rights, civil liberties, international law, and for the rule of law itself have been stunning. In a few short years Bush—installed in office by the Supreme Court and without a popular mandate—has managed to drag the nation into two interminable wars, subvert the Constitution, unilaterally revoke several longstanding international treaties, run up mind-bogglingly huge trade and budget deficits, violate basic American rights of citizenship, undo longstanding bans on domestic spying by the CIA and the military, endorse official policies of torture and extraordinary rendition, undo decades of environmental protection legislation, and subvert the very process of free and fair elections. It's a wild spree of abuses that makes this president the Willie Sutton of Constitution wreckers. Yet even before Bush took office, there were clear signs, both in his own record and in those of his key advisers and backers, of what was coming.

### *Early History: Shortcuts, Important Connections, and Dirty Tricks*

Nobody would accuse George Bush of being a born leader. No one, in fact, would accuse him of having been a man driven to succeed through intelligence and hard work. His early history—Phillips Academy party boy and cheerleader, Yale frat boy, Vietnam War service dodger, Texas Air National Guard AWOL, admitted drunk driver, and later, after an undistinguished year at Harvard Business School, a stint as failed businessman and corporate board figurehead—does not hint of anything resembling presidential timber, or even of gubernatorial kindling for that matter. Yet as the eldest son of George H. W. Bush, America's forty-first president, and the first of the next generation of the Connecticut-based blue-blooded Bush clan, the man known as Dubya was nonetheless destined, however improbably, for bigger things.

Bush gained his early political experience by working on his father's various campaigns. In 1964, just as Dubya was starting college, he helped on "Poppy's" unsuccessful bid for a Texas House seat, a role he reprised when George H. W. Bush ran a second losing campaign for the House in 1970. In 1978, young George W. Bush tried for the same seat himself, losing to a legislator from the state senate.

Perhaps frustrated by those losing efforts, Bush turned to business, where success proved equally elusive. If his remarkable record of getting into and graduating from some of the top schools in the nation despite mediocre academic performance hadn't taught him the importance of having powerful connections, his lackluster entrepreneurial record certainly did. Despite showing a singular lack of business acumen as he partied and glad-handed his way through a string of failed companies, Bush managed to prosper handily thanks to family connections. In 1977, he founded Arbusto Energy (Arbusto is "Bush" in Spanish), an oil-and-gas exploration company. A sizeable chunk of Bush's initial investment capital for Arbusto was provided by James Bath, who was also a business agent for, among others, Saudi billionaire Salem bin Laden,[1] business colleague of the elder Bush and older brother of Osama bin Laden (a man who would years later come to play a far bigger role in Bush's fortunes). Arbusto went bust-o, and then, after a series of corporate name changes and continued losses, was rescued by Harken Energy. As part of that deal, Bush became a Harken director. He had no role in running the company other than lending his family name to the company's prospectus, but that chore earned him a fat "consulting fee," which ranged from $42,000 to $120,000, depending on whether or not he showed up for meetings.

Bush's next venture was to become a 2-percent investor in a consortium that bought major league baseball's Texas Rangers in a $75-million deal. Bush's ante was financed by a friendly $500,000 bank loan (from a bank of which he had been a director). He repaid that debt by selling $848,000 worth of Harken Energy stock—eight days before the company announced a $23.2 million loss and its shares tanked. The SEC investigated Bush's suspiciously timed deal, and the fact that he had been on the board's audit committee—so he would have known about the forthcoming report—but with the SEC then headed by an appointee of his president/father, the conclusion—"no evidence of insider trading"—was predictable. Bush's role at the Rangers was handling media and governmental relations—a job at which he proved adept as the owners wangled a sweetheart deal to have the taxpayers of Arlington, Texas, pay for a new stadium and use the powers of eminent domain to obtain the land on which the stadium and shopping centers were built. When he left to run for governor of Texas, he sold his stake in the then much-inflated team, a deal that earned him a cool $14 million.

Bush's run for governor might seem curious at first glance. Even he had scoffed at the idea only a few years earlier. Back in 1989, when Karl Rove, the man who would later come to be known as "The Architect,"* was pressing him to run for governor in the upcoming 1990 race, Bush said:

> You know, I could run for governor, but I'm basically a media creation. I've never done anything. I've worked for my dad. I've worked in the oil business. But that's not the kind of profile you have to have to get elected to public office.[2]

Rove, who had cultivated the Bush family and saw George W. as his ticket to the White House, clearly didn't agree.

The two men had met in Washington in 1973. At that time, Rove was chairman of the College Republicans organization, and in that capacity began working with the Republican National Committee, which was then headed by Bush's father. A consummate behind-the-scenes player, Rove quickly recognized the potential of both father and son. In 1977, he began working on the senior Bush's program to win the 1980 Republican presidential nomination. Reagan won that contest, but picked Bush as his running mate. While working for the elder Bush, Rove also ran his son's failed 1978 congressional campaign. Later, after failing to convince the younger Bush to run for governor in 1990, Rove convinced him to try for the post in 1994.

That race, against incumbent Ann Richards, featured the kind of dirty tricks that have become Rove's trademark—most notably his furtive use of "whisper" campaigns to spread untrue rumors, both door-to-door and via skillful use of media contacts. During that cam-

---

*Bush famously likes to give nicknames to all his staff. Rove's, besides "The Architect," is reportedly "Turd Blossom."

paign, some Texas voters reported that people posing as pollsters were calling them and asking if they would vote for Richards if they knew that her staff was "dominated by lesbians." There were also damaging and unfounded rumors, reportedly planted by Bush campaign operatives, that Richards herself was homosexual. Bush won that race with 53 percent of the vote. His later Rove-run campaigns have continued to feature such devious tactics: during the crucial 2000 Republican primary in South Carolina a whisper campaign spread the despicable rumors that Bush rival Senator John McCain had gone round the bend as a Vietnamese POW, and that he had fathered a black child. The relationship between the two men—one, an entitled preppy with an elite education, standing out front, and the other, a college dropout working behind the scenes—was sealed. Also established was their political MO: Do and say whatever it takes to win. Win at all costs.

## *Faux Populist: Bush Prefers to Keep the Public at a Distance*

George W. Bush campaigned for president in 2000, posing as a man of the people—and as a "uniter." Famously favoring cowboy boots, an adopted Texas drawl, and a bowlegged swagger, no one should be deceived by this man who grew up mostly in Washington, D.C., and New England. Long before the Republican convention anointed him as the GOP nominee in August 2000, Bush and his handlers had gone to unprecedented lengths to cultivate his image as a Texas good ol' boy, while making sure that he was exposed only to adoring fans, at a comfortable distance. During preparations for that convention, the Bush campaign and the Republican National Committee extorted the city of Philadelphia (desperate at the time to win convention business for its underbooked new facilities) into granting the GOP permits for every available outdoor assembly venue in the entire metropolitan area. During convention week, it was literally impossible to hold a legal protest rally anywhere in the heart of the very city where the Declaration of Independence, the Constitution, and the Bill of Rights had been created. In response to the howls of protest from those who wanted to make their dissent heard, the city established a sunken space in a park skating rink, half a mile from the convention site, and offered protest organizations, on a lottery basis, fifteen-minute slots in what became known as the "protest pit." When various groups attempted to be heard by demonstrating where they wanted without permits, they were jumped on by Philadelphia police, with hundreds rounded up, often brutally, at the urging of the Secret Service. Nearly every one of those arrests was voided by the courts months later, but the damage was done. The blackout of dissent during the Bush nomination was almost total.

The insulation of the president from any hint of public protest has continued through five years, actually getting worse over time. Secret Service and White House advance teams go to any venue where Bush or Vice President Dick Cheney are to appear in public and instruct local police to remove all potential protesters—even people just wearing a T-shirt critical of the president or his policies—from caravan routes and or speaking venues.[3] Against all regulations two women wearing T-shirts—one of them in support of American troops in Iraq—were removed from the House gallery during the President's 2006 State of the Union speech. Officials later apologized publicly to both women, but once again the Bush bubble had been maintained. Protesters are typically given a choice: go to a fenced-in "free speech zone" set up far from the president and the accompanying media gaggle, or face arrest. For the most part, by 2004 the president was only speaking at controlled gatherings where the attendees are certain to be supportive—a reason he tends to favor military bases. Tickets to attend other presidential events are available only to known supporters through the offices of select Republican elected officials—despite the fact that these are not partisan events and are paid for with public funds. Democratic elected officials say they aren't even provided with tickets to give out to constituents.[4]

## Core Values: Secrecy, Deception, and Lies

At the same time that the president and vice president were deliberately encapsulating themselves in a White House bubble, they also began taking steps, even before inauguration day, to seal off the Bush presidency from public, media, or even congressional scrutiny. As John Dean notes,[5] Bush set the tone on secrecy even before taking office. While still governor of Texas, he tried to pull an end-run on Texas's open records law, shipping off all the records from his governorship to his father's presidential library at Texas A&M, instead of to another Texas library. His intention was to ensure that access to the files would be controlled by his father and by federal law on presidential archives, instead of the much more permissive state law. This trend continued after the inauguration, with Bush returning the favor to his father by issuing an executive order early in his first term that sealed presidential documents dating from 1980—including the Reagan and Bush administrations—and giving authority over them jointly to former presidents or their heirs and to the sitting president.

Here it becomes necessary to speak not of the Bush presidency, but of the Bush/Cheney presidency, for much of the administration's obsession with secrecy, and the record of deception and distortion, can be traced to the vice president. Cheney displayed his contempt for public accountability dramatically when he accidentally shot a quail-hunting companion in February 2006. He waited a day before having the incident reported to the media, and then another three days before he personally spoke about it publicly. Following the shooting, which was serious enough that one of the pellets he fired damaged the heart of the seventy-eight-year-old victim, causing a "mild heart attack," Cheney had his Secret Service detail delay local sheriff's deputies from doing their job and questioning him for a period of over fourteen hours. This vice president and the people around him have a long history of disdaining the whole notion of open government. Yet it is widely believed that most of the political and intellectual heavy lifting in this White House is actually being done by the man in the shadows, Vice President Cheney, perhaps from his mysterious "undisclosed location."

As John Dean—who came to know Cheney personally during the Nixon years, when both worked for that famously deceptive and secrecy-obsessed chief executive—writes in his analysis of the Bush/Cheney administration:

> George W. Bush and Richard B. Cheney have created the most secretive presidency of my lifetime. Their secrecy is far worse than during

Watergate, and it bodes even more serious consequences. Their secrecy is extreme—not merely unjustified and obsessive. It has created a White House that hides its president's weaknesses as well as its vice president's strengths. It has given us a presidency that operates on hidden agendas. To protect their secrets, Bush and Cheney dissemble as a matter of policy. In fact, the Bush-Cheney presidency is strikingly Nixonian, only with regard to secrecy far worse . . . To say their secret presidency is undemocratic is an understatement.[6]

The efforts to seal off the White House from outside scrutiny began even before the Florida election battle had ended. Assuming he would win, Bush had Cheney set about constructing a new administration right away. Cheney, who as chief of staff of the Ford White House knew a fair amount about both running the West Wing and about leaks—much to journalists' delight and Cheney's annoyance the Ford administration, with its competing groups of Nixon hangers-on and Ford congressional cronies, had been a sieve—made it clear that there would be no *unauthorized* leaking in the new Bush White House. At least until the Iraq War began to go seriously sour and the Bush administration started sinking in the polls, the strategy worked.*

But plugging leaks was just the beginning. Bush and Cheney also essentially shut down the Freedom of Information Act (FOIA), with the Justice Department of John Ashcroft issuing an order to all executive departments and agencies that requests from journalists and the public under FOIA were to be responded to as minimally as possible. Since 1993, federal guidelines required government agencies to respond to FOIA requests by releasing everything except that material which legally could not be released for reasons of privacy or national security. But in Ashcroft's order, which went out October 12, 2001, with no public announcement, agencies were told to withhold information

---

*That's not to say there were no White House leaks, just that the leaks that occurred—such as the notorious one (from Cheney's office and possibly from the White House) to Judith Miller, Matt Cooper, Bob Woodward, Robert Novak, and other reporters about the secret undercover identity of CIA operative Valerie Plame—were deliberate, approved leaks, not the work of dissident bureaucrats.

whenever "institutional, commercial, and personal privacy interests could be implicated by disclosure of the information."[7]*

Not content with just blocking outside access to what had previously been considered public records, the administration effectively ended a program of reviewing and declassifying old government documents, and added new layers of restrictive classifications to keep new records secret. It also began browbeating and threatening legal action against government civil servants who provided information to journalists and even to Congress.

To make certain that federal employees got the message that unauthorized leaking by federal workers would not be tolerated by the Bush/Cheney White House, the Ashcroft Justice Department established an interagency anti-leak task force. If the mere existence of that operation didn't have a major chilling effect on would-be leakers and whistleblowers, there were also prosecutions. The message was received. Journalists widely agree that this has been the most leakproof administration in memory.

It has also been the most manipulative and combative in terms of the media. Besides setting a new record for fewest press conferences, Bush has run those few he has held like scripted scenes from a shooting of *West Wing*. At the rostrum, he keeps a map of where reporters are seated, and chooses his questioners based upon presubmitted and vetted questions. Reporters who don't want to play this charade—waving their hands, shouting, and asking to be called on to make it look as if it were

---

*While working on a book in 2002, I needed to obtain the FBI file of a deceased Philadelphia police officer, Daniel Faulkner. I filed an FOIA request with the FBI and received in return six pages, nearly two-thirds of which were whited out completely. The reasons given, absurdly, were "privacy" and "national security." Since this was just a young Philadelphia police officer, the national security claim was ludicrous. As for privacy, the information sought, regarding the officer's professional activities as an officer, and the circumstances of his death twenty-one years earlier could not in any way have interfered with anyone's privacy. When I filed an appeal, some portions of the missing material were provided. It turned out that their deletion had had nothing to do with either reason given. About a third of the file was never provided.—Dave Lindorff

a real press conference—are simply left out in the cold. Helen Thomas, the dean of the White House press corps, who traditionally has been seated front and center, and who by tradition should get the opening question, has been unceremoniously moved to the back of the room and ignored by Bush (without protest from her colleagues) because she dared to ask a tough question and referred to him in print as the worst president in history.

Bush's handlers took manipulation several steps further, though. They got caught planting a shill, GOP operative James Guckert (aka Jeff Gannon), who had previously worked as a male escort, to pose as a White House reporter. The idea was to allow Bush, or Bush press spokesman Scott McClellan during his regular press briefings, to call on the fake reporter for a diversionary softball query if the real press pack started asking tough questions. For the most part, though, such deceitful tactics weren't even needed. The administration's hardball intimidation of reporters, and its threat to freeze out those journalists who got too feisty or inquisitive, had worked so well that for several months nobody noticed the Guckert/Gannon ruse. It seems his sycophantic questions were so similar to the ones emanating from some of the real reporters seated around him, no one noticed him for a while. The White House also secretly and illegally spent millions of dollars paying columnists to write propaganda pieces, and even produced fake "news" videos that were broadcast by local TV stations with no acknowledgement that they had been made and distributed by the Bush administration.

## Restoring the Imperial Presidency

Bush and Cheney may have had to cut a few corners to win the White House, but they came into office with a bonus: Republican control of both houses of Congress (at least until Republican Senator Jim Jeffords of Vermont declared himself an Independent and began voting mostly with the Democrats in June, 2001). With a narrow Republican majority in the House and an evenly divided Senate, which became a fifty-one-seat majority whenever Cheney, as president of the Senate, added his vote, Bush had the support to push his agenda that no Republican president had enjoyed since before the 1920s. Key agenda items could be passed without the vote of a single Democrat and no nosy committees were going to question the administration very hard about anything.

But that was not enough.

Cheney in particular, who had served six terms as a congressman from Wyoming, had never liked the idea of Congress interfering in the prerogatives of presidents, particularly in foreign policy. As a member of the House Intelligence Committee in 1988 during the Iran-Contra scandal investigation (which looked into the secret sale by Oliver North of weapons to Iran to finance a guerilla war in Nicaragua), he had taken a lead role in opposing a bill that would have required a president to notify Congress within forty-eight hours of the initiation of any covert operation. Despite the clear illegality of Reagan's scheme, Cheney wrote in a *Wall Street Journal* op-ed article at the time:

> On the scale of risks, there is more reason to be concerned about depriving the president of his ability to act than about Congress's alleged inability to respond.[8]

It might seem counterintuitive that a member of Congress would argue against the right of legislative oversight, but Cheney's dark and brittle heart was always across the Mall at the White House, even when he was serving in the Capitol. As ranking minority member of the House committee that investigated Iran-Contra, Cheney had penned a minority report opposing the committee's conclusion. Rejecting the committee's finding that Reagan's secret deal to sell Stinger missiles to Iran to raise money for the banned Contras in Nicaragua had been duplicitous and illegal, Cheney wrote that this blatant—and clearly unconstitutional—violation of laws had been "mistakes in judgment and nothing more."[9] It's a view of executive power Cheney has long harbored and continues to hold as Bush's vice president.

In fact, Bush and Cheney had a far bolder vision of presidential power. Both viewed the presidencies of Gerald Ford and Bush's father (which they had experienced personally), and certainly of Carter and Clinton, as having been weak and overly deferential to Congress. They wanted to go back to a fabled time when presidents were like emperors:

the Franklin Roosevelt, Lyndon Johnson, and especially the pre-Watergate Nixon-Kissinger years. Just days into Bush's first term they initiated their plan with the establishment of the National Energy Policy Development Group—a secret assembly rumored to have been comprised of leaders of the major energy corporations, and chaired by the vice president. Like Bush, Cheney was an oil man; having served as president and CEO of Halliburton, a giant oil services conglomerate, before joining the Bush team. Contrary to his initial claims, Cheney has continued to receive annual compensation from the company while serving as vice president. Cheney's energy policy group reeked of a payoff for the millions of dollars in campaign contributions that oil companies had poured into the Bush presidential race. Wanting to know exactly what deals were being made behind the locked White House doors, two Democratic congressmen, Henry Waxman (D-CA), ranking minority member of the House Committee on Government Reform, and John Dingell (D-MI), ranking minority member of the House Energy and Commerce Committee, took advantage of their authority to request details about Cheney's group from the General Accounting Office (GAO), Congress's investigative and auditing arm.

It was a simple request. All they asked for were the names of the participants and a description of the group's activities. They specifically did not request possibly privileged information about the actual deliberations. But Bush and Cheney, establishing a pattern they have repeated throughout their administration, stonewalled. They flatly refused to provide any information at all, claiming they had no obligation to answer GAO inquiries about the policy group, not even after the GAO limited its request to only the names of the people who attended this meeting. The head of the GAO, Controller General David Walker, filed suit, but ultimately lost in federal court to a judge, John Bates, who had served on the staff of Clinton sex scandal special prosecutor Kenneth Starr, and who had recently been appointed by Bush to the federal bench. Unwilling to risk setting a bad precedent at an even higher court level, the agency did not appeal. It was a major victory for presidential secrecy—and for politicized judicial rulings—supporting Bush's and Cheney's claim that their actions should be beyond congressional scrutiny. Four years later, it was finally discovered that Cheney had indeed met with the top executives of the major oil companies. Little wonder that he had been so anxious to keep these tête-à-têtes behind closed doors. Still unknown is what he and the oilmen discussed, what deals were cut, and how much their collusive plotting would cost the American public after all hell broke loose.

## Hidden Agendas, Overreaching, and a Sinking Ship

Why is the Bush/Cheney administration so obsessed with secrecy? While both the president and the vice president have always been secretive by nature, a key reason for their desire to wall off the White House from scrutiny is that their whole presidency was based upon a central deception. The Rove strategy had always been to simultaneously lock in support from the conservative, fundamentalist wing of the Republican Party by having the president endorse signature "values" issues like limiting abortion, endorsing prayer in schools, and opposing gay marriage, while luring mainstream voters with carefully market-researched catchphrases like "compassionate conservative," or "fiscal responsibility," or his signature slogan, "No Child Left Behind."

In fact, though, the "product" was always something quite different from the commercials: to reestablish an all-powerful unitary executive; to pour billions into the military; to assert an aggressive, unilateralist foreign policy; to starve domestic social programs through a Stockmanesque program of slashing taxes*—especially for corporations and higher-income individuals—and to gut regulations controlling pollution, worker safety, transportation, communications, agriculture, and food and drug safety. Managing such a massive bait-and-switch deception has required not just secrecy, but endless dissembling. As John Dean, who witnessed considerable lying in the Nixon administration, puts it:

*David Stockman, the head of Reagan's Office of Management and Budget, eventually spilled the beans that the huge budget deficits caused by that president's tax cuts had been a deliberate effort to create a budget crisis, which would lead to a slashing of entitlement spending, especially on programs for the poor.

with the Bush-Cheney presidency, it appears that mendacity has become policy. Their lying relates to matters large and small. Lies are told to hide, to mislead, and to gain political advantage.[10]

On the topic of the alleged threat posed by Saddam Hussein, Congressman Henry Waxman has gathered up 237 "specific misleading statements" made by Bush administration officials as they engaged in a massive propaganda campaign to convince Americans to support an invasion of Iraq.

Much of the foreign policy component of the Bush-Cheney hidden agenda was laid out in a document called *Rebuilding America's Defenses: Strategy, Forces and Resources for a New Century*, which was produced by a neoconservative think tank named The Project for a New American Century. Many of the authors of that document—among them Cheney, Donald Rumsfeld, Paul Wolfowitz, Richard Perle, and I. Lewis "Scooter" Libby—ended up working in the new Bush administration. Published in September 2000, its main premise was stated concisely:

> The United States is the world's only superpower, combining preeminent military power, global technological leadership, and the world's largest economy. Moreover, America stands at the head of a system of alliances which includes the world's other leading democratic powers. At present the United States faces no global rival. America's grand strategy should aim to preserve and extend this advantageous position as far into the future as possible.[11]

This grandiose and staggeringly expensive imperial plan was really a restatement and expansion of an earlier report produced, during the waning days of the first President Bush's administration, at the direction of then Secretary of Defense Dick Cheney. The PNAC report glowingly recalls that earlier Cheney study, saying:

> The Defense Policy Guidance (DPG) drafted in the early months of 1992 provided a blueprint for maintaining U.S. preeminence, precluding the rise of a great power rival, and shaping the international security order in line with American principles and interests.[12]

Clearly this was not the message that had been presented to Americans by Bush and Cheney on the campaign trail, when in speech after speech and during the debates they mocked the "nation-building" efforts of President Clinton and Democratic presidential candidate Al Gore.

On the domestic side, the administration began aggressively pushing its agenda of hard-right measures, featuring increased military spending, cuts in social programs, and a record-shattering $1.35 trillion tax cut. This tax cut that strongly benefited the wealthiest Americans passed, but it led directly to the defection from Republican ranks of Senator Jeffords, and with him, at least briefly, Republican control of the Senate.

Far from being the "uniter" he had campaigned as, Bush in office had become a hard-right ideologue, and his poll numbers began to show it.

All during August of 2001, stories were running in the media suggesting that President Bush had blown his opening act, and that his presidency was sinking. Typical was a CBS News poll on September 5, less than a week before the 9/11 attacks, which found the president's approval rating at 50 percent, down from 53 percent on June 1 and 60 percent on March 1. Worse, from the White House's perspective, was the finding that 52 percent of Americans and 56 percent of independent voters, agreed that Bush was "out of touch with what average Americans think."[13]

As the network's accompanying news report put it:

Disapproval of President Bush's handling of the economy has . . . risen while his overall approval rating has dropped to a new low. In addition, Mr. Bush faces public opposition to several of his priorities, including his energy plan and increased military spending.

Even Bush's signature tax cut was causing problems, as the CBS report noted:

While most Americans don't see the Bush tax cut as the primary culprit behind the shrinking budget surplus, the White House is not viewed as a credible authority on the actual state of the federal budget. And more Americans say it's the Democrats in Congress, not President Bush, who are more likely to make the right decisions about that budget, the economy, and government spending.[14]

This was not what Karl Rove, a man who lived his whole life in a campaign mode, wanted to be hearing as the 2002 off-year congressional contests approached. Indeed, as CNN senior White House correspondent John King, in an August 6 CNN chatroom commentary on the president's sinking poll numbers, reported, "Bush has high personal approval ratings, but people have doubts about his agenda and leadership skills." He reported that White House strategists—meaning Rove—were advising that Bush should shift gears, backpedal on his conservative agenda, and do more to reach out to middle-of-the-road voters.[15]

## *Pearl Harbor Redux*

In 1940, with war raging in Europe and Asia, Franklin Roosevelt had run for a third presidential term promising that he would keep America out of those conflicts. But historians have reported that within his inner circle at the White House he had already been gearing up for war, and was just looking for the right political opportunity to join our allies in the fight against fascism. When the Japanese attacked Pearl Harbor on December 7, 1941, he immediately asked Congress for a declaration of war against the Axis powers. George Bush got his Pearl Harbor at 8:46 on the morning of September 11, 2001, when American Airlines Flight 11 slammed into the north tower of the World Trade Center in New York City. And however genuine their horror at the carnage must have been, it would be hard not to conclude that the White House wasn't opportunistic about the timing—on the level of political strategy, anyhow. Not only was the president in a political slump, but his administration's big goals—a transformation of the presidency, a dramatic rollback of the welfare state, and a new foreign policy built around the concept of imperial dominance—were foundering under the weight of recession, mounting political opposition, and the public's growing disenchantment with their new president.

That notorious PNAC document had made it clear as early as 2000, that the major work of "transforming" the U.S. military, ensuring U.S. global hegemony into the indefinite future, and actively preventing other nations from challenging U.S military dominance, at the estimated cost of a third of a trillion taxpayer dollars a year, would take an unacceptably long time to accomplish, "absent some catastrophic and catalyzing event—like a new Pearl Harbor."[16]

On September 11, 2001, they got their "new Pearl Harbor." Four massive airliners had been commandeered by radical Muslim terrorists and transformed into fuel-laden missiles. Two of those planes hit the World Trade Center in downtown Manhattan, the nation's financial capital, obliterating three massive buildings and killing almost three thousand people. In Washington, D.C., the Pentagon, headquarters of the most mighty military machine the world had ever known, had been severely damaged. And only the extraordinarily heroic actions of the passengers aboard the fourth plane, which crashed in rural Pennsylvania, prevented it from hitting the Capitol or White House.

It was a once-in-a-century opportunity for a president to take charge, and even if the president himself initially seemed a bit daunted and incapable of responding, his administration grabbed this opportunity with a vengeance.

With evidence pointing to Osama bin Laden and his terrorist organization Al Qaeda—an Arabic word meaning "the base"—as the source of the attacks, plans were immediately made to attack their training camps in Afghanistan. Bin Laden and the mujahadeen volunteer forces had long been helping that nation's ruling Taliban government in its fight against Russian-backed warlords. Within a few weeks, on October 7, the United States was at war with both the Taliban forces and Al Qaeda in Afghanistan. But Afghanistan was only small change for the Bush-Cheney team. According to Paul O'Neill, the administration's first treasury secretary and a member of the National Security Council (NSC) from day one of the Bush presidency, Iraq and its dictator, Saddam Hussein, were the real target. O'Neill, later dumped by Bush for questioning the staggering size of the administration's tax cuts, says invading Iraq and overthrowing Saddam were on the agenda of the very first meeting of the Bush NSC, held in the first days of the new administration. According to O'Neill, no one at the session questioned the reason for such an invasion. As he remembers:

> It was all about finding a way to do it. That was the tone of it. The president saying, "Go find me a way to do this."[17]

Iraq had nothing to do with the attacks on 9/11: not a single member of the hijack teams was Iraqi, and no connection was ever found between Hussein and the 9/11 plot. But the administration, and especially the president and vice president, continued to revise history by linking Hussein and 9/11. For Bush and Cheney this was a necessary lie—it provided the excuse they needed to attack Iraq.

As journalist William Rivers Pitt wrote less than a month before the U.S. invasion of Iraq began:

> On September 11th, the fellows from PNAC saw a door of opportunity open wide before them, and stormed right through it.[19]

Karl Rove saw that same open door, and stormed through with them. For Rove, though, the issue wasn't a geopolitical realignment aimed at consolidating American hegemony in the world. Rather, it was a domestic realignment aimed at consolidating Republican hegemony in the United States.

This explains the whole approach of the Bush administration over the following years—the concerted efforts to push for war against Iraq, despite the negative effect this had almost immediately upon the military's effort to catch or kill Osama bin Laden in Afghanistan. Even pro-administration military leaders in charge of that mission grumbled that their troops were being drained. And when bin Laden was finally cornered in the rugged mountains of Tora Bora there were insufficient American troops to pursue him, allowing him to escape. It explains the whole color-coded scheme of terror alerts created by the newly created Department of Homeland Security, alerts which did absolutely nothing to prevent attacks, but which were seemingly raised to a more dangerous color every time the White House found its policies under attack. It explains the harsh political attacks on Democrats—with charges of "aiding the enemy" or "aiding terrorists" bandied about regularly during the 2002 congressional campaign—at a time when, normally, one would have expected the administration to be seeking unity at home.

Putting it all together, it seems clear in retrospect that 9/11 was seen by the Bush-Cheney administration as a golden opportunity to overcome their failure to win the 2000 election outright, and to manufacture a "mandate" for virtually unchallenged rule where none had existed. Furthermore, it seems clear that White House strategists, notably Rove and Cheney, realized, too, that the short attention span of the public meant they needed something longer term than just 9/11. The Afghanistan conflict wouldn't do it—the Taliban collapsed in weeks, and once the U.S. military had captured Osama bin Laden, that convenient scapegoat would be history, too. Even the "War on Terror" would wear thin once Ashcroft's federal authorities had rounded up and deported several thousand Islamic-named aliens and tried and convicted a few terrorist suspects. It would become just another "War on . . ." like the War on Drugs and the War on Poverty. What they needed was a *real* war—a war that would transform their lackluster and tongue-tied President Bush into the nation's snappy-saluting, tough-talking commander in chief, and the public into an unthinking, unquestioning, jingoistic mass of troop-supporting patriots.

It was the urgency of needing to achieve all these things, while the horror of 9/11 and the weird and never solved Anthrax postal attacks on Congress and several other locations that soon followed were fresh in the consciousness of the American people, that led to the overreaching. They had to take action while the people, the Congress, and the judges on the federal bench were all ready to give the administration a free pass, while fear, anger, and patriotic fervor were at their height. It was this desire to opportunistically grab power while the nation was feeling vulnerable that led to the lies about the threat posed by Iraq, to the potentially criminal outing of an undercover CIA agent, to the undermining of the integrity of the nation's voting system, and to efforts to undermine the Constitution itself. It was this urgency to take advantage of 9/11, finally, which led to the administration's abuse of power, and to a whole series of high crimes and misdemeanors.

Some of those high crimes and misdemeanors may be very twenty-first century, involving high-tech spying, international intrigue, and issues of global survival, but the answer for how to respond to such threats to democracy, liberty, and public safety were developed centuries ago by our British ancestors and the nation's founders: impeachment.

# THREE

## *The Origins of Impeachment*

Judgment in Cases of Impeachment shall not extend further than to removal from Office, and disqualification to
hold and enjoy any Office of honor, Trust, or Profit under
the United States; but the Party convicted shall nevertheless be liable and subject to Indictment, Trial, Judgment,
and Punishment, according to the Law.
          —*Constitution of the United States, Article I, Section 4*

### *What Do We Know About This Unusual Political Process?*

As the public and the Congress become increasingly ill-at-ease with the
administration's claims that the president may at will violate the Constitution, forsake the Bill of Rights, and disavow binding international
treaties, a debate is growing over whether now is the time for Congress
to consider invoking the Impeachment Clause of the Constitution. For
such a discussion to be of value to all of us—*the People*—we must first
have an understanding of what impeachment was intended to achieve,
how the process was intended to be used, how it has been used in American history, and what its use now would mean for the future.

Historians, legal scholars, and social studies teachers point out that the Framers, steeped in English history as they were debating and drafting the clauses of the Constitution, were haunted by visions of despotic kings and scheming ministers.[1] In particular, the specter of authoritarianism was ever present during the constitutional debates and engendered the fear that the new republic might create an executive who could, engorged with tyrannical power, rain abuses down upon the populace. The president was not to be a king in the new republic. It was to allay these concerns that the Framers awarded to Congress the power to remove the president and his cabinet members. The colonies' partiality to Congress among the three branches of the federal government "sprang from the fact that the Assemblies were their own, whereas Governors and Judges had been saddled on the Colonists by the King and his minions."[2]

The constitutional grant to Congress of the power to impeach makes sense as part of the Framers' plan for a system of checks and balances intended to ensure that no branch could overtake the others and use its accumulated powers to oppress the people. But while the motivation in adopting the impeachment device may be very clear, even today the scope of that power and how and when it is properly invoked have remained much more opaque. For example, are members of Congress subject to impeachment as well as the president and federal judges? What offenses constitute appropriate bases for impeachment? Is impeachment reserved only for those governmental officers who commit criminal offenses, or does the Impeachment Clause include political conduct that may not be punishable as a crime? Does the Impeachment Clause also address situations in which the president may be unable to lead because of a physical or psychiatric disability? Does it apply to personal, nonofficial misconduct? The answers to most of these questions can't be found in the Constitution. Ironically, the clearest picture that we may be able to get of the meaning and scope of the impeachment process and its place in our present constitutional scheme is one that comes from piecing together the history of its development in England, the Framers' interpretation of that historical use, and Congress's practices when it has invoked the process from the early 1800s until now.

The historical use of the impeachment mechanism can provide us with an understanding of its current political role and the powerful potential it has for determining our course in the future.

## The Historical Origins of Impeachment

In England, impeachment was considered "the chief instrument for the preservation of government,"[3] and was used originally for the removal of corrupt judges.[4] As a result of long and bitter struggles between the king and Parliament for political supremacy, impeachment eventually became the means by which Parliament held the king's ministers accountable to it rather than to the Crown.[5] With the rise of the Tudor family, however, impeachment fell into disuse for more than 160 years, until royal excesses compelled Parliament to revive the process in order to remove oppressive ministers and restore some balance of power between itself and the Crown.

From the time of its origin and first use in England in 1386, impeachment has been a political proceeding, and impeachable offenses have been political crimes. Examples abound illustrating the types of misconduct that were seen as involving "High Crimes and Misdemeanors." The Earl of Suffolk suffered impeachment proceedings in 1386 because he "applied appropriated funds to purposes other than those specified."[6] Proceedings were brought in 1450 against the Duke of Suffolk for "procure[ing] offices for persons who were unfit and unworthy of them and delay[ing] justice by stopping writs of appeal (private criminal prosecutions) for the deaths of complainants' husbands," and in 1642 against Sir Richard Burney, Lord Mayor of London, who "thwarted Parliament's order to store arms and ammunitions in storehouses;" and in 1660 against Viscount Mordaunt, who "prevented Tayleur from standing for election as a burgess to serve in Parliament, [and who] caused his illegal arrest and detention;" and against Chief Justice North "[who] assisted the Attorney General in drawing a proclamation to suppress petitions to the King to call a Parliament."[7]

Indeed, there is a broad consensus among constitutional scholars that the Framers chose the phrase "other high crimes or misdemeanors" as the basis for impeachable offenses because it was the term of art used in eighteenth-century England to refer specifically to "political crimes."[8] This phrase did not necessarily mean indictable criminal offenses but, rather, abuses of power or injuries to the State that could only be committed by public officials by virtue of the positions of power they held.[9] Thus, the English impeachment process treated "high crimes and misdemeanors [as] a category of political crimes against the state,"[10] with the critical showing of injury to the State required to prove that a "high crime" had been committed.[11] Impeachable conduct consisted of political offenses that caused injury to the state "in its political character" and "breach[ed] the public's trust."[12]

In the colonies, impeachment was intended to act as one of the many structural safeguards included in the national Constitution to ensure that the officers of the new federal government would act with integrity. The possibility of removal from office would guarantee that the president and other officials would remain honest, faithful to the law, and accountable to *the People*.[13] John Jay, one of the authors of the Federalist Papers—the series of essays written about the Constitution in 1787–88 immediately following its drafting at the 1787 Convention—states plainly that the Framers anticipated that the Constitution's structure would ensure that presidents and senators would live up to their expectations regarding truthfulness, accountability, trustworthiness, and honor:

> With respect to their responsibility, it is difficult to conceive how it could be increased. Every consideration that can influence the human mind, such as honor, oaths, reputations, conscience, the love of country, and family affections and attachments, afford security for their fidelity. In short, as the Constitution has taken care [by means of indirect elections] that they shall be men of talents, and integrity, we have reason to be persuaded that the treaties they make will be advantageous as, all circumstances considered, could be made; *and so far as the fear of punishment and disgrace can operate, that motive to good behavior is amply afforded by the article on the subject of impeachments.*[14]

The question of whether the impeachment process in America should be a political proceeding aimed at addressing executive misconduct in the nature of political offenses was debated both at the Constitutional Convention and at the subsequent state ratification conventions. The delegates spoke of impeachment as a remedy when an official "deviates from his duty" or "abuses the power vested in him by the people."[15]

This understanding drew on both the centuries of practice in England and the more recent practices in colonial America where the process was also a political one.[16]

History shows that the English concept of impeachment as a device intended to remedy momentous political offenses or serious injuries to the state made its way across the ocean with the Founders and was incorporated by the Framers into the laws of the new republic. According to Alexander Hamilton, impeachable offenses were considered to be those "which proceed from the misconduct of public men, or, in other words, from the abuse or violation of some public trust. They are of a nature which may with peculiar propriety be denominated Political, as they relate chiefly to injuries done immediately to society itself."[17] James Madison concurred with Hamilton's view, stating that impeachment was "indispensable" to protect the State from the "incapacity, negligence or perfidy to the chief Magistrate."[18] And Justice James Wilson, one of the fathers of the Constitution, confirmed this view, noting that "impeachments are confined to political characters, to political crimes and misdemeanors, and to political punishments."[19] Addressing both the nature of the offense and the proper sanction to be imposed upon conviction, Justice Joseph Story wrote that:

> the jurisdiction is to be exercised over offences, which are committed by public men in violation of their public trust and duties. Those duties are, in many cases, political. . . . Strictly speaking, then, the power partakes of a political character, as it respects injuries to society in its political character. . . . [Limiting] punishment to such modes of redress [as removal and disqualification], as are peculiarly fit for a political tribunal to administer [would] secure the public against political injuries.[20]

While the delegates to the conventions had this shared understanding of impeachment as a political proceeding and impeachable offenses as abuses of power that injured the State or the Constitution, the language they included in the state and federal constitutions did not identify a category of "great" offenses or "abuses of the State" that would constitute impeachment offenses.[21] Some participants, like Hamilton and Story, believed that creating such a category was simply not possible.

Justice Story thought that impeachable offenses would have to be decided on a case-by-case basis because, as he put it, "political offenses are of so various and complex a character, so utterly incapable of being defined or classified, that the task of positive legislation would be impracticable, if it were not almost absurd to attempt it."[22]

But there can be no question that under the conservative belief that judges must strictly interpret the Constitution based on the expressed intentions of the Framers, a president could be impeached for political reasons in addition to criminal actions.

## What Is Our Current Understanding of Impeachable Conduct?

The Framers provided no list of impeachable offenses. Instead, they left to each future Congress the task of determining what would constitute an impeachable offense based on the Framers' commentary, the republic's practices, and the judgment of the legislators. So, within the very broad boundaries set by the Framers, how *does* a contemporary Congress identify the political crimes that may constitute impeachable offenses?

Well, plainly, the Framers' inclusion of treason and bribery as grounds for impeachment was intended to deal with acts that undermine the government or our constitutional system. "Treason" is defined in the Constitution as "levying War against [the United States], or in adhering to their Enemies, giving them Aid and Comfort."[23] The essence of the offense of treason is the idea that the accused has betrayed his own people by making war or conspiring against them. "Bribery," too, involves a betrayal—of integrity and virtue—and a refusal to operate in the service of the best interests of the people. In both offenses then, the wrongdoer subverts the interests of the people who entrusted him with power to his own selfish interests, ignoring the duties with which he has been charged.

During the ratification debates concerns arose about how to protect the new republic against presidential behavior that might undermine the constitutional order by other, less drastic, and not necessarily criminal means. One delegate, George Mason, suggested adding the term "maladministration" to cover these types of political offenses.[24] But James Madison complained that this term was too vague and might put the president at the mercy of the Senate because of the broad swath of political action it would be able to overrule by threat of impeachment.[25] In response, Mason replaced the word "mal-administration" with the phrase "or other high crimes and misdemeanors against the state," and so the language of the clause was essentially set.[26]

With the written record of the debates, the evidence of historical practices, and the constitutional text to guide them, each Congress that has convened from 1787 until the present has formed and applied its own conception of impeachment. The factual historical record, together with the Founders' notion that the category of impeachable political offenses would be shaped by congressional judgments over time, has led to scholars' persistent efforts to divine impeachment trends by surveying Congress's impeachment decisions over the years.

According to Professor Michael Gerhardt, a leading constitutional scholar who has analyzed the history of the American impeachment process, there are several patterns evident in Congress's past impeachment proceedings. One is that "members of Congress, particularly in the Senate, have agreed with the view that impeachable offenses are not necessarily *indictable crimes* but, rather, are political crimes in which a critical element is serious injury to the political order or the constitutional system."[27] The principles are now widely accepted that an offense need not be a violation of criminal law at all in order for it to be properly impeachable under the Constitution, or that even when a crime has been committed it will not necessarily be deemed to warrant impeachment. As the famous constitutional law professor Laurence Tribe noted in the 1998 House Judiciary Hearing on the Background and History of Impeachment:

> A president who completely neglects his duties by showing up at work intoxicated every day, or by lounging on the beach rather than signing bills or delivering the State of the Union address, would be guilty of no crime but would certainly have committed an impeachable offense. Similarly, a president who had oral sex with his or her spouse in the Lincoln Bedroom prior to May 23, 1995 (the date on which the D.C. statute was repealed), or in a hotel room in Georgia,

Louisiana, or Virginia at any time, would be guilty of a felony but surely would have committed no impeachable offense.[28]

This pattern, identified by Gerhardt and Tribe, is visible in the historical record of House impeachments and Senate convictions and removals. Of the seventeen men impeached by the House, *only five* were impeached on grounds that constituted criminal offenses: Secretary of War William Belknap for accepting bribes; Judge Harry Claiborne for knowingly making false tax statements; Judge Alcee Hastings for conspiring to solicit a bribe and perjury; Judge Walter Nixon for committing perjury; and President William Clinton for perjury.[29] The other twelve proceedings were based on allegations of misuses of power that did not constitute federal criminal offenses.[30] Similarly, only three of the seven men who were actually convicted and removed by the Senate had been found guilty of indictable crimes: Judges Claiborne (income tax evasion), Hastings (bribery and perjury), and Nixon (making false statements to a grand jury).

Another pattern is also revealed by the historical record: that when Congress determines that an alleged crime reflects an egregious breach of the public trust, serious abuse of the privileges of office, significant disrespect for the constitutional system, or serious injury to the republic, the accused official is likely to be found to have committed misconduct meriting impeachment and removal.[31] Underlying this trend is the principle that impeachment and removal should occur when an official's misconduct is closely related to his formal duties and his misdeeds are fundamentally incompatible with the responsibilities of his office. This principle anchors the modern boundaries of the category of impeachable offenses in the Framers' notion that abuses of power constitute the type of political crimes warranting impeachment and removal from office. It also concomitantly illustrates the paradigmatic case for impeachment. The paradigm is well represented by the House of Representative's articles of impeachment filed against President Richard Nixon. The three charges—obstruction of justice, abuse of powers, and refusal to comply with a House subpoena for records—all stemmed from Nixon's misuse of the privileges of his office to undermine his political opponents and facilitate his reelection, and to thwart all attempts to investigate his misconduct.[32] Decisions by the House *not* to pursue impeachment in certain cases also lend support to this characterization of the paradigmatic case. So, for example, then Congressman

Gerald Ford's resolution intended to start an impeachment action against Justice William O. Douglas foundered because a majority of House members did not accept the idea that either the justice's lifestyle or the content of his judicial decisions constituted a proper subject for an impeachment inquiry. The House's decision not to impeach President Tyler for abusing his powers by refusing to divulge whom he was thinking of nominating for certain positions and by vetoing many different pieces of the opposing party's legislation, makes clear that erroneous policy judgments do not rise to the level of impeachable offenses. In the final analysis, the majority of the officials impeached by the House and convicted by the Senate were found to have breached the public trust by misusing their federal position, and in doing so seriously injured the republic.[33] Thus, while impeachment proceedings may begin with partisan accusations, the process has historically operated to reach and punish only those offenses that the Framers intended for it to reach.

In 1974, the House Judiciary Committee examined the history of federal impeachment proceedings and issued a report describing three categories of impeachable offenses.[34] The first included actions that involved exceeding or abusing the constitutional limits on the powers of the office at the expense of the powers of another branch of government.[35] The second included conduct that is fundamentally incompatible with the function and purpose of the office of the offender.[36] The third category covered actions that involved using the power and authority of the offender's office for an improper purpose or for personal gain.[37] The breadth of these categories illustrates the difficulty Congress would face if it attempted to define a limited set of impeachable offenses. Nevertheless, the three categories cover the quintessential misdeeds considered impeachable by the Framers, because such acts subvert the constitutional structure of the federal government, the process of government, and the country's faith in the integrity of leadership.

## Just How Broad Is Congress's Impeachment Authority?

Without a codified list of impeachable offenses, Congress has complete discretion in defining what constitutes impeachable conduct. Gerald Ford's famous pronouncement in the impeachment proceedings brought against Supreme Court Justice William O. Douglas, that an impeachable offense "is whatever a majority of the House [considers it] to be at any given moment in history,"[38] may reflect the practical reality of the impeachment process, even though it ignores the role of history and precedent in influencing Congress's actions.[39]

The power of the House of Representatives to decide for itself what kinds of conduct should lead to an impeachment proceeding is even more awesome than it first appears because Congress's actions in this process are not reviewable by any other branch of government. Unlike almost any other legislative action, impeachment is not subject to presidential veto or judicial review.[40] Congress's decision is final.

Why is this worth mentioning? Because the impeachment clause is one of the cornerstones of the Constitution's architecture; it embodies a key feature of our form of government: the balancing of the branches. The correct calibration of that balance means that we can rely upon the government to defend the rights of individuals, while an incorrect one may move the nation closer either "to an imperial presidency or to parliamentary system."[41] It is up to Congress to keep the balance true.

Justice Story characterized the English practice of impeachment, noting that: "Lord chancellors and judges and other magistrates have not only been impeached for bribery, and acting grossly contrary to the duties of their office, but for misleading the sovereign by unconstitutional opinions and for attempts to subvert the fundamental laws and introduce arbitrary power."[42] This notion of impeachment has survived until today and takes on even greater relevance in the context of President Bush's unilateral declaration of a "war on terror" and his assertion of powers beyond those constitutionally granted to the office of the presidency.

With the president claiming that his role as commander in chief, combined with a supposed war without end, trumps the traditional constitutional division of power among the three branches by putting him at the "zenith" of his powers, it is clearly time for Congress to recalibrate the balance of power.

# FOUR

# *Impeachment, Trial, and Removal*

## *How Do We Impeach a President Today?*

Although "impeachment" begins with the commencement of a House of Representatives inquiry regarding the conduct of a public officer, most people today use the term to refer to the whole, complex set of steps and procedures undertaken by Congress from the initial investigation in the House Judiciary Committee to the full-blown trial in the Senate. The Constitution itself sets forth the basic framework for the process: The House of Representatives has the power to indict, and a majority vote of the House on any charge (an article of impeachment) is enough to place the accused official on trial.[1] The trial of the impeached official is held in the Senate; a two-thirds majority is required to convict.[2] If convicted, the officer is removed from office, and, if the Senate chooses to do so, the officer may also be disqualified from any future office of "honor, trust, or profit under the United States."[3]

The impeachment process is guided by a 140-year-old set of rules, compiled from rulings in the more than fourteen Senate impeachment trials held, and the decisions and judgments made by the one hundred members of the Senate and the Chief Justice of the Supreme Court who sits as the presiding officer at the trial. Detailed impeachment rules were drafted for the first time in 1868 for the trial of President Andrew Johnson and were later revised in 1974 in anticipation of the impeachment trial of President Nixon.[4] This set of rules was formally adopted in 1986, when the Senate was preparing for the impeachment of Judge Harry Claiborne. In addition to these rules, both the House and the Senate set rules (by resolution) for each specific impeachment trial.[5]

In a nutshell, the process in Congress actually looks like this: The House Judiciary Committee deliberates over whether to initiate an impeachment inquiry, and adopts a resolution seeking authority from the entire House. After debate, a majority vote of the House approving the resolution is required. The Judiciary Committee then conducts its impeachment inquiry, sometimes by means of public hearings, and if warranted, prepares the articles of impeachment. After a majority of the Committee approves the articles, the House of Representatives as a whole considers and debates them. Once a majority vote of the House approves a single article of impeachment, the president is technically "impeached," meaning that he is subject to trial in the Senate. President Richard Nixon resigned after the House Judiciary Committee voted to recommend impeachment, but before the full House could act. History will thus record the end of Nixon's term as a resignation; he was never "impeached" by the House.

At the trial, the Senate sits as a jury with the chief justice presiding, ruling on all questions of evidence. Unlike the situation in a normal court of law, however, the Senate can reverse a ruling made by the presiding officer by a majority vote. During the trial, the Senate debates and votes on any motions made by the two sides—the House impeachment managers and the president and his defense team—regarding the evidence to be presented and the procedures to be used. The House then makes its presentation in support of the articles of impeachment and the president's presentation follows. The Senate is permitted to question both sides. At the conclusion of this inquiry, any motion to dismiss will be argued. During this phase of the trial, both the House side and the president may call witnesses to testify and present evidence. Under the questioning procedure used in the trial, senators may pose questions to the thirteen House managers, the White House lawyers, or any potential witnesses, but only in writing. The questions are delivered by a page to the chief justice, who, under the rules, is required to ask whatever questions the senators pose, but who may not pose questions himself. The senators' questions are subject to objection by the lawyers and under recent rules to objections by other senators as well. If the Senate does not dismiss the case, the two sides then proceed to present their full case at trial.

During the trial, the senators, unlike jurors in an ordinary trial, are not prohibited from reading newspapers, listening to the media, or discussing the case. In fact, there are no written rules of evidence which guide the trial; the senators are instead expected to rely upon their knowledge of the federal rules of evidence, common law principles, and the rules developed in past impeachment trials. Nor are the senators required to weigh the evidence presented against any particular burden of proof such as "preponderance of the evidence" or "reasonable doubt." Although the lawyers for Judge Claiborne argued that the House managers should be required to prove their guilt "beyond a reasonable doubt," the Senate rejected that motion in Judge Claiborne's trial. To date, it appears that no definitive rule has been set adopting a particular standard for the determination of guilt.

The jury of the Senate deliberates behind closed doors. At the end of the deliberations, the senators vote on each article of impeachment. If the accused is found guilty by a two-thirds vote of the Senate of the acts alleged in any article, then upon the pronouncement of the judgment, he automatically ceases to hold office. A bar from holding any office in the future is also within the Senate's discretion.[6]

## Some Thoughts About Why the Process Might Be Structured This Way

First, the Framers plainly vested the impeachment power in Congress, rather than in the Supreme Court, because they undoubtedly wanted to ensure a measure of accountability to *the People*. The need to make sure that a political body close to *the ordinary citizens* would be intimately involved in the process is likely the reason that the House of Representatives (where all representatives face the electorate every two years) was included in the impeachment plan from the beginning of the discussions at the Constitutional Convention.[7] Indeed, Alexander Hamilton, describing the House of Representatives' responsibilities in the impeachment process, stated that House members were the "representatives of the people, [the] accusers."[8]

The concern over ensuring accountability to the broader public, and not just to the political establishment, has gained in importance as the independence of the electoral college declines and the presidency becomes more of a populist institution than it had been in an earlier era. The dilemma is that Congress is required to take *the People*'s voice into consideration, while rendering a decision to remove a president that those same people chose, which would seem to directly unravel the people's choice. Yet, conversely, Congress's failure to consider a public clamor for the removal of a president would equally undermine the constitutional process. "Grand juries and prosecutors (the House in this context), as well as judges and juries (the Senate), are all supposed to discharge their duties consistent with the public interest."[9]

Second, the Framers injected the strong constitutional preference for the status quo into the impeachment design, to be relied upon, of course, only if the status quo was legitimate from the outset. Thus, presidents who have prevailed in honest and uncontested elections have traditionally been seen as having a strong claim to legitimacy. And this legitimacy has "grown stronger as the role of the People in directly electing their President has itself grown."[10] For these reasons, the impeachment process was also designed to favor the status quo. The two-thirds supermajority requirement for conviction by the Senate jury provides significant protection for the president; and a failure to convict, even if it is by the slimmest margin below the two thirds requirement, ends the matter completely. There is no opportunity for retrial as there is in the criminal context, where, when the jury as a whole cannot agree on a result a hung jury is called, and the case may be retried. So, for example, in the impeachment context, when fewer than sixty-seven Senators vote to convict, the impeached person is acquitted, even though only thirty-four senators may have voted to acquit. Nor can a trial be commenced by another sovereign in the impeachment context, as is possible with state and federal criminal prosecutions. The supermajority requirement has been in place from the beginning of the republic to the Senate's most recent pronouncement that it had acquitted Bill Clinton.

Interestingly, contrary to ultra-right-wing pundit Ann Coulter's observations about the impeachment process, which she suggests mandates impeachment after the House investigation is complete no matter how minor the transgression, the text of Article I of the Constitution makes clear that the House is not obligated to impeach nor is the Senate obligated to convict, even if there is conduct that may constitute "high crimes and misdemeanors."[11] The language of the Constitution speaks only of the powers that the two houses of the legislature have; it says nothing of their duty to enforce them in a particular manner.[12] According to a well-respected constitutional scholar, the manner in which other congressional powers are constitutionally conferred and interpreted—such as the power to regulate interstate commerce—leads to the conclusion that the House and Senate have considerable discretion where impeachment is concerned. The House, for instance, has the discretion to decide whether or not to prosecute all high crimes and misdemeanors. The Senate, for its part, has the authority to not try all of the cases that the House places before it.[13] Furthermore, the Constitution does not prevent the congressional prosecutors from using their discretion to offer the accused a plea bargain. As long as the congressional offer of conditional amnesty constitutes an exercise of mercy and not the imposition of punishment, it is not forbidden by the Constitution's Bill of Attainder provision.* A congressional or one-house censure of the President—such as that currently proposed by House Judiciary Committee Minority Leader Representative John Conyers (D-MI)—or a publication of the Senate's findings of fact would likely fall in this category.[14]

## So What Have Impeachment Proceedings Actually Looked Like?

Impeachment proceedings appear to be as varied as the times and the individuals involved in them. President Andrew Johnson's confronta-

---

*Bills of attainder are laws enacted specifically to punish specific individuals. Only those bills with punitive ends, rather than merciful ones, are forbidden under Bill of Attainder jurisprudence.

tion with the Radical Republican–controlled Congress in 1868 reflected a partisan battle over a substantive policy issue: the Reconstruction plans for the Confederate states.[15] The Radical Republicans favored a strong plan for rehabilitation and pushed vigorously for all seceded states to mandate black suffrage. In contrast, Johnson's plans for organizing the new governments of seceded states included backing individuals for office who had supported the Confederacy. Many of these officials in turn pushed through legislation intended to impose prohibitions on blacks so that they could not rent land or give testimony against whites in court.[16] Johnson's position became clearer when he vetoed the Civil Rights Act of 1866, which acknowledged the rights of blacks to hold national citizenship, to acquire property, and make contracts. When both houses of Congress overrode the veto, the die was cast. Johnson's subsequent opposition to the Fourteenth Amendment—which provides that a state cannot deny to any person the equal protection of the laws, nor deprive any person of life, liberty, or property without due process of law—further widened the divide. By the fall of 1866, when the congressional elections put the Republicans in control of both houses, with the ability to override any presidential veto, talk had already begun of impeachment.[17]

To the dismay of the Radicals, the Judiciary Committee's investigation proceeded very slowly, spanning the terms of two Congresses. By the time that the Judiciary Committee's report came before the entire House for debate and vote in December 1867, Congress had passed over Johnson's veto a number of laws designed to circumscribe the power of the president. Despite this wide gap, however, the December 1867 motion to impeach Johnson failed. A second effort by the House succeeded only after Johnson unilaterally removed Edwin Stanton, Secretary of the War Department, which angered many in the Senate. After Johnson had a note delivered to Stanton stating that he was being removed from the Cabinet, the Senate advised Stanton to hold his ground. While Stanton barricaded himself in his office, the House Reconstruction Committee reported the Impeachment Resolution to the full House for debate. The resolution that the House passed stated only the following: "Resolved, That Andrew Johnson, President of the United States, be impeached of high crimes and misdemeanors in office."[18] The eleven articles of impeachment reported to the House were all—save three—based upon Johnson's removal of Stanton from his cabinet post. And even those three related to Johnson's removal decision: the first alleging that Johnson's appointment of an interim Secretary of War was a high misdemeanor; the second criticizing Johnson's conversation with a military officer about the constitutionality of a bill provision which limited the president's removal power;[19] and the third seeking Johnson's removal for making disparaging public statements about members of Congress and Congress as a whole in various speeches.[20]

By all accounts, the Senate trial was a painfully long proceeding. Closing arguments alone on each side lasted for three days. The critical question seems to have been whether the president had a right to have the constitutionality of an act determined by the courts—the Tenure of Office Act, which was enacted to prevent Johnson from removing people from offices for which Senate confirmation was required for appointment.[21] In the end, the roll was called for votes only on three of the eleven articles, and after it was clear that conviction had not been carried on these, a motion to adjourn the session of the Senate sitting as a court of impeachment was carried.[22] Impeachment scholars now seem of the mind that it would have been an extraordinary act "to remove from office a president who violated a law when the meaning of the law [w]as at best ambiguous, and when his Cabinet had unanimously advised him that it was unconstitutional."[23]

The next in line to be considered for impeachment after Andrew Johnson was Richard Nixon. The House investigation, in October 1973, commenced its investigation of whether Nixon should be impeached, but the precipitating events began the year before, just prior to the Democratic Convention, when burglars broke into the headquarters of the Democratic National Committee located in the Watergate complex in Washington, D.C. At first it was seen as a two-bit break-in of no political consequence. But that changed dramatically when one of the perpetrators of the burglary, James McCord, the Security Coordinator for the Committee to Re-elect the President, was implicated in the plan to bug the Democratic Committee offices. When it became apparent that the Republican Party and White House staff had actively sought to frustrate the investigation, fearful it would involve President Nixon, the impeachment train began gathering speed. After testimony in a Senate inquiry revealed that Nixon had secretly recorded all conversations in the presidential offices, a special Justice Department prosecutor subpoenaed the tapes.[24] The tipping point was reached when Nixon refused to produce the tapes, claiming they were protected by executive privilege, and then preceded to fire the special prosecutor. The articles of impeachment included, among others, a count based on Nixon's obstruction of the investigation of the burglary, his refusal to honor the subpoenas issued by the Judiciary Committee, his abuse of power in ordering the Internal Revenue Service to audit the tax returns of his enemies, and the false statements he made to Congress about the bombing of Cambodia during the Vietnam War.[25] Before the Judiciary Committee could make its report to the House, the Supreme Court determined that the special prosecutor was entitled to access to the White House tapes. When the tapes were turned over, one recording provided strong evidence concerning the obstruction of justice charge. Within four days of the publication of the contents of the tape, Nixon resigned.

## What Are Considered Truly Impeachable Offenses in the Twenty-first Century?

History has made clear that even where there may have been partisan manipulation of the impeachment process—the prospect of which greatly concerned the Framers*—the constitutional penalty of removal from office generally has not been carried out unless the misconduct involved a grave breach of official duties or a serious abuse of power. The evidence is incontrovertible that the Framers viewed impeachment as a

---

*In *The Federalist* No. 65, Alexander Hamilton wrote that "There will always be the greatest danger that the decision [to impeach] will be regulated more by the comparative strength of the parties than by the real demonstration of innocence or guilt." *The Federalist* No. 65, 396–97 (Alexander Hamilton) (Clinton Rossiter ed., 1961). Hamilton abhorred "the demon of faction" and the Framers were concerned that the impeachment process might be dominated by "faction" and thus deny the process legitimacy (ibid., 401).

remedy for momentous offenses against the Constitution, "great injuries" to the state,[26] or "formidable abuses of official authority."[27]

So, while a president's misdeeds in his private life might be disgraceful—and perhaps even a cause for national embarrassment—they generally have not been found to be impeachable offenses. For example, even though strong evidence was presented in 1974 that President Richard Nixon had participated in the backdating of documents that resulted in tax fraud, the House Judiciary Committee dropped the charge on the ground that this type of personal misconduct was not an impeachable offense, because it did not involve a political offense against the state. According to the House Committee report, "tax fraud . . . was not the type of abuse of power at which the remedy of impeachment is directed."[28] Of course, there are instances of wholly private misconduct that Congress would most definitely find rising to the constitutional level of impeachable offenses, because such acts—like murder, for instance—would make the president's "continuance in office dangerous to the public order."[29]

How consistent has Congress been in drawing the lines between impeachable and nonimpeachable *private* conduct? Not very. The Democratically controlled House of Representatives in 1974 held that President Nixon's lies on his tax documents were not impeachable offenses because they involved neither an abuse of executive power nor a violation of the Take Care Clause of the Constitution,[30] the provision requiring the president to "take Care that the Laws be faithfully executed."[31] In President Clinton's case, however, the Republican-run House of Representatives in 1999 determined that the president's lies about his sex life in order to hide personal misconduct indeed constituted impeachable offenses. Surely this was not what the Framers meant when they referred in the Constitution to "Treason, Bribery, or other high Crimes and Misdemeanors."[32] That is not to say, of course, that there are not some lies—such as lying about whether the United States is bombing another country—that would constitute a serious abuse of office and therefore likely be considered an impeachable offense, but failing to confess to your staff or the public that you had an inappropriate liaison with an intern does not threaten to undermine the constitutional scheme of the country.

So, one president's public lie about his personal misbehavior was deemed an impeachable offense while another's was not, even though neither act of misconduct involved an official action that constituted either a serious abuse of the power of the office or a grave breach of official duties. What explains the drastically different treatment afforded President Clinton? Experts have offered many different theories, including the degree of partisan politics, personal dislike of President Clinton by key members of Congress, or the moral offense taken by certain officials.[33] Citing the fact that the independent counsel's charges all derived entirely from the president's lies about his sexual escapades with Monica Lewinsky, constitutional law experts and political analysts have expressed the concern that the Clinton impeachment proceedings "trivialized" the impeachment process and implicitly rejected the standard set by the Framers.[34]

The difficulty we have in identifying an objective basis for treating so differently these two instances of private presidential misconduct is enhanced by Congress's action—or rather its *inaction*—in the face of President Ronald Reagan's role in the Iran-Contra affair. On November 6, 1986, President Reagan publicly denied the existence of the arms for hostages deal, stating that the story of the trade "has no foundation."[35] Eight days later, Reagan again called the story "utterly false" and firmly stated that "We did not—repeat—did not trade weapons or anything else for hostages."[36] These patent lies plainly were an integral part of his official duties, not his private business.

The Iran-Contra affair was in fact the product of two foreign policy directives issued by President Reagan that were specifically intended to evade the law, and that were implemented by the NSC staff.[37] Officials high in the CIA, the State Department, and the Department of Defense also knew about and supported the scheme. In October 1984, Congress had passed the Boland Amendment, which banned the use of appropriated funds to support the Contras. The Reagan administration's two secret policies were designed to circumvent Congress and the law by selling arms to Iran in order to procure the release of American hostages, and equally important, to use the proceeds to keep the Contras in operation.[38] The thought was that any post-Watergate rules governing the conduct of national security agents would not apply if the agents were participating in a private operation supported by privately generated funds.[39] More significantly, this process was intended to—and did—successfully evade legislative oversight and control. Congress's appropriation restrictions were circumvented while Congress continued to believe that the administration was following the law. And after the affair was revealed, the Reagan administration undermined many congressional inquiries "through false testimony and the destruction and concealment of government records,"[40] in addition to pre-issuing pardons to participants. Yet somehow, despite President Reagan's extreme dereliction of his executive responsibility,[41] his deliberate decision to undermine the legislative branch and defy Congress's appropriations restrictions, and his ordering of the destruction and concealment of government records and information regarding the executive's clandestine activities throughout the entirety of the investigation, only one member of Congress stood up and made the call for impeachment.

How does impeachment affect our view of the political process? What is the legacy of an impeachment? Bill Clinton was the first elected president to be impeached, tried, and then acquitted by the Senate of charges arising from the scandal surrounding his adultery. Although it is too early for us to claim an historical perspective, it seems clear that the episode revealed a continuing problem in our political culture: the inability to forge a compromise. That the process was taken so far in order to address what was essentially a private moral failing is disturbing. What does it say about our national government that the people comprising it could not work together to address problems that arose from an individual's personal weakness? The bitter partisan atmosphere in the House and Senate created the current that powered a runaway train, and seemingly nothing could be done to stop it. How important is the Clinton impeachment incident in terms of affecting the strength of the office of the presidency? Experts seem to agree that there is not likely to be any long-term diminishment of presidential authority in the eyes of either the American public or the nations of the world. Indeed, presidential historians Doris Kearns Goodwin and Michael Beschloss have opined that the stain of impeachment proceedings becomes attached to the accused individual rather than the office, and that the process does not affect the power of the office.[42]

The results of the Clinton impeachment trial likely attest to both the popularity of the president at the time of trial and the fact that the senators sitting in judgment felt that the Framers' vision was not one in which a president should be removed for an insubstantial offense or a mistake of judgment. But what would history make of a president who, rather than merely exhibiting human frailties, violates the highest level of public trust? How should we—*the People*—view a chief executive who has violated the Geneva Conventions, a treaty signed and ratified by the United States, by compelling our participation in a war of unprovoked aggression? How should we view a chief executive whose administration expressly authorized the use of indefinite detention and torture on people in military custody in violation of both the Constitution, and military laws, including those embodying treaties adopted by the United States and the community of nations to prevent any repeat of the barbarous acts committed in the two World Wars? How should we view a president who authorized intelligence agencies to create secret prisons beyond the law to conceal the government's actions from public scrutiny and to escape evaluation by our nation's courts, and who authorized the seizure and incommunicado detention of American citizens for years without charge or access to a court? And how should we view a president who specifically authorized the violation of a law (ironically designed to *facilitate* the authorization of government surveillance of foreign intelligence activities) in order to permit an agency to spy on the protected political activities of Americans?

## What Can We Glean from Our Impeachment History?

Our current concept of impeachment has been shaped by its history as a part of our legal inheritance from Great Britain, by the Framers' effort to distinguish American democracy from the British parliamentary monarchy, and by Congress's interpretation of the grounds for removal from office spelled out in the Constitution. Thus, eighteenth-century discussions regarding the meaning of words considered for, and ultimately used in, the impeachment provisions of the Constitution portray only a tiny part of the much larger debates of that time. To truly under-stand the nature of the process and its intended use, we need to look at where impeachment fits within the broader constitutional scheme.

The impeachment process was plainly intended to assist in main-taining the balance of power among the three coequal branches of gov-ernment. Its use requires careful consideration. We risk creating a dangerous precedent if we invoke the process too readily. If we lower the threshold of conduct that constitutes impeachable offenses, we could end up with something more like the parliamentary system, in which the president would serve at the pleasure of Congress. A system in which a weak president could easily be recalled by Congress would threaten the separation of powers principle, a key cornerstone of our democracy.

Similarly, a system in which a weak Congress failed to impeach a president who was abusing his power would also threaten the separa-tion of powers principle. Furthermore, each of these opposing dangers would be heightened if the impeachment process were to become solely a partisan tool.[43] For these reasons scholars, from the Framers them-selves to contemporary constitutional law experts, have admonished us—*the People*—to make sure that when Congress invokes (or fails to invoke) the Impeachment Clause, it does so with a sense of great re-sponsibility and with the awareness that its decisions will set precedents for future cases that will affect the balance of powers among the three branches of government and ultimately the vitality of the democratic principles and moral values embedded in our Constitution.

In the following chapters, we will look at the impeachable crimes of President George W. Bush and his administration. It is our contention that these crimes, transgressions and abuses of power rise above the common fray of political dispute, meet the standards which the Found-ers had in mind as they wrote Article II of the Constitution, and cry out for the men and women of principle in the House to act. And we—the *People*—must make sure this happens.

# FIVE

## *Deadly Lies and an Illegal War*

ARTICLE I: In his conduct of the office of President of the United States, George W. Bush, contrary to his oath faithfully to execute the office of the President of the United States, and to the best of his ability preserve, protect, and defend the Constitution of the United States, and in violation of his constitutional duty to take care that the laws be faithfully executed, acting without a specific authorization from Congress as required under Article II of the Constitution and under the terms of the War Powers Act, did order the U.S. military to invade the nation of Iraq. The President and his agents made false and misleading statements to Congress and to the people of the United States for the purpose of deceiving them into believing that a war against Iraq was urgent and necessary and that Iraq had weapons capable of striking and causing serious death and damage in the United States.

> My fellow citizens, at this hour, American and coalition forces are in the early stages of military operations to disarm Iraq, to free its people and to defend the world from grave danger.
>
> On my orders, coalition forces have begun striking selected targets of military importance to undermine Saddam Hussein's ability to wage war.
>
> —*President George W. Bush, announcing the start of the American invasion of Iraq*

THERE WERE two disturbing things about the opening two sentences of President Bush's March 19, 2003, address to the nation announcing the start of the U.S. invasion of Iraq. First was his enormous lie that the purpose of the invasion was "to defend the world from grave danger," for it was already clear to most of the world that Iraq wasn't even a threat to its neighbors, much less to the United States. This lie was the last in a long string of lies and dissembling regarding Iraq's alleged weapons of mass destruction and Saddam Hussein's alleged links to Al Qaeda terrorists, which the administration fed to friendly journalists at venues like *The New York Times* and Fox TV, repeated on conservative talk shows, and testified about in Congress. Second was his factually correct statement that it was on *his* orders the invasion had begun. The problem is that under the Constitution it is Congress, not the president, who is supposed to decide to go to war, and there remains a major question as to whether there ever was a congressional authorization for this attack. This is because when Congress gave Bush the authority to "use force" against Iraq in October 2002, many members had assumed he would get approval from the United Nations before any invasion. The president never received, or even seriously sought, such approval. Both of these matters are potentially impeachable offenses.

## *A War Based Upon Lies*

There is no decision the leader of a country can make that is more deadly, expensive, and far-reaching than to send a nation and its young men and women into war.

A generation ago, in Indochina, America learned the price that is to be paid when instead of openly presenting and arguing the case for war to the American people and to Congress, a series of administrations puts the country at war through deception and then keeps enlarging the conflict, at ever higher cost in both money and blood. In the end, the American people rebelled against that war, demanding an end to a conflict they never really understood or wanted in the first place, and the United States suffered its first major defeat in history. The Bush administration, only twenty-five years after the Vietnam debacle, forgot that lesson and, obsessed with a desire to attack Iraq, used lies and deceit to start another seemingly endless war, at terrible cost to the nation.

The Iraqi adventure is not the first war to be started with the help of White House lies. Lyndon Johnson used a lie that a U.S. destroyer innocently sailing in the Gulf of Tonkin, the *Maddox,* had been attacked by North Vietnamese gunboats, as a pretext for escalating what had been a relatively limited defense of South Vietnam into what became a full-scale war against the Communist North. The truth, as revealed in the Pentagon Papers and more recently in new documents released from the National Archives, was that first of all the *Maddox* was hardly innocent. It had been operating for some time inside North Vietnamese territorial waters and had been provocatively shelling Vietnamese boats and shore installations. Moreover, it never was actually attacked by Vietnamese torpedo boats as claimed. The whole incident, which sparked a war that ended up killing millions of Vietnamese and over 58,000 American troops, had been based upon a faked report.

In the case of the first Gulf War, the administration of George H. W. Bush ginned up stories of atrocities allegedly committed by Iraqi forces in Kuwait—most notably the supposed dumping of dozens of premature infants from incubators in Kuwaiti hospitals—when in truth it knew no such thing had happened (an ad agency with close ties to Bush had gotten the fifteen-year-old daughter of the Kuwaiti U.S. ambassador to pose as a witness to the alleged atrocity).[1] The Bush Pentagon also warned that Iraq would use massive air-fuel bombs to attack American forces—exactly the same bombs we later used in that conflict. The first Bush administration, in making its bid for a war resolution, also failed to mention to Congress that a central grievance of Iraq's was a claim that Kuwait was slant drilling from its territory to steal from oil deposits that were actually well inside Iraq. As well, the first Bush kept to himself information that his own state department had twice hinted to Iraqi diplomats that the United States would not respond militarily if Iraq moved into Kuwait over the drilling issue.

These were all serious deceptions, with serious ramifications, and both Bushes, father and son, set a terrible precedent by lying to Congress about inducing the country into war. In fact, the late Rep. Henry Gonzalez (D-TX) was so outraged at the highly controversial Gulf War that he filed an impeachment resolution in the House. In the patriotic fervor of the moment, with U.S. soldiers marching into battle across the Saudi border, Gonzalez's resolution died. But nothing the first Bush's administration concocted compares to the lying of the current administration, an extraordinary propaganda effort designed to gain public and congressional support for an outright invasion, conquest, and long-term occupation of Iraq. Representative Gonzalez retired from the House in 1998, and died in November 2000, in the midst of the battle over the Bush-Gore presidential election results. So far, none of his old Democratic colleagues or his successors in the House has had the courage to take the step he took in 1991.

## *Making War*

Within hours of the 9/11 attacks on the World Trade Center and the Pentagon, the Bush administration began behind-the-scenes planning to launch a war against Iraq. Their true objective had nothing to do with tracking down and killing the terrorists responsible for the attacks; instead it was aimed at "regime change"—the overthrow of dictator Saddam Hussein.

There was absolutely no evidence linking Iraq to the September 2001 attacks. Not one of the nineteen hijackers of the four planes, or even of the people in Al Qaeda identified as having organized their elaborate project, was Iraqi. That didn't matter to President Bush, Vice President Cheney, or Defense Secretary Rumsfeld, as they immediately began looking for ways to expand their military response to the events to include not just Afghanistan, where Al Qaeda's leaders were hiding, but also Iraq.

Richard Clarke, then head of the National Security Council's counterterrorism program, remembers being called into a meeting with Bush the day after the attack. During that meeting the president made it clear to him that he wanted Clarke and others to find a link to Iraq.[2] Within days Rumsfeld ordered his generals to began preparations for an attack on Iraq. Later, as the war in Afghanistan was being fought, and the pursuit of the Al Qaeda leadership was beginning to achieve results, General Tommy Franks found himself being handicapped in that campaign by the Pentagon's decision to begin pulling troops and equipment out of that country and moving them to staging areas around Iraq.

None of this maneuvering toward a war against Iraq during late 2001 and early 2002 was known to the American public or to Congress, who were still being assured that there was an all-out campaign to get Osama bin Laden, as Bush put it in his faux cowboy lingo, "dead or alive."

In fact, Afghanistan was never the Bush administration's primary target. The target was Iraq. Bob Woodward, who had been granted extraordinary access to Bush and other administration officials following 9/11, recounted in a CBS *60 Minutes* interview:

There's this low boil on Iraq until the day before Thanksgiving, November 21, 2001. This is seventy-two days after 9/11. This is part of the secret story. President Bush, after a National Security Council meeting, takes Don Rumsfeld aside, collars him physically, and takes him into a little cubbyhole room and closes the door and says, "What have you got in terms of plans for Iraq? What is the status of the war plan? I want you to get on it. I want you to keep it secret."

Six days after the president's request for the Iraq war plan, Rumsfeld flew to see General Tommy Franks at CENTCOM [central command] headquarters in Tampa.

"Pull the Iraq planning out and let's see where we are," Rumsfeld told Franks when they were alone. . . .

"Let's put together a group that can just think outside the box completely," Rumsfeld ordered.[3]

But this plan to attack Iraq had to be kept secret, not just from Saddam Hussein, but from the American public, the media, and the Congress. As General Franks writes in his book *American Soldier,* when he next met with Rumsfeld, on December 12, 2001, to report on his plan for war with Iraq, Rumsfeld's big concern was secrecy:

"General Franks," Rumsfeld asked when I'd completed the briefing, "what's next?"

Aware that we might move from the conceptual to the practical at any time, I chose my words carefully. "Mr. Secretary," I said, "we want to begin now to improve our force posture in the region."

"How visible will these activities be?" Rumsfeld asked.

"Mr. Secretary, the troop increases in Kuwait will be seen as training exercises, and we can time the carrier cruises to draw minimum attention. I don't envision any CNN moments, but there is no guarantee."[4]

That buildup proceeded apace, and took an obvious toll on the effectiveness of the Afghanistan campaign. In early 2002, the Pentagon reportedly pulled the Fifth Special Forces Group out of Afghanistan and sent it to Iraq—a major blow to the pursuit of bin Laden, since members of that unit, unique in the U.S. military, spoke Arabic, Pashto, and Dari, and, after operating in Afghanistan for half a year had developed a network of sources and allegiances with local groups—the kinds of contacts that could really prove invaluable in tracking down Al Qaeda leaders. The unit's transfer signaled a significant downgrading of the campaign to snare bin Laden. This decision has been singled out by retired Florida Senator Bob Graham, who at the time was chairman of the

Senate Intelligence Committee, as an impeachable offense by the president. As Graham emphasized in his book *Intelligence Matters*, this decision was made "in spite of the specific congressional authority the President had sought and received to conduct war on al-Qaeda and the Afghanistan government."[5]

All the while, even as the War in Afghanistan and the hunt for bin Laden were being quietly wound down, the administration and the Pentagon continued to deny that there was a plan for war against Iraq. At a press briefing at the Pentagon on March 29, 2002, when General Franks was asked if men and materiel were being pre-positioned for a war against Iraq, he said flatly, "No. We have not—we have not positioned assets in any region in anticipation of an action any place, with the exception of what we have talked about in Yemen, in terms of providing support to President Ali Abdullah Saleh in his efforts to reduce terrorism inside Yemen."

It was a blatant lie. By September 2002, one full year after the 9/11 attacks, bin Laden was still free and sending taunting messages to Bush, the pressure on him had eased up, and the Taliban were regrouping. But the United States had positioned nearly 50,000 troops and a complete command structure in Saudi Arabia, Bahrain, Kuwait, and the Kurdish areas of Northern Iraq. The administration was actively planning and preparing for a new and much bigger and more complex war, but the nation was not being told about what was in store.

### Fixing the Facts Around the Policy: The Downing Street Memo

As it turns out, by the summer of 2002, the Bush administration and the Pentagon were way past the point of no return in planning an invasion. In May 2005, the *Sunday Times* of London published an internal memorandum dated July 23, 2002, from Matthew Rycroft, a foreign policy aide to Tony Blair, British prime minister, to Blair's chief foreign policy adviser David Manning (the U.K. equivalent to then National Security Adviser Condoleezza Rice). (See appendix A—Downing Street Memo.) This document recounted a visit to the White House by "C," the code name for Sir Richard Dearlove, the head of Britain's spy agency, MI6, which included a lengthy private meeting between Dearlove and his U.S. counterpart, CIA Director George Tenet.

The memo, classified as "secret," and "extremely sensitive," caused a scandal in Britain but initially was ignored by the U.S. media. The document made it clear that Dearlove, fresh from meeting with high-ranking administration officials, was convinced that Bush had already decided to invade Iraq, and that if necessary the American government would "fix" the intelligence and the facts as needed to get there. As the memo related, Dearlove had found in Washington

> a perceptible shift in attitude. Military action was now seen as in-evitable. Bush wanted to remove Saddam, through military action, justified by the conjunction of terrorism and WMD. But the intelli-gence and facts were being fixed around the policy. The NSC had no patience with the UN route, and no enthusiasm for publishing mate-rial on the Iraqi regime's record. There was little discussion in Wash-ington of the aftermath after military action.[6]

Lending credence to the authenticity of both the memo (which was never challenged by Downing Street) and the accuracy of Dearlove's rec-ollections of his White House meeting, was the report that

> the Defense Secretary [Rumsfeld] said that the U.S. had already begun "spikes of activity" to put pressure on the regime. No decisions had been taken, but he thought the most likely timing in U.S. minds for military action to begin was January, with the timeline beginning 30 days before the U.S. congressional elections.

The terminology "spikes of activity" had been used by Rumsfeld in the account General Franks gave of his conversation with Rumsfeld in talking about the buildup of U.S. forces in the Gulf region.[7]

The Downing Street memo went on to make it clear that despite what Bush, Cheney, and Rumsfeld were telling the American public, members of Congress, and the world at large about wanting to answer peacefully the question of whether or not Saddam Hussein possessed weapons of mass destruction, the White House had already decided on war, and knew that the reasons being given for attacking Iraq were being hyped or "fixed." It also suggested that—as later came to pass—an ultimatum could be made to Saddam Hussein to allow WMD inspectors back in, as a way to create a justification for an invasion. As the memo recounts, Dearlove said:

> it seemed clear that Bush had made up his mind to take military action, even if the timing was not yet decided. But the case was thin. Saddam was not threatening his neighbors, and his WMD capability was less than that of Libya, North Korea, or Iran. We should work up a plan for an ultimatum to Saddam to allow back in the UN weapons inspectors. This would also help with the legal justification for the use of force.

In late January 2006, the *Guardian* newspaper in the United Kingdom obtained another damning memo, initially discovered by Phillipe Sands, a professor of international law at University College of London. This memo, a summation of a two-hour meeting between Prime Minister Blair and President Bush at the White House on January 31, 2003, reveals that Bush told Blair the United States planned to invade Iraq, whether or not it got a second resolution endorsing an invasion by the United Nations. It states that the president told Blair "the diplomatic strategy had to be arranged around the military planning," but it goes on to report that:

> Mr. Bush told Mr. Blair that the U.S. was so worried about the failure to find hard evidence against Saddam that it thought of "flying U2 reconnaissance aircraft planes with fighter cover over Iraq, painted in UN colours." Mr. Bush added: "If Saddam fired on them, he would be in breach [of UN resolutions]."[8]

While he was apparently discussing his war plans with his British ally, Bush, as late as February and early March 2003, was still publicly claiming he was trying to *avoid* war with Iraq, and that America would go to war only as a last resort, and only, as National Security Adviser

Condoleezza Rice warned, to prevent "the smoking gun (being) a mush-room cloud."

The impact of the Downing Street memo, once it was finally re-ported in the United States in May 2005, * was electrifying. In Congress, open opposition to the war began to grow, and included a few congres-sional Republicans. Public opinion, which was already starting to show signs of war-weariness as the number of U.S. soldiers killed in action climbed toward two thousand, began to turn against the war. Now even the president's integrity regarding the reasons for the war itself began to be seriously challenged. Had this memo been disclosed three years earlier, it seems likely that the president would have had a hard time even getting Congress to approve the measure he later claimed was a war authoriza-tion vote. As it is, the memo started Bush's and Cheney's poll numbers on a long downward spiral. But the big lie exposed by the Downing Street memo was only one of many. It had become apparent that as the White House began marching to war, the march of lies quickened, too.

And lying, whether to Congress or to the American people, is some-thing that both the Founding Fathers and several Congresses have deter-mined to be an impeachable offense, particularly when it is about going to war.

## *Marketing a War*

As the 2002 congressional election approached, the Bush administra-tion had what it perceived as a perfect opportunity to achieve two goals at once: a congressional go-ahead for an invasion of Iraq, and a big pickup in seats in both House and Senate. It managed to achieve both.

The strategy was simple and characteristic of Karl Rove, Bush's longtime campaign strategist. In addition to tying Hussein to the at-tack on 9/11, the White House would portray Iraq as a looming and deadly serious threat, based on claims that Saddam Hussein had

---

*The American media ignored the story for days and even weeks, and those news organizations that did initially report on the memo treated it initially as a British election story, not an American scandal.

weapons of mass destruction capable of harming Americans, and would ask for a congressional resolution authorizing the president to take decisive action against him. By hyping Iraq as a terror threat, scarcely a year after the 9/11 attacks, any Democrat who raised questions or who stood in opposition to administration war planning could be cast as weak on defense and as unpatriotic, making him or her vulnerable on Election Day.

And so began the marketing campaign for war with Iraq.

In September 2002, Secretary of Defense Rumsfeld created the Office of Special Plans (OSP), which was run by neoconservative Douglas Feith. This was a sort of in-house pseudo-intelligence operation that had the job of "cherry picking" intelligence about Iraq to make the case that Hussein was developing and stockpiling weapons of mass destruction and that he was linked to the 9/11 terror attack.

With a huge $40-billion intelligence operation that included spy satellites, spy planes, and a network of undercover agents and analysts all focusing on Iraq, a small coterie of "intelligence operatives" in a Pentagon office wasn't going to add anything in the way of new information. But that was not the purpose of the new unit. This was quite clearly a propaganda operation aimed at shaping public opinion and helping to build a case for war. As one former CIA officer, Larry Johnson, put it, the OSP:

> lied and manipulated intelligence to further its agenda of removing Saddam. It's a group of ideologues with pre-determined notions of truth and reality. They take bits of intelligence to support their agenda and ignore anything contrary.[9]

The OSP was aided in this secret propaganda campaign by another new office established by the White House, called the White House Iraq Group (WHIG). Created in August 2002 by White House Chief of Staff Andrew Card and Karl Rove, the goal of WHIG, which included among its members then National Security Adviser Condoleezza Rice, Cheney's chief of staff "Scooter" Libby, and Bush media maven Karen Hughes, was to shape public opinion in favor of war.

As *The Washington Post* described the operation, in an investigative article that appeared a year later:

> The escalation of nuclear rhetoric a year ago, including the introduction of the term "mushroom cloud" into the debate, coincided with the formation of a White House Iraq Group, or WHIG, a task force assigned to "educate the public" about the threat from Saddam Hussein, as a participant put it.
>
> Systematic coordination began in August 2002, when Chief of Staff Andrew H. Card, Jr. formed . . . WHIG, to set strategy for each stage of the confrontation with Baghdad.[10]

The role of WHIG as a propaganda operation was made clear by Card, who, when asked by a reporter why the administration had waited until September to begin pressing the case for war against Iraq, said, "From a marketing point of view, you don't introduce new products in August."[11]

In the course of special counsel Patrick Fitzgerald's investigation to determine exactly who in the administration had leaked the identity of undercover CIA operative Valerie Plame Wilson, (see chapter 8), it became clear that WHIG played a key role. This ad hoc group of White House propagandists worked the media through contacts like *New York Times* reporter Judith Miller, planting scare stories about an alleged Iraqi nuclear weapons development program, germ warfare production facilities, and chemical arms, as well as alleged links to Al Qaeda. Card's WHIG team was also working hand-in-glove with Rumsfeld's OSP to win over Congress to pass a war authorization resolution.

## *Conning Congress*

Throughout September, the OSP and WHIG did their job. The OSP sifted through all the intelligence out of and about Iraq (including a lot of highly questionable information generated by the Iraqi National Congress, a CIA-created body headed by convicted bank swindler Ahmed Chalabi). Rumsfeld's in-house intelligence unit was then handing over to the White

House spinmeisters only that material that made Iraq look the most dangerous, and was removing any caveats that the professional intelligence community had included in their assessments. The most tenuous connections between anything Iraqi and Al Qaeda were portrayed as potent links. Aluminum tubes purchased, most likely, for short-range rocket bodies were characterized as "only suitable as" components for a uranium enrichment centrifuge, which was necessary to build atomic weapons, though scientists immediately said they were too short for the purpose. A clumsily forged document supposedly showing that Iraq had been trying to purchase uranium ore from Niger was touted as proof of an Iraqi nuclear weapons program, though such raw material is years and billions of dollars away from the enriched uranium and the advanced technology needed to construct such an atomic bomb.

No matter. The U.S. media were full of stories, most of them planted by administration sources with friendly reporters, of Iraqi WMD threats. There were harrowing tales of pilotless Iraqi drones that could allegedly deliver poison gas over U.S. cities, reports of mobile germ-weapons labs that could move around the Iraq countryside dodging UN arms inspectors, stories of thousands of tons of stored sarin gas weapons, anthrax bombs, and even smallpox virus stockpiles. Not one bit of it was true. UN arms inspectors said over and over that Iraq no longer had any WMD arms caches. The International Atomic Energy Commission said there was no nuclear weapons program in Iraq. And the alleged links between Iraq and Al Qaeda were nonexistent as well as politically ludicrous—Osama and his fundamentalist Islamic comrades loathed Arab secularists like Saddam Hussein almost as much as they despised Western society.

The truth did not matter to the Bush White House. The administration clearly intended to keep pushing the fear button, and to push it often and hard. The events of 9/11 were only a year old, and American nerves were frayed, not least because the new Department of Homeland Security, under Secretary Tom Ridge, was raising and lowering the color alert flags as though it was a naval signal corps exercise. In October, only days before Congress was to vote on a bill providing authorization for the president to take action against Iraq, Bush went on national television from Cincinnati, Ohio, and pushed all these buttons:

Tonight I want to take a few minutes to discuss a grave threat to peace, and America's determination to lead the world in confronting that threat.

The threat comes from Iraq. It arises directly from the Iraqi regime's own actions—its history of aggression, and its drive toward an arsenal of terror.

Now that he had everyone's undivided attention, the president launched into a series of lies and distortions about the alleged threat posed by Saddam Hussein. Iraq, he said,

possesses and produces chemical and biological weapons. It is seeking nuclear weapons. It has given shelter and support to terrorism, and practices terror against its own people.

. . . If we know Saddam Hussein has dangerous weapons today—and we do—does it make any sense for the world to wait to confront him as he grows even stronger and develops even more dangerous weapons?

In 1995, after several years of deceit by the Iraqi regime, the head of Iraq's military industries defected. It was then that the regime was forced to admit that it had produced more than 30,000 liters of anthrax and other deadly biological agents. The inspectors, however, concluded that Iraq had likely produced two to four times that amount. This is a massive stockpile of biological weapons that has never been accounted for, and capable of killing millions.

We know that the regime has produced thousands of tons of chemical agents, including mustard gas, sarin nerve gas, VX nerve gas. Saddam Hussein also has experience in using chemical weapons. He has ordered chemical attacks on Iran, and on more than forty villages in his own country. These actions killed or injured at least 20,000 people, more than six times the number of people who died in the attacks of September the 11th.

And surveillance photos reveal that the regime is rebuilding facilities that it had used to produce chemical and biological weapons.

If that wasn't enough, Bush went on to link Iraq to the dreaded Al Qaeda, saying:

> We know that Iraq and the al Qaeda terrorist network share a common enemy—the United States of America. We know that Iraq and al Qaeda have had high-level contacts that go back a decade. Some al Qaeda leaders who fled Afghanistan went to Iraq. These include one very senior al Qaeda leader who received medical treatment in Baghdad this year, and who has been associated with planning for chemical and biological attacks. We've learned that Iraq has trained al Qaeda members in bomb-making and poisons and deadly gases. And we know that after September the 11th, Saddam Hussein's regime gleefully celebrated the terrorist attacks on America.
>
> Iraq could decide on any given day to provide a biological or chemical weapon to a terrorist group or individual terrorists. Alliance with terrorists could allow the Iraqi regime to attack America without leaving any fingerprints.[12]

Almost none of this was true, and the few things that were at least partially fact-based, such as the charge that Hussein had used poison gas on his own people, were exaggerated or incomplete. In fact, the United States had supplied some of the material for those attacks, and, far from condemning his criminal action, had at the time been helping Hussein in his war with Iran by, among other things, providing him with satellite photos of Iranian positions. There was no alliance between Hussein and Al Qaeda, no training of Al Qaeda terrorists by Iraq, and no evidence Hussein planned to arm terrorists against the United States. But the steady drumbeat linking 9/11 to Iraq coming from the president and his underlings had its intended effect. Pollsters reported that by Election Day in November 2004, a majority of Americans had been *convinced* that Iraq was *behind* the 9/11 attacks.

Again it must be pointed out that lying *to the American people,* not just to Congress and not just under oath, can be and in the past has been considered an impeachable offense. It is one of the charges that was leveled against President Richard M. Nixon, and is one of the charges that was voted out of the House Judiciary Committee considering his impeachment.

Not everyone was fooled by Bush's lies. As Senator Russell Feingold (D-WI) said during the floor debate on October 11, 2002, over the Joint Resolution to Authorize the Use of U.S. Armed Forces Against Iraq:

> The Administration's arguments just don't add up. They don't add up to a coherent basis for a new major war in the middle of our current challenging fight against the terrorism of al Qaeda and related organizations.
>
> . . . I am increasingly troubled by the seemingly shifting justifications for an invasion at this time. My colleagues, I'm not suggesting there has to be only one justification for such a dramatic action. But when the Administration moves back and forth from one argument to another, I think it undercuts the credibility of the case and the belief in its urgency. I believe that this practice of shifting justifications has much to do with the troubling phenomenon of many Americans questioning the Administration's motives in insisting on action at this particular time.
>
> What am I talking about? I'm talking about the spectacle of the President and senior Administration officials citing a purported connection to al Qaeda one day, weapons of mass destruction the next day, Saddam Hussein's treatment of his own people on another day, and then on some days the issue of Kuwaiti prisoners of war.[13]

Nonetheless, the fateful resolution passed by 296–133 in the Republican-led House, and by 77–23 in the Democratic-led Senate (where 23, or nearly half, of the 50 Democratic senators voted for it). The threat of being called "soft on defense" or unpatriotic, less than a month before voters went to the polls, was too great a risk for most members of Congress facing election. It was easier, and politically safer, just to go along with the majority.

Even that wasn't the end of the story. In order to win over those few wavering members of Congress concerned about another war in Iraq— one aimed at toppling Saddam Hussein this time—the Bush administration had to deny that it was committed to an invasion. Instead, the administration contended that it needed the congressional resolution passed to put additional pressure on Hussein to comply with international demands that he rid his country of WMDs. This meant more lies, because, as the administration was being told by UN inspectors and its own intelligence analysts at the CIA, Iraq didn't actually *have* any WMDs to get rid of. Indeed, the pretense that the joint resolution was only being sought to strengthen America's and the United Nation's hand in convincing Iraq to disarm was itself a lie, as the Downing Street memo later made clear. The reality was that the administration was already committed to an invasion and was busy "fixing the facts" to make it happen.

## Going Nuclear: The Big Lie

The lies were many and ugly, but they just weren't doing the job. As war with Iraq became increasingly likely, opposition was growing. Massive demonstrations in which millions of people took to the streets were taking place in Europe among America's NATO allies. Inside the United States, dozens of Internet-based lobbying campaigns and marches in Washington and other major cities were intended to pressure members of Congress to oppose an invasion. And so, the administration responded with even bolder falsehoods.

The first of these came in the State of the Union message on January 28, 2003. The second came in a "letter of determination" to Congress delivered by the president on March 18, explaining why he was launching his invasion Iraq the following day.

A State of the Union speech is unique because it is the only message to Congress by the president that is mandated by the Constitution. As such, it is an official action of profound legal significance. Presidents have traditionally used the occasion to set the agenda for the next year, and to lay out broad themes and new programs at the one time every member of Congress, and a significant percentage of the American public, are listening. President Bush used this particular occasion to make the case for going to war against Iraq:

The United Nations concluded in 1999 that Saddam Hussein had biological weapons sufficient to produce over 25,000 liters of anthrax—enough doses to kill several million people. He hasn't accounted for that material. He's given no evidence that he has destroyed it.

The United Nations concluded that Saddam Hussein had materials sufficient to produce more than 38,000 liters of botulinum toxin—enough to subject millions of people to death by respiratory failure. He hasn't accounted for that material. He's given no evidence that he has destroyed it.

Our intelligence officials estimate that Saddam Hussein had the materials to produce as much as 500 tons of sarin, mustard, and VX nerve agent. In such quantities, these chemical agents could also kill untold thousands. He's not accounted for these materials. He has given no evidence that he has destroyed them.

U.S. intelligence indicates that Saddam Hussein had upwards of 30,000 munitions capable of delivering chemical agents. Inspectors recently turned up sixteen of them—despite Iraq's recent declaration denying their existence. Saddam Hussein has not accounted for the remaining 29,984 of these prohibited munitions. He's given no evidence that he has destroyed them.

From three Iraqi defectors we know that Iraq, in the late 1990s, had several mobile biological weapons labs. These are designed to produce germ warfare agents, and can be moved from place to place to evade inspectors. Saddam Hussein has not disclosed these facilities. He's given no evidence that he has destroyed them.

The International Atomic Energy Agency confirmed in the 1990s that Saddam Hussein had an advanced nuclear weapons development program, had a design for a nuclear weapon, and was working on five different methods of enriching uranium for a bomb. The British government has learned that Saddam Hussein recently sought significant quantities of uranium from Africa. Our intelligence sources tell us that he has attempted to purchase high-strength aluminum tubes suitable for nuclear weapons production. Saddam Hussein has not credibly explained these activities. He clearly has much to hide.

. . . And this Congress and the America people must recognize another threat. Evidence from intelligence sources, secret communications, and statements by people now in custody reveal that Saddam Hussein aids and protects terrorists, including members of al Qaeda. Secretly, and without fingerprints, he could provide one of his hidden weapons to terrorists, or help them develop their own.[14]

The lies and misinformation in this section of the address were numerous and serious. As mentioned earlier, the CIA had already alerted the White House that the information from Iraqi exile sources claiming Hussein links to Al Qaeda was unreliable at best (the administration never admitted in public that its only evidence often came from these biased and unreliable sources). The aluminum tubes had been demonstrably shown to be useless for centrifuges, and most significantly, the CIA had informed the administration that a report claiming Hussein had sought to buy uranium yellow-cake ore from Niger was bogus and the document on which it was based clearly forged. (See appendix B—Niger Forgeries.) Moreover, at the time the president was speaking, contrary to his assertions, the UN inspectors were reporting that there were no WMDs in Iraq, no biological and chemical weapons labs or manufacturing facilities, and that there was no active nuclear program.

According to some constitutional attorneys, President Bush's State of the Union address containing these lies was a clear violation of the False Statements Accountability Act of 1996, which makes it a felony to knowingly make false statements to Congress. John Bonifaz, a constitutional law expert who brought a lawsuit against the U.S. government days before the Iraq invasion began on behalf of several soldiers who claimed they were being sent off to an illegal war, a suit that was rejected by a federal court on technical grounds, says, "If the president knew that the intelligence he was citing was fabricated, that would be a felony. It didn't have to be a statement under oath." Bonifaz says that the State of the Union address also appears to have violated the federal anticonspiracy statute, which makes it a felony to defraud any U.S. agency for any purpose, including the Congress.

But the president didn't just break these laws once, Bonifaz argues. He did it again, even more seriously perhaps, on March 18, 2003, in his letter to Congress. That curt and dramatic missive read:

Dear Mr. Speaker: (Dear Mr. President:)

Consistent with section 3(b) of the Authorization for Use of Military Force Against Iraq Resolution of 2002 (Public Law 107-243), and based on information available to me, including that in the enclosed document, I determine that:

(1) reliance by the United States on further diplomatic and other peaceful means alone will neither (A) adequately protect the national security of the United States against the continuing threat posed by Iraq nor (B) likely lead to enforcement of all relevant United Nations Security Council resolutions regarding Iraq; and

(2) acting pursuant to the Constitution and Public Law 107-243 is consistent with the United States and other countries continuing to take the necessary actions against international terrorists and terrorist organizations, including those nations, organizations, or persons who planned, authorized, committed, or aided the terrorist attacks that occurred on September 11, 2001.

> Sincerely,
> GEORGE W. BUSH[15]

As Bonifaz commented in an interview, "The president was asserting in that letter that the national security of the United States was threatened by Iraq, which he knew simply was not true. He also asserted in that letter that he was going to war against Iraq as part of continued actions against international terrorists and those who had aided the terrorist attacks of 9/11, which he also knew was not true." He argues that in both cases the president was therefore "defrauding Congress" and thus committing a felony.

John Dean agrees, writing in *Worse than Watergate* that the president's March 18 letter "is closer to a blatant fraud than to a fulfillment of the president's constitutional responsibility to faithfully execute the law."[16]

Not all constitutional scholars are ready to agree with Bonifaz that the untruthful assertions in the State of the Union address and the letter to Congress reach the level of an impeachable offense. Cass Sunstein, a professor of law at the University of Chicago who was one of four experts asked by Sen. Barbara Boxer (D-CA), in December 2005, to advise her on whether impeachable offenses had been committed by the White House, says the impeachment effort against President Clinton, which he calls "blatantly unconstitutional," leads him to set a very high bar for impeachment actions:

"I think that if the president hyped the evidence for war, it would not be close to impeachable. If he knowingly said things that were untrue, that's closer, but even then you'd need to know the context. There'd have to be a systematic pattern of intentional misstatements of fact to get the country into a war, which could then constitute a misdemeanor, or 'bad act' in the old English usage that the Constitution refers to, and I'm not sure I've seen it."

Bonifaz disagrees strongly. "There is certainly enough evidence of deliberate lying about the causes for war to justify demanding an impeachment investigation," he insists.

Representative John Conyers, the ranking minority member of the House Judiciary Committee (and the man who would chair that committee if the Democrats were to regain the majority in the House in 2006), clearly agrees with Bonifaz's view. On December 18, 2005, Representative Conyers introduced censure motions for both Bush and Cheney in the House of Representatives, and also a resolution, HR 365, calling for creation of a select committee modeled on the Senate Watergate Committee to

> investigate the Administration's intent to go to war before congressional authorization, manipulation of pre-war intelligence, encouraging and countenancing torture, and retaliating against critics, and to make recommendations regarding grounds for possible impeachment.[17]

Conyers, a soft-spoken and low-key veteran of the House, took action after receiving a report of the minority staff of the Judiciary Committee, which concluded after a detailed investigation:

> that there is substantial evidence the President, the Vice President and other high-ranking members of the Bush Administration misled Con-

gress and the American people regarding the decision to go to war with Iraq [and] misstated and manipulated intelligence information regarding the justification for such war.

The staff report went on to assert:

There is a prima facie case that these actions by the President, Vice-President, and other members of the Bush Administration violated a number of federal laws, including (1) Committing a Fraud against the United States; (2) Making False Statements to Congress; (3) The War Powers Resolution; (4) Misuse of Government Funds; (5) federal laws and international treaties prohibiting torture and cruel, inhuman, and degrading treatment; (6) federal laws concerning retaliating against witnesses and other individuals; and (7) federal laws and regulations concerning leaking and other misuse of intelligence.[18]

There is a substantial difference between impeaching a president for political gain, as the Republicans did to Clinton, and seeking impeachment for actual transgressions against the Constitution. The difficulty in the present situation is that any attempt to impeach President Bush would be seen by some as political retribution. For that reason the evidence against President Bush has to be unassailable. By this time though, there no longer could be any question about the illegality of the president's actions. And having constructed this illegal and blatantly false foundation, he persisted in building his argument for going to war on top of it.

## Violating the War Powers Act and the Constitution

As despicable and devious Bush's lying was before the war, and as terrible have been the consequences of those lies, this was not the only, or perhaps even the most egregious, of presidential crimes relating to the Iraq War. The very act of invading Iraq itself takes that honor. For in deciding to invade Iraq in March 2003, the president may well have engaged in a constitutional abuse of power and a violation of the War

Powers Act of 1973. This possibility is discussed in the congressional staff report cited above.

So momentous is the issue of going to war that the founders of the United States of America made it clear in the Constitution that they didn't want that decision to ever be made by any president. They felt that a president was inherently too removed from the popular will. Instead, they opted to make declaring war the responsibility of the Congress (except in the case of immediately responding to an attack upon the country). Over the years, however, that protective barrier to wanton or politically motivated militarism has broken down. Advances in the technology of war, which make it possible for enemies anywhere in the world to strike almost without warning, combined with a marked tendency on the part of congressional officials to pass the buck on any issue of real importance or controversy, have weakened the constraints on bellicose presidents. Indeed, while the United States has been involved in many wars large and small since 1945, World War II is the last time that Congress has actually made a formal declaration of war. Incredibly, although about 58,000 Americans died in Korea and 58,000 were killed in Vietnam, constitutionally neither one of those military involvements was a declared war.*

Even so, except in the case of very short-term "police" actions involving minimal numbers of troops for a short duration, presidents planning military actions have usually still felt the need for a congressional cover. Thus, they have generally sought some kind of vote from Congress authorizing them to go to war against another nation—a kind of virtual declaration of war, if you will. President Lyndon Johnson got his Gulf of Tonkin Resolution before attacking North Vietnam, George H. W. Bush got a war resolution from Congress before attacking Iraq and driving Saddam Hussein's army out of Kuwait, and his son George W. Bush sought Congress's approval before invading Iraq in 2003. (And, it should be noted, Nixon almost faced an impeachment article for his invasion of Cambodia,

---

*That said, both were wars under international law in that they involved armed conflicts between two or more high contracting parties to the Geneva Conventions, as is also clearly the case with the fighting in Iraq and Afghanistan. Just because a president ignores the War Powers Act does not mean a military action does not fall under the Geneva Conventions.

which was done *without* his going to Congress for permission—one of the reasons Congress passed the War Powers Act of 1973.)\*

But the younger Bush's "war authorization," which passed in October of 2002, *more than six months before* the Iraq invasion, raises many questions. It certainly was not on a par with its predecessors, which led to almost immediate onset of hostilities. Moreover, as many members of Congress have noted, including the unofficial Senate historian Robert Byrd (D-WV), the Joint Resolution, cited by Bush as his alleged war authorization to attack Iraq, actually had only been passed by Congress following assurances from the White House that the measure would *not* be the last word on the subject. The White House had promised Congress during debate on the resolution that before engaging in any military action the administration would first seek the support of a UN Security Council Resolution, which would have made an invasion a sanctioned UN action, like the first Gulf War, not a unilateral American action. The White House and its supporters in Congress had further argued that the October 11 resolution would serve to strengthen the United Nation's hand in winning compliance from Iraq with arms inspection requirements, thus obviating any need for an invasion. In the end, those arguments both turned out to be lies of sorts, too. Indeed, if the Downing Street memo is a true and accurate account of administration planning in 2002, the administration, far from trying to avoid war, was looking for a way to "set up" Saddam by tricking him into expelling the arms inspectors, thereby providing an excuse for an invasion. True, Bush dispatched Secretary of State Colin Powell to the UN Security Council, where he presented the same misinformation about alleged WMDs in Iraq—evidence that Powell himself has subsequently disavowed—all in hopes of winning a Security Council Resolution to support an invasion. But after the Security Council refused to authorize an invasion, the president went ahead and attacked Iraq, dragging with

---

\*A proposed article of impeachment on the issue of Nixon's secret war against Cambodia was prepared by the House Judiciary Committee, but the measure was dropped from the final list of three articles, which were voted out of committee and presented to the full House of Representatives, allegedly as part of a deal to gain Republican votes for the remaining articles.

him Great Britain, Italy, Spain, and a ragtag group of small nations that were bribed or threatened into providing token troop commitments and that were, with astonishing cynicism, referred to by Bush as "The Coalition of the Willing."

The invasion of Iraq did not have the support of the United Nations. It would appear also not to have had the support of a true resolution by the two houses of Congress either. As such, the American war against Iraq was both a constitutional abuse of power and a violation of the UN Charter and the Nuremberg Charter. As such, the decision by the president to invade Iraq is an impeachable crime.

Like the Vietnam War before it, the War in Iraq, founded on lies and tricks, never had the solid or enthusiastic support of the American people. Many of those who supported it did so believing the carefully constructed Bush administration lie that Iraq was somehow to blame for 9/11, though their numbers are diminishing. For those people the war was seen as retribution. Meanwhile, opposition to the invasion was widespread around the world even *before* the war began. That opposition only has grown as the body bags and flag-draped coffins—hidden at first by the administration—have been flown home. And as the quick march on Baghdad was replaced by a grinding occupation and counter-insurgency, with Iraq turning into a chaotic zone of tribal and religious feuds, Iranian meddling, and violence, always more violence.

The political ground in America by the beginning of 2006 had begun to shift, with pundits even starting to talk about the possibility of a Democratic takeover of one or both houses of Congress in the November midterm elections. In the wake of the attacks of 9/11 in 2001, a panicked and terrified nation was canceling public school field trips, prophylactically "nuking" mail in microwave ovens, and canceling air travel to the point that major airlines, bankrupt, needed federal bailouts. Bush was riding high, with at one point an approval rating of 90 percent. Less than five years later, America had moved to the point that the president's integrity and even his fitness to serve out his second term of office were being openly questioned by at least some members of Congress, and two-thirds of Americans wanted the United States to quit Iraq and bring the troops home. This political change was particularly surprising, given that the country has remained bogged down in several bloody wars that might ordinarily be expected to rally people around their leaders. Even more surprisingly, impeachment, which had been joked about at anti-war marches as late as 2005, was beginning to be discussed seriously, not just on the Internet, but on mainstream editorial pages and talk shows, in Congress, and on the campaign trail.

★ ★ ★ ★ ★ ★ ★ ★ ★ ★ ★ ★ ★ ★

# SIX

★ ★ ★ ★ ★ ★ ★ ★ ★ ★ ★ ★ ★ ★

## *Dark Questions About a Dark Day*

ARTICLE II: In his conduct of the office of President of the United States, George W. Bush, contrary to his oath faithfully to execute the office of the President of the United States, and to the best of his ability preserve, protect, and defend the Constitution of the United States, and in violation of his constitutional duty to take care that the laws be faithfully executed, did knowingly ignore grave warnings of an impending enemy attack on the territory of the U.S., resulting in the deaths of thousands of American citizens, and thereafter did conspire to obstruct investigations by Congress and by an independent commission of inquiry into both the events leading up to the attacks of September 11, 2001, and to the government's response to those attacks. These actions by the President and his subordinates constitute the crime of criminal negligence at a minimum, threaten the security of the nation, and may constitute obstruction of justice.

**THE HORRIFYING** attacks on the World Trade Center and Pentagon on September 11, 2001, replayed endlessly on television, were probably watched by more people in the United States and around the globe than was the famous 1969 Apollo Moon landing. Yet, for all that public attention and scrutiny those images received, and the multiple investigations into why 9/11 happened, there remain more troubling questions about that dark, watershed day in American history than there are concerning the 1963 assassination of President John F. Kennedy. Little wonder that in 2004 one poll found that 90 percent of Americans suspected a White House cover-up of 9/11.[1] As James Ridgeway, one of America's leading investigative reporters, writes:

> How could this have happened?
> Of the unanswered questions about 9/11, this is the question that encompasses all the others. It is the question most of us asked ourselves while we watched, in shock and near disbelief, as the Twin Towers burned and collapsed. . . . It is the question most of us, in one way or another, are still asking.[2]

There are other more pointed questions Americans are asking, too. Among them:

*How could such a massive conspiracy, involving not just the nineteen terrorist hijackers who commandeered those three planes, as well as a fourth plane that crashed in the Pennsylvania countryside, but also those countless more who trained them, financed them, and helped them enter the United States, have escaped the notice of America's sprawling $40-billion intelligence apparatus, and the even larger domestic law-enforcement establishment?*

In fact, it didn't. As Eleanor Hill, staff director for the joint House-Senate inquiry into alleged intelligence failures ahead of the September 11 attacks, wrote in a thirty-page report issued a year after the attacks, there were dozens of warnings that came into the government in the months preceding 9/11. While these didn't give a time, date, and description of the plan of attack, there were warnings about the use of planes as weapons. And one, presented to "senior government officials" in July, just two months before the attacks, said

> . . . that [bin Laden] will launch a significant attack against U.S. and/or Israeli interests in the coming weeks. . . . The attack will be spectacular and designed to inflict mass casualties against U.S. facilities or interests.
>
> Attack preparations have been made. Attack will occur with little or no warning.[3]

And yet, at the 9/11 Commission hearing President Bush's national security adviser Condoleezza Rice insisted that the administration had had "no warning" of the attacks, and had no idea that planes would be used as missiles.

It's not that the messages being picked up by the CIA, the FBI, and the State Department weren't getting delivered to the top people in the administration, including Bush himself. A presidential briefing by the CIA, delivered to the president while he was on vacation at his Crawford, Texas, ranch on August 6, 2001, just over a month before the attacks, was pretty unambiguous. Titled "Bin Laden Determined to Strike in United States," it specifically mentioned the possibility of hijackings of planes. Yet, astonishingly, that warning to the president led to no heightened security measures or other efforts by the administration. In her testimony before the 9/11 Commission, National Security Adviser Rice (whom the White House had tried mightily to prevent from having to testify at all), tried to downplay the August 6 memo's significance. She claimed it was "nothing new" and was just "historical" information. But in fact the memo, later partially declassified, included the following anything-but-historical warning:

> FBI information since that time indicates patterns of suspicious activity in this country consistent with preparations for hijackings or other types of attacks, including recent surveillance of federal buildings in New York.[4]

How can the president and his advisers have been so disinterested in the face of these warnings?

*Did intelligence agencies and diplomats from other countries, including
Germany, France, Israel, Russia, Morocco, Jordan, and Egypt, warn
the United States of the attack?*

There are a number of reports that each of those countries' intelligence services provided warnings that something was going to happen around the time of September 11, some of them chillingly close in their details to the actual attack. For example, Mossad, Israel's security agency, reportedly warned the CIA of an impending, unspecified major attack on the United States. The U.S. embassy in Japan was also warned, and passed word along to Washington of an attack on a U.S. military target.[5] If there were all these warnings, why was nothing done in response? Why, for instance, were airports and airlines not immediately put on higher alert?

As Ridgeway points out, Pakistan's intelligence service almost certainly knew something was about to happen. That agency had *set up* the Taliban in Afghanistan, and knew all the players. He says:

> Through its powerful intelligence service, Pakistan basically created the Taliban in Afghanistan, and its agents stationed around that country cooperated with Al Qaeda. It ignored the Taliban's support of Al Qaeda. There is little doubt that members of Pakistani intelligence knew that 9/11 was going to happen, including the details. But today, Pakistan is our best friend in the region, receiving a significant increase in U.S. aid.[6]

Ridgeway notes that the current Saudi ambassador to the United States, Prince Turki, was the head of Saudi intelligence at the time of 9/11. Turki was the man who recruited Osama bin Laden in the mid 1980s to go with a group of Saudi fundamentalist mujahadeen to fight the Soviets in Afghanistan.

Richard Clarke, in his memoir of the events of 2001, recalls that CIA Director George Tenet was becoming increasingly alarmed about Al Qaeda as the first year of President Bush's first term of office progressed:

> For years George Tenet had called me directly when he read a piece of raw intelligence about a threat. Often when I checked out these re-

ports with CIA experts, they would point out that the source was untrustworthy or the report was contradicted by more reliable information. Now Tenet's calls to me about threatening intelligence reports became more frequent and the information was good. There were a growing number of reports that al Qaeda's operational pace was picking up. Cells were discovered and rounded up by security services in Italy, France, and Germany. There were reliable reports of a threat to the U.S. Navy in Bahrain. . . . The Italians had credible reports that there would be an attempt to attack the G-7 Summit in Genoa . . . [7]

Again, how could the administration have ignored such warnings?

*Why were Saudis who were living or visiting in the United States, including members of the bin Laden family, immediately picked up and flown out of the U.S. by chartered jet without being subjected to FBI questioning immediately after the 9/11 attacks? Particularly since all other nonmilitary air traffic had been grounded? Who ordered their hasty evacuation?*

The explanation that they were being protected is ludicrous. The government could as easily have offered them protection if it feared problems from angry citizens, while it conducted a thorough investigation into what each of these people knew of the people involved in the attacks.

Former Florida Senator Bob Graham, who sat on the Senate Intelligence Committee until 2004, and chaired that committee until November 2002, says he suspects the White House is covering up much deeper and closer involvement by the Saudi government or key Saudi officials in the 9/11 attacks than is already known. "We know that Saudi officials were providing money to two of the hijackers in San Diego," says Graham in an interview. "It doesn't seem likely that if Saudi money was going to two of the hijackers, it wasn't going to more of them." He notes that most of the hijackers were from Saudi Arabia. "I suspect the White House doesn't want Americans to know the real truth about Saudi involvement in 9/11 because they know if it were common knowledge, people would be incensed and it would create a major problem in relations with a major supplier of American oil," says Graham. In his book, *Intelligence Matters,* Graham charges that Bush has actively interfered with investigations into Saudi and other foreign government assistance to the 9/11 plotters, writing:

> Throughout 2002, the president directed the FBI to restrain and obfuscate the investigation of the foreign government support that some and possibly all the September 11 hijackers received.[8]

Richard Clarke is skeptical about theories linking senior Saudi leaders to the 9/11 plot, but he suggests that they may nonetheless have helped the plotters:

> . . . it must be said that Ministers and members of the royal family did knowingly support the global spread of Wahhabist Islam, jihads, and anti-Israeli activities. . . . As long as the royal family and its rule were not the obvious targets, some undoubtedly turned a blind eye to a host of things that made al Qaeda's life easier.[9]

All this may be profoundly embarrassing and potentially politically damaging to Bush, whose family has long had close relations and business ties with both the Saudi royal family and the bin Laden family, but that is no justification for the administration's continued obstruction of efforts to investigate the Saudi connection to the 9/11 disaster. And yet the Bush administration has gone out of its way to prevent any public awareness of the Saudi links to 9/11. The administration insisted on blacking out twenty-eight pages of material related to Saudi Arabia from the Senate Intelligence Committee's final report on 9/11. Graham says that, on reviewing that material, he could find no national security justification for withholding 95 percent of the material. His conclusion was that "these pages were being kept secret for reasons other than national security."[10]

Nor was that the only information the administration has kept secret on questionable grounds. As *The New Republic* reports:

> About 15 percent of the [Senate Intelligence Committee] report is bathed in black ink, redacted because the CIA deemed the information classified. But those redactions are highly suspect. First, the CIA

tried to black out about half of the report. Then, after protests from Congress, the Agency yielded, to no demonstrable harm. Second, many of the heavily redacted sections deal with the most politically sensitive topics, such as whether intelligence analysts were pressured by administration officials, and the story behind President Bush's claim that Saddam Hussein sought uranium from Africa.[11]

That kind of obstruction alone, falsely presented by the administration as being based upon national security concerns, should be considered grounds for impeachment.

*Why was the U.S. military's Able Danger intelligence unit, which had discovered the activities of Al Qaeda cells in the United States and possibly lead hijacker Muhammed Atta, prevented from alerting the FBI?*

Former FBI Director Louis Freeh believes the answer to this question alone could lead to a "smoking gun" in the mystery of 9/11. Clearly he is not talking about an Arab-held gun. Freeh is not alone. Congressman Curt Weldon, a Republican from Pennsylvania, has blasted both the 9/11 Commission and the White House for what he calls a "cover-up worse than Watergate." Weldon charges that the White House has blocked officers from the Able Danger unit from testifying about what they had learned about Al Qaeda's activities in advance of the attacks. He further charges that the administration has been conducting a smear campaign against the officers who have blown the whistle about the bureaucratic intelligence screw-up that kept them from reporting what they knew about Al Qaeda to the FBI before 9/11.

Likewise, why did senior FBI officials fail to act on a report from Special Agent Coleen Rowley, a staff lawyer at the agency's Twin Cities bureau in Minneapolis, who informed Washington that her office was holding a man, Zacarias Moussaoui (for a while he was considered to be the twentieth hijacker), on immigration charges, who had been taking flying lessons and might be a terrorist? Why was she denied the chance to get a warrant to check out his apartment and his computer? Journalist Seymour Hersh writes that the agency felt at the time that Rowley didn't have sufficient "probable cause" for a search warrant. But then, this wasn't the only evidence about terrorists training to fly. FBI headquarters had been advised in July 2001 by the Phoenix bureau office that several suspicious Arabs were training at U.S. flight schools. That memo had urged that all flight schools be canvassed to see who they were training. Why was nothing was done about that warning until after 9/11?[12]

*What was the White House told about these warning signs of trouble? After the August 6 presidential briefing by the CIA, was the FBI asked what it knew? If not, why not?*

In fact, these and many other bizarre questions hang more like a smoking cloud over this epic disaster. A big one might be this: If it is true, as the administration has been trying to claim, that the failure to anticipate 9/11 and to mobilize and try to prevent it was the result of a massive intelligence breakdown, why has no one been punished? Look at the record: The head of the CIA, George Tenet, did warn of growing threats from Al Qaeda, but failed to identify any of the nineteen hijackers or to predict the first massive, coordinated attack on the country since World War II, yet he was awarded a Presidential Medal of Freedom; Condoleezza Rice, who as national security adviser completely missed the Al Qaeda threat, was promoted in Bush's second term to secretary of state; Michael Chertoff, who as head of terrorism prosecutions under John Ashcroft only managed a few minor convictions (some badly botched), was promoted first to federal judge and then to Secretary of Homeland Security (where he also thoroughly botched the Katrina disaster crisis in New Orleans); Paul Wolfowitz, who as deputy secretary of defense played a key role in downplaying concerns about Al Qaeda during the first eight months of Bush's presidency (and who prominently pushed the idea that an invasion of Iraq would be a "cakewalk"), was nominated for the presidency of the World Bank. Those who have criticized the way the administration handled pre–9/11 intelligence, on the other hand, like Clarke, Rowley, and many others, have been smeared, or marginalized and driven to leave the government.

A major reason for the paucity of answers about 9/11, and for the widespread and growing suspicion among the public that something is amiss, is that the White House, in what qualifies as an impeachable crime of obstruction of justice, has stubbornly refused to provide requested information to the 9/11 Commission and to other investigative agencies, including Congress. Nor would the president and vice president agree to answer commission questions under oath, as other witnesses were required to do.

The Internet is awash in theories about 9/11, touting everything from alien subversion to convoluted plots by Israeli and even American intelligence. It's not necessary to develop elaborate conspiracy theories linking the 9/11 attack to the Oklahoma City bombing, the Kennedy assassination, and the late Elvis Presley, though, to recognize that there are many valid questions about this modernday Pearl Harbor attack on America—questions that not only have unacceptably remained unanswered, but that even more unacceptably aren't even being asked. The key ones fall into the category of who knew what about the attacks, when did they know it, and why didn't the government act on the warnings it was getting? A second set of questions involves how the government responded to the attacks once they began. Why, for example, did the president continue reading to an elementary school class after the first plane had struck instead of immediately taking charge of an emergency response? Surely, a loaded jumbo jet slamming during working hours into the largest building in New York in the heart of the financial district should have been seen as a disaster of epic proportions, even if terrorism wasn't involved. (Then again, the president's and his administration's detached and belated response to the Katrina strike on New Orleans four years later suggests there may be a pattern here.)

At this point, we should know answers to these and many other questions, but we don't. The key reason is that the administration has refused to provide them. As John Dean wrote in *Worse than Watergate,* instead of wanting to get to the bottom of this first major attack on the United States since the War of 1812 by asking and by answering all these hard questions,

> Bush and Cheney have stonewalled all of them. As a result the conspiracy theories continue. . . . The irresponsible secrecy of Bush and Cheney and their efforts to keep that truth of 9/11 from being revealed are enabling, if not encouraging such conspiracy theories to flourish.[13]

Is the White House stonewalling to hide its gross incompetence and criminal negligence in failing to take action to prevent the attacks? That might be politically understandable, but it's not correct or legal. It's not ethical or patriotic either, since only by thoroughly understanding how 9/11 happened can the nation hope to prevent another such attack.

Incompetence alone is not an impeachable offense, though as we will see in chapter 10, *gross* incompetence could be, if it rises to the level of criminal negligence. As Ridgeway writes:

> The fact that I see no smoking gun—in the form of a well-defined and purposeful conspiracy to support or permit the attacks—doesn't mean that no crime has taken place. Negligence, after all, can be criminal. And sometimes it can be impossible to see a smoking gun, because the air is already so thick with smoke.[14]

Unfortunately, the 9/11 Commission, Congress, and even most of the media have shown that they lack the courage, in the face of administration stonewalling, secrecy, and belligerence, to aggressively investigate, or in some cases even ask impolite questions about some of these issues. None of those groups or organizations has called the president and vice president on the carpet in the face of obstruction and demanded answers.

There are indications that as doubts grow among average Americans about the truthfulness and integrity of this administration, and about whether it has been honest about the causes of the war in Iraq, doubts are also growing about the official explanations surrounding 9/11. Representative Weldon has been highly critical of the administration and the Pentagon, under Secretary of Defense Donald Rumsfeld, for barring Pentagon personnel from testifying in Congress regarding the pre–9/11 Able Danger information about Al Qaeda and Muhammed Atta. Senator Arlen Specter (R-PA), chair of the Senate Judiciary Committee, has accused the administration of obstruction, for refusing to allow witnesses to testify.[15] Senator Barbara Boxer (D-CA) has also raised questions about the 9/11 Commission's findings, saying, "We need to pursue the truth about 9/11, wherever it may lead. The truth should be the only priority."[16]

"If I were a member of the House today, and I were submitting an impeachment bill, I would certainly include an article concerning the administration's obstruction regarding 9/11 information," adds former Senator Graham.

The mounting doubts and growing questions about the veracity of administration explanations concerning what was known and what was done leading up to, during, and after the 9/11 attacks on the United States, and the growing disenchantment with the wars started in retaliation for those attacks, have created a new crisis of legitimacy for the American government. This kind of crisis, which resembles the one that followed the Kennedy assassination and the subsequent Warren Commission Report (another commission whose conclusions were widely disputed, disbelieved, and discredited), breeds a cynicism about American government that is itself dangerous to democracy.

The charitable explanation for the administration's incredible ineptness in the period prior to 9/11, and to its subsequent years of obfuscation, denial, and obstruction, is that there is shame and profound embarrassment in the White House, as well as political concern about how the public would respond to an admission of failure. Such a reaction is surely understandable. But 9/11 was more than just a giant governmental screw-up. It was the biggest and costliest intelligence failure since Pearl Harbor. Moreover, the results of that failure have been used shamelessly by this administration to aggrandize power, even as its efforts to hide its failings have left the United States vulnerable to future attacks.

The proper solution is an aggressive demand for honest answers from the White House and key federal agencies—the kind of demand that could probably only be made by a House Judiciary Committee impeachment inquiry. For this reason, the president should be impeached on charges of obstruction of justice, violation of his oath of office, and jeopardizing national security in relation to the 9/11 attacks and the administration's response to those attacks.

✫ ✫ ✫ ✫ ✫ ✫ ✫ ✫ ✫ ✫ ✫ ✫ ✫

# SEVEN

✫ ✫ ✫ ✫ ✫ ✫ ✫ ✫ ✫ ✫ ✫ ✫ ✫

## *Taking Liberties*

ARTICLE III: In his conduct of the office of President of the United States, George W. Bush, contrary to his oath faithfully to execute the office of the President of the United States, and to the best of his ability preserve, protect, and defend the Constitution of the United States, and in violation of his constitutional duty to take care that the laws be faithfully executed, repeatedly did violate the constitutional rights of citizens and residents of the United States by detaining them without charge, depriving them of the right to a fair and speedy trial, denying them the fundamental right of habeas corpus, and misusing the National Security Agency to spy on citizens, in violation of the Fourth Amendment to the Constitution and the Foreign Surveillance Intelligence Act passed by Congress in 1978.

Youngster, let that show you what it is to be without a family, without a home, and without a country. And if you are ever tempted to say a word or to do a thing that shall put a bar between you and your family, your home and your country, pray God in His mercy to take you that instant home to His own heaven.

—*Philip Nolan, in Edward Everett Hale's*
Man Without a Country

**SHORTLY AFTER** special counsel Patrick Fitzgerald announced his indictment of Vice President Dick Cheney's chief of staff I. Lewis "Scooter" Libby, in the fall of 2004 on perjury charges relating to the outing of CIA agent Valerie Plame Wilson, President Bush tried to escape the bad news in Washington by hiding at Camp David. When he found himself besieged en route to his helicopter by a gaggle of Washington reporters demanding a comment, the president did his best to come to the defense of Libby, who had played so key a role in pushing Iraq scare stories into the media and in propelling the country into war.

"In our system," the president intoned solemnly, "each individual is presumed innocent and entitled to due process and a fair trial."

Five years into a presidency that has been built on lies, deceit, and overt and furtive actions that undermine those very rights, we should not be surprised at President Bush's ability to utter that line with a straight face. Nor, after five years of puffball questions and pro-government cheerleading from the mainstream media, should we be surprised that not one reporter in the press pack rose to ask how the president could make such a statement when he himself had summarily revoked the citizenship rights of some Americans and denied constitutional protections to hundreds of legal residents.

What is shocking is the extent to which the Bush-Cheney administration has run roughshod over civil liberties. This administration has successfully attacked the right to assemble and speak against the government and the right to travel freely, the right to the privacy of one's conversations, and even the right to a fair trial and to be able to face one's accuser. One by one, this administration has undermined almost all of the articles in the Constitution's Bill of Rights, and even fundamental rights like habeas corpus—the absolute right to have one's incarceration and punishment reviewed by a court—which dates back to the earliest days of British Common Law, and perhaps earlier.

## Guilty by Presidential Fiat

At the same moment Bush mouthed those time-honored sentiments about the presumption of innocence and the right to a fair trial for an administration staffer, two other less well-connected American citizens were being denied both rights on orders of the president. Jose Padilla, a young Brooklyn-born American arrested in Chicago and accused of being associated with Al Qaeda, was locked away in solitary confinement in a military brig in South Carolina, held for years without charge, barred from seeing family, friends, or even a lawyer. For most of that time Padilla was deliberately prevented from knowing why he was being held and was unable to appeal to the federal courts or even face his accusers. A second native-born American, Yaser Hamdi, who had been captured in Afghanistan,* was in Saudi Arabia. Although he was a native-born American, the U.S. government, after holding him in isolation for a similar period of captivity without charge, had deported him to the country of his parents. Hamdi had been offered a grim choice:

---

*There has never been any evidence presented to suggest that Hamdi, or another American arrested in Afghanistan, John Walker Lindh, had gone to Afghanistan to fight America. In fact, both young men had traveled there to help the Taliban before 9/11, at a time when the Taliban government was fighting warlord armies backed by Russia, and when it was receiving aid from the United States. Both men appear to have been caught in a difficult spot when 9/11 happened and the United States went to war against the Taliban. Yet both were treated as traitors fighting against their country. Raising doubts about the seriousness of government concern about Hamdi, the government agreed to let him return with his family to visit Disneyland in ten years!

remain imprisoned indefinitely without charge in a military brig in Virginia, or renounce his citizenship and be deported to Saudi Arabia.

As the president was declaiming about the importance of due process, thousands more people, most of them legal residents working in the United States, were confined—often in brutal conditions—in Immigration and Naturalization Service prison cells awaiting deportation. Others were already in distant lands, to which they had been summarily deported without trial after being snatched from their families and swept up in a mass roundup of aliens ordered by the president and his attorney general in the wake of 9/11. Many of these people were taken in the dead of night by heavily armed INS agents who refused to identify themselves, or tell family members why the arrested family members—usually fathers or older sons—were being taken or held. These people simply "disappeared," in a tactic all too reminiscent of the behavior of the military juntas that brought terror during the 1970s and '80s to citizens of a number of Latin American countries,

A third group consisting of hundreds of men—and even boys as young as seven, most, but not all of them captured in Afghanistan—is being held without trial in Guantanamo Bay, Cuba.* "Gitmo" is a U.S. naval base that sits on territory technically leased from Cuba but wholly under U.S. jurisdiction, where the government was claiming these prisoners had no right to a trial or even to prisoner of war status. The base, by the president/commander in chief's tortured logic, supposedly is not a part of the United States (though crimes by personnel committed there have traditionally been tried in U.S. courts).

The Founding Fathers of the United States began the Constitution

---

*As details began finally to emerge about the identities of the captives held at Guantanamo in March 2006, it has become evident that many of them had nothing to do with Afghanistan, with people having been captured in places like Gambia, Belgium, Bosnia, Zambia, and elsewhere, and sent or rendered to Guantanamo, sometimes via a stop for torture and interrogation in Afghanistan. Those captured in Afghanistan should have, under the Geneva Convention protocols, been given an in-country status determination as to whether they were POWs. Those captured elsewhere should have received due process as arrested suspects under the U.S. criminal code.

with the stirring words that "all men are created equal" and that they enjoy "inalienable rights." Shortly after its adoption they added the Bill of Rights, with its guarantees of freedom of speech and assembly, and its prohibitions against illegal searches or detention without trial. Those founders would surely not recognize the new reality of Bush's America. Indeed they warned about just such abuses in the discussions that led them to include, in the very article of the Constitution defining the powers of the president, an impeachment clause for removing a president who engaged in them.

What would Thomas Jefferson, Alexander Hamilton, Benjamin Franklin, or James Madison have said about the treatment of Jose Padilla? Picked up at Chicago's O'Hare International Airport on May 8, 2002, on a flight from Pakistan, Brooklyn-born Padilla essentially had his citizenship snatched away from him, simply because President Bush has claimed the right, on his sole authority as commander in chief, to declare any American citizen to be an "enemy combatant" and to revoke that individual's constitutional rights and citizenship.

For three and a half years no charges were filed against Padilla, but that didn't stop the White House and Justice Department from making wild and unsubstantiated assertions to the media that this alleged former gang member (who lacked even a high school education) had been sent by Al Qaeda to build and detonate a so-called "dirty" nuclear bomb.* As that outlandish claim began to lose credibility, the government shifted to a new one—also never formally introduced as an indictment—that Padilla had planned to blow up apartment buildings by opening gas mains in basements and igniting the ensuing clouds of natural gas. Again there was widespread skepticism. When a federal court finally took note of this presidential affront to the Constitution and ordered the administration to either charge Padilla or release him, the Justice Department had a Florida federal prosecutor indict him. Curiously, in that indictment all reference to bomb plots, dirty nuke or otherwise, vanished and was replaced by a

---

*The government also always carefully referred to Padilla as a "Puerto Rican," as if to stress that he is an alien. In fact, not only are all Puerto Ricans American citizens, but Padilla himself was born in Brooklyn, making him a native New Yorker and a native-born American.

vague charge of allegedly assisting a group to raise money for Islamic terrorist activities overseas. One reason the Bush Justice Department dropped the bombing allegations against Padilla when it came to actually indicting him is that their "evidence" was obtained through the use of torture. One of those torture victims, the alleged 9/11 mastermind Khalid Sheikh Mohammed, had been repeatedly subjected to "water-boarding," a medieval technique of near-drowning. The other, Binyan Muhammed, had been "renditioned" (kidnapped and smuggled abroad) by the CIA to Morocco, where he too, was reportedly tortured.[1] Such evidence would not be admissable in a trial.

Actually, the Founding Fathers—who had considerable experience with indefinite detention without charge under British colonial rule—did have a few things to say about precisely the kind of treatment meted out by the Bush administration to Padilla and Hamdi and other American captives. "Freedom of the person under the protection of the habeas corpus I deem [one of the] essential principles of our government," said Jefferson in his first inaugural address as president. Jefferson also wrote, in an 1819 letter to Isaac H. Tiffany, "Law is often but the tyrant's will, and always so when it violates the right of an individual."

Jefferson's intellectual and political rival, Alexander Hamilton (a man none could accuse of mushy liberalism) said "To bereave a man of life or by violence to confiscate his estate, without accusation or trial, would be so gross and notorious an act of despotism, as must at once convey the alarm of tyranny throughout the whole nation; but confinement of the person by secretly hurrying him to gaol, where his sufferings are unknown or forgotten, is a less public, a less striking, and therefore a more dangerous engine of arbitrary government."[2]

James Madison, for his part, said "The accumulation of all powers, legislative, executive, and judiciary, in the same hands, whether of one, a few, or many, and whether hereditary, self-appointed, or elective, may justly be pronounced the very definition of tyranny."[3]

It was left to Benjamin Franklin to offer up the most uncompromising and characteristically pithy warning against such measures: "Those who would give up essential liberties to obtain a little temporary security deserve neither liberty nor security."

But stirring words from the founders about fundamental American rights carry little weight in the thinking of our nation's forty-third president or of his regent, Vice President Cheney. Indeed, one journalist, Doug Thompson, editor and publisher of the widely read Washington-based journal *Capital Hill Blue,* reports that three Republican congressmen went to the president to warn him that some of his extraconstitutional actions were causing him problems among his core conservative backers. All reportedly told Thompson, a former House aide, they were treated to an astonishing outburst from the president, who allegedly shouted at them, referring to the Constitution as "just a goddamned piece of paper"[4] If the president has such a low opinion of the document he swore to uphold and defend, impeachment is surely in order.

## *Big Brother Bush*

The president's disdain for constitutional limitations and the rule of law became even more evident on December 16, 2005, when *The New York Times,* after holding the information back from publication for almost a year at the request of the White House, published an exposé of a vast government domestic spying campaign conducted by the National Security Agency. This huge, ultrasecret high-tech spy agency (it manages the nation's spy satellites) has been specifically barred from domestic spying without court authorization since 1978. Upon publication of the *Times* stories, President Bush admitted that he had issued executive orders only days after 9/11, and renewed them thirty times thereafter, authorizing the agency to monitor telephone and Internet communications on thousands of people, without any court oversight or warrants.

Citing advice given to him by his attorney general and former White House legal counsel Alberto Gonzales, the president claimed that he had the authority to ignore federal law in ordering the domestic spying on the strength of a congressional resolution passed on September 14, 2001, which authorized him to use "all necessary and appropriate force" against the terrorists who had attacked the country on September 11, 2001. His assistant attorney general, William Moschella, in a letter to Congress, went further, arguing that Congress had in effect authorized granting the president warrantless domestic surveillance authority, the rationale being that surveillance could be considered an integral part of military force.

Most civil liberties legal scholars were unconvinced or outraged. David Cole, a staff attorney with the Center for Constitutional Rights, skewers the argument made by Bush and his attorney general Gonzales that somehow Congress, in authorizing the use of force against Al Qaeda terrorists in Afghanistan, had also authorized domestic spying:

> Attorney General Gonzales contends that the authorization by Congress to use military force somehow implicitly gave the president power to wiretap Americans at home. But nothing in the authorization even mentions wiretaps. And that claim is directly contrary to the express language in FISA limiting any such authority. While intercepting the enemy's communications on the battlefield may well be an incident of the war power, wiretapping hundreds of people inside the United States who are not known to be members of Al Qaeda in no way qualifies as an incidental wartime authority.
>
> . . . To uphold the president here would require finding that Congress has no authority at all to regulate domestic wiretaps of Americans—a proposition that would require overturning decades of established federal law built on congressional regulation of electronic surveillance.[5]

To John Dean, the former counsel to President Richard Nixon (a man whose own domestic spying scandal was the subject of one of three impeachment counts voted out against him by the House Judiciary Committee, and as such led to his resignation from office), Bush's secret spying operation crossed the line into illegality. "There can be no serious question that warrantless wiretapping, in violation of the law, is impeachable," he wrote in a column for the online journal *Findlaw.com*. He went on to call Bush's attempts to justify his transgressions laughable:

> He claims that implicit in Congress' authorization of his use of force against the Taliban in Afghanistan, following the 9/11 attack, was an exemption from FISA.
>
> No sane member of Congress believes that the Authorization of

Military Force provided such an authorization. No first year law student would mistakenly make such a claim. It is not merely a stretch; it is ludicrous.

But the core of Bush's defense is to rely on the very argument made by Nixon: that the president is merely exercising his "commander-in-chief" power under Article II of the Constitution. This, too, is a dubious argument.[6]

Meanwhile, Tom Daschle, the former Democratic senator from South Dakota who had been Senate Majority Leader when the force resolution was passed, weighed in. He recalled that only minutes before that resolution was put to a vote, he had been asked by the White House to amend the bill to include not just Afghanistan and other international jurisdictions, but also the domestic United States within the terms of the resolution. As Daschle said:

> Literally minutes before the Senate cast its vote, the administration sought to add the words "in the United States and" after "appropriate force" in the agreed-upon text. . . . This last-minute change would have given the president broad authority to exercise expansive powers not just overseas—where we all understood he wanted authority to act—but right here in the United States, potentially against American citizens. I could see no justification for Congress to accede to this extraordinary request for additional authority. I refused.

As a *Washington Post* article on Daschle's account noted:

> Daschle's disclosure challenges a central legal argument offered by the White House in defense of the National Security Agency's warrantless wiretapping of U.S. citizens and permanent residents. It suggests that Congress refused explicitly to grant authority that the Bush administration now asserts is implicit in the resolution.[7]

This type of spying is illegal according to the Congressional Research Service, a nonpartisan research arm of Congress. The CRS, in a report requested by several members of Congress and released in the first week of 2006, said that the legal rationale for the secret, warrantless spying by the NSA offered by Bush and his attorneys in the Justice Department "does not seem to be as well grounded" as the administration claims. It pointedly disputes the president's assertion that in granting the president the authority to use all appropriate force against the terrorists behind the 9/11 attacks, Congress had also meant to include domestic wiretapping of Americans. Congress "does not appear to have authorized or acquiesced in such surveillance," the report's authors state.[8]

The Congressional Research Service also concluded that what the White House described as "informing Congress" was in reality a violation of federal law, since federal law requires the administration to keep "all the members" of the House and Senate Intelligence Committees "fully and currently informed" of such activities by the NSA and other intelligence agencies of the government.[9]

This spying program clearly constitutes a willful violation of the law by the president of the United States—one, moreover, which the president has openly admitted to in what amounts to a dare to Congress to do something about it. On its face it is an impeachable crime. As Senator Russell Feingold (D-WI), a member of the Senate Judiciary Committee, says, "We have a system of law. He just can't make up the law . . . It would turn George Bush not into President George Bush, but King George Bush."

Laurence Tribe, a leading constitutional scholar and law professor at Harvard University, goes further. In a letter addressed to Rep. Conyers, Tribe writes:

> Some have defended the NSA program as though it involved nothing beyond computer-enhanced data mining used to trace the electronic paths followed by phone calls and e-mails either originating from or terminating at points overseas associated with terrorists or their affiliates or supporters . . . but that type of intelligence gathering . . . typically entails little or no interception of communicative content that would make it a "search" or "seizure" . . . for Fourth Amendment purposes. . . . Unfortunately, as Attorney general Gonzales candidly conceded . . . the program under discussion here authorized precisely such interception of "contents of communications."

Tribe's evisceration of the administration's argument that Congress' post 9/11 Authorization for the Use of Military Force (AUMF) gave the president the authority to violate FISA is withering:

> It is telling that Attorney General Gonzales, when asked . . . why the administration hadn't simply proposed to congress, in closed session if necessary, that it amend FISA to grant legislative permission for the kind of domestic surveillance program the President deemed essential to the nation's security, replied that the administration had concluded such a request would probably have been futile because Congress would most likely have denied the authority sought! To argue that one couldn't have gotten congressional authorization (in late 2001 when the NSA program was secretly launched) after arguing that, by the way, one did get congressional authorization (in late 2001, when the AUMF[10] was enacted) takes some nerve . . .
>
> The inescapable conclusion is that the AUMF did not implicitly authorize what the FISA expressly prohibited. It follows that the presidential program of surveillance at issue here is a violation of the separation of powers—as grave an abuse of executive authority as I can recall ever having studied.[11]

The NSA spy scandal adds a new dimension to the Bush-Cheney impeachment debate, because concerns about privacy and government threats to Fourth Amendment rights are felt across the political spectrum. In arbitrarily asserting a claim of presidential authority to monitor domestic electronic communications without a court warrant and without establishing a case of probable cause, and in asserting a right to blatantly violate a law passed by Congress outlawing such monitoring, the administration has outraged civil libertarians on both the right and the left.

Said Paul M. Weyrich, a leader of the Free Congress Foundation, a conservative think tank:

> My criteria for judging this stuff is what would a President Hillary do with these same powers. And if I'm troubled by what she would do, then I have to be troubled by what Bush could do, even though I have more trust in Bush than I do in Hillary.[12]

Grover Norquist, a leader of the archconservative group Americans for Tax Reform, and a longtime Bush backer, scoffs at Bush administration legal arguments trying to justify the commander in chief's power to violate a law of Congress, as claimed by Bush and Attorney General Gonzales, saying:

> There is no excuse for violating the rule of law. You can listen to [suspects] and get the warrant afterward. Not to do that appears to be an expression of contempt for the idea of warrants.[13]

The president clearly recognized the danger in publicly admitting that the government is spying on American citizens, for until caught in the act he was careful to insist that his administration was strictly adhering to traditional constitutional requirements. As alarms were being raised in red and blue states about the new Uniting and Strengthening America by Providing Appropriate Tools Required to Intercept and Obstruct Terrorism (USA PATRIOT) Act, Bush—even as he was secretly authorizing the NSA to monitor communications without a warrant—said reassuringly:

> Now, by the way, any time you hear the United States government talking about [a wiretap], it requires—a wiretap requires a court order. Nothing has changed, by the way. When we're talking about chasing down terrorists, we're talking about getting a court order before we do so. It's important for our fellow citizens to understand, when you think Patriot Act, constitutional guarantees are in place when it comes to doing what is necessary to protect our homeland, because we value the Constitution.[14]

We know at this point that this was an outrageous lie. As the president well knew, at the moment he spoke those words, thousands of people were being monitored and tapped without any warrant being obtained to do so, and in deliberate contravention of established federal law. Instead of "valuing the Constitution," President Bush has taken the position that as commander in chief he has the power to ignore federal laws, Congress, and the courts as he sees fit. It is a claim, as Senator

Robert Byrd (D-WV) told his Senate colleagues in a speech from the floor after word of the NSA spying broke out, that is more appropriate to despots than to an elected president. It is also a claim that, on its face, is a violation of the president's oath of office and an impeachable crime.

As Byrd observed, the Constitution established the presidential role of commander in chief to ensure that a civilian would always be in charge of the nation's military, but this role is strictly limited to the military during hostilities (and in no event does it imply using the military in a role against U.S. citizens):

> The President claims that these powers [to spy on American citizens without a court order] are within his role as Commander in Chief. Make no mistake, the powers granted to the Commander in Chief are specifically those as head of the Armed Forces. These warrantless searches are conducted not against a foreign power, but against unsuspecting and unknowing American citizens. They are conducted against individuals living on American soil, not in Iraq or Afghanistan. There is nothing within the powers granted in the Commander in Chief clause that grants the President the ability to conduct clandestine surveillance of American civilians. We must not allow such groundless, foolish claims to stand.[15]

But while Senator Byrd is right that the Constitution's assigning of the role of commander in chief to the president does not grant him the power to spy on the citizenry, Bush's actions are anything but foolish. The whole point of his executive order allowing NSA domestic spying was to avoid having to go before a federal judge sitting in a court established specifically for this purpose for approval. This begs the question: What has he been so anxious to hide? Absent a serious independent investigation, with witnesses subpoenaed to testify under oath, we can at the time of this writing only speculate as to why the president was so willing to risk yet another scandal in order to avoid a court as compliant about wire tapping as the FISA court. After all, that special secret court turned down only four of 19,000 requests for warrants between 1978 and 2005! An impeachment panel should, as an initial step, call Federal District Judge James Robinson, who resigned in early 2006 from the FISA court citing the president's end run of the secret FISA court process.

Reasonable speculation leads in an extremely disturbing direction. Surely the NSA was not just being asked to spy on Al Qaeda suspects, for the FISA judges would have no problem approving such activities in a flash. It seems almost as unlikely that it could have been about spying on the anti-war movement, as unconstitutional as such an action might be. Attorney General John Ashcroft, in office through 2004, on a number of occasions equated opposition to the Iraq War to terrorism, while others have called it treason—sentiments that may be shared by some conservative federal judges. Again it seems probable the administration would have had little difficulty winning approval to wiretap anti-war activists—especially those who were communicating with fellow peace activists overseas.

Yet *The New York Times* reported in late 2005 that the warrantless spying, which Bush's executive order said needed to be approved by the attorney general's office, apparently ran into difficulty getting that approval. *The Times* reported that James B. Comey, who was acting attorney general in 2004 when Ashcroft fell ill with an inflamed gall bladder, was reluctant to sign his name to an extension of the spying program for unspecified reasons. The administration ended up dispatching White House Chief of Staff Andrew Card and White House counsel Alberto Gonzales (who later replaced Ashcroft as attorney general) to the seriously ailing Ashcroft's bedside to get his approval. And reportedly even Ashcroft balked, before finally signing off on the spying.[16]

What was it about this spy program that made Comey and Ashcroft so anxious about being complicit? While both men have refused to explain their actions, the answer could possibly be that the spying involved more than tracking suspected terrorists. For example, it might have included White House political targets, and in 2004, a presidential election year, that recalls the actions of the Nixon White House in the 1972 election year—the year of the Watergate burglary and the notorious White House "plumbers."

As longtime Washington investigative reporter Jim Ridgeway writes:

Given all that's happened, the only explanation for the Bush domestic spying is that it's political. There are no crimes involved here. But there is an overweaning desire by this so-called conservative government to establish and institutionalize a Big Brother regime that tolerates no dissent and wrecks constitutional government.[17]

Far-fetched? Just look back to the origins of the 1978 Foreign Intelligence Surveillance Act itself, which was enacted by Congress following the revelations of the Church Hearings into NSA spying abuses by the Nixon administration, which had used the NSA to monitor political opponents and to gain electoral advantage.

While the Senate Judiciary, as this volume was going to press, was continuing to dig into what the president's secret and Fourth Amendment–subverting spying was all about, and how extensive an operation it was, the Senate Intelligence Committee, headed by the profoundly incurious Sen. Pat Roberts (R-KA), was simultaneously cutting a deal with the White House designed to retroactively okay the president's circumvention of the FISA Court, and to allow his warrantless spying to continue. The deal, which would require the Justice Department only to notify the notoriously compliant Intelligence Committee of its spying activities, even if adopted, would not absolve the president from having committed an impeachable offense, however. As constitutional attorney Francis Boyle explains, "The NSA spying on American citizens without any showing of probable cause is a clear offense under the Fourth Amendment. It really doesn't matter what the Senate does, because the Senate has no right to repeal the Fourth Amendment."

Like the body of lies leading up to the war against Iraq and the outing of Valerie Plame Wilson, the Bush domestic spying scandal is not likely to fade away. Rather, it seems destined to grow as more information inevitably comes out about the program's scope and intentions. In early January 2006, one former NSA intelligence officer, Russell Tice, who was fired from the agency in May 2005 for raising concerns about intelligence security breaches, told the Pacifica Radio program *Democracy Now!* that many of his former colleagues at the NSA were upset at the breach of the rules. Most NSA operatives, he said, take seriously the agency dictum "No spying on Americans." Tice continued:

It's not very difficult to get something through a FISA court. I kind of liken the FISA court to a monkey with a rubber stamp. The monkey sees a name, the monkey sees a word justification with a block of information. It can't read the block, but it just stamps "affirmed" on the block, and a banana chip rolls out, and then the next paper rolls in front of the monkey. When you have like 20,000 requests and only, I think, four were turned down, you can't look at the FISA court as anything different.

So, you have to ask yourself the question: Why would someone want to go around the FISA court in something like this? I would think the answer could be that this thing is a lot bigger than even the President has been told it is, and that ultimately a vacuum-cleaner approach [that] may have been used, in which case you don't get names, and that's ultimately why you wouldn't go to the FISA court. And I think that's something Congress needs to address. They need to find out exactly how this system was operated and ultimately determine whether this was indeed a very focused effort or whether this was a vacuum-cleaner-type scenario.

Tice went on to warn that when this type of broad-based spying campaign is combined with a situation in which the president claims the right to declare anyone an "enemy combatant" and remove their constitutional rights, as Bush did to Padilla and Hamdi, no one is safe:

Anytime where you have a situation where U.S. citizens are being arrested and thrown in jail with the key being thrown away, you know, potentially being sent overseas to be tortured, U.S. citizens being spied on, you know, and it doesn't even go to the court that deals with these secret things, you know, I mean, think about it, you could have potentially somebody getting the wrong phone call from a terrorist and having him spirited away to some back-alley country to get the rubber hose treatment and who knows what else. I think that would kind of qualify as a police state, in my judgment.

I certainly hope that Congress or somebody sort of does something about this, because, for Americans just to say, "Oh, well, we have to do this because of terrorism," you know, it's the same argument that we used with communism years ago: take away your civil liberties, but use some threat that's been out there for a long time.

Terrorism has been there for—certainly before 9/11 we had terrorism problems, and I have a feeling it's going to be around for quite some time after whatever we deem is a victory in what we're doing now in the Middle East. But it's just something that has to be addressed. We just can't continue to see our civil liberties degraded.[18]

Interestingly, the response from political conservatives in Congress and across the country to the spy scandal has been mixed. Many Republicans have rallied around their president, but others have become alarmed. For example, conservative former Congressman Bob Barr, one of the leaders of the Clinton impeachment effort, said "Do we truly remain a society that believes that . . . every president must abide by the laws of this country? I, as a conservative, say yes." In response, the Bush Justice Department ordered an immediate investigation—not of the violation of the FISA Act, but rather how the existence of the program was leaked to *The New York Times*—a move that was applauded by many Republicans in Congress. This suggests that any serious investigation of the NSA spying operation and of the White House role in it is unlikely in the current Republican-led Congress.

Still, at least some conservative voices were calling for some action. As an editorial in the arch-conservative *Deseret News* in Utah put it:

> The president would have Americans believe that Congress authorized him to tap into the phone calls and e-mails people in America send overseas when it authorized him to fight terrorism before the war in Afghanistan. He said Monday that the Constitution grants him the authority to approve such spying, but he never elaborated as to exactly where in the Constitution such authority is granted.
>
> The issue here is not so much whether the federal government should be allowed to listen in on communications it suspects involve terrorist plots. Clearly, the government has a duty to protect national security, and it has a right to obtain vital information that aids in performing that duty.

No, the issue has to do with following the process that is in place to protect the American people from abuses by a president and his investigators. The Foreign Intelligence Surveillance Act allows the government to wiretap in defense of national interests. But it also sets up a special secret court, available on a moment's notice, to hear the government's pleas and to grant a warrant for such searches.

That safeguard is a necessary check on power. Otherwise, the president would have absolute authority to spy on Americans as he pleases.[19]

Another view of the scandal was offered by Bruce Fein, a politically conservative constitutional scholar and former deputy attorney general during the Reagan administration. He said:

> On its face, if President Bush is totally unapologetic and says "I continue to maintain that as a wartime President I can do anything I want—I don't need to consult any other branches"—that is an impeachable offense. It's more dangerous than Clinton's lying under oath because it jeopardizes our democratic dispensation and civil liberties for the ages. It would set a precedent that . . . would lie around like a loaded gun, able to be used indefinitely for any future occupant.[20]

Or by the current one, who seems to have no qualms about violating constitutional rights and traditions of checks and balances, unless stopped by an impeachment proceeding.

Indeed, even as questions were continuing to grow about the warrantless NSA spying program exposed by *The New York Times,* the administration was hinting that it might not have fully come clean with either Congress or the American public about the extent of that program. In a letter of clarification sent by Attorney General Gonzales to the Senate and made public on February 28, 2006, Gonzales seemed to be trying to explain that he might have not been entirely forthcoming in his February 6 testimony before the Senate Judiciary Committee, either about the extent of the domestic spying or about its justification. Before that committee, Gonzales had declared that the warrantless wiretapping had been authorized by President Bush "and that is all that he has authorized." But in his later letter he wrote:

> I did not and could not address . . . any other classified intelligence
> activities . . . I was confining my remarks to the Terrorist Surveillance
> Program [the name the administration belatedly bestowed on the program] as described by the President, the legality of which was the subject [of the Feb. 6 hearing].[21]

As former White House lawyer Bruce Fein, who had also testified at that hearing, commented dryly,

> It seems to me he is conceding that there are other NSA surveillance
> programs ongoing that the president hasn't told anyone about.[22]

In his letter to the Senate, Gonzales also cast some doubt on his and the administration's earlier claim that it had taken the September 2001 congressional force authorization resolution as its justification for the spying program. In the letter he wrote,

> These statements may give the misimpression that the Department's
> legal analysis has been static over time.[23]

The new information suggests that the AUMF resolution argument was used by the administration as an ex post facto justification for its FISA-violating spying program, perhaps developed *after* the program was exposed. As attorney Fein suggests, the administration's legal justification for the warrantless spying appears to have "evolved over time."

## *Disappearing Act*

It is often said that one can judge a society by how it treats its weakest members. It is also true that a society's justness can be judged by how well it protects the rights and freedom of its citizens when it feels itself under threat.

By that standard, the United States came up short during World War II when it interned over 110,000 Japanese men, women, and children living in this country, the vast majority of them U.S. citizens. Many of those people lost businesses, farms, and homes during their enforced confinement in these remote internment camps. Once again during the current crisis the nation has come up short, as thousands of immigrants, foreign visitors, students of Arab, South Asian, and Muslim backgrounds were rounded up, imprisoned, mistreated, subjected to secret deportation hearings, and often deported to their native countries, where some of them may have been tortured or killed by the repressive governments they had earlier fled.*

In the immediate aftermath of the 9/11 attacks, the U.S. government began a mass roundup of thousands of males from Arab, South Asian, and Islamic nations. The actual number of people who have been detained is not known, as the government refuses to divulge that information, but it easily could exceed five thousand. Some people were detained after local police stopped them for minor traffic violations—a broken taillight or an expired registration sticker. Others were held when they went into an INS office to correct a late green card renewal, or to comply with a post-9/11 order requiring males from Islamic nations to register with the INS. Almost all of these people were law-abiding residents of this country, with families. Many of them were married to American citizens and had American-born children, had legitimate businesses or jobs, and had simply come to the attention of law enforcement in a run-of-the-mill way. In ordinary times, they might have had to hire an attorney to fix the problem or it might have simply been waived. But things had turned ugly. Many hundreds of those rounded up found themselves packed off to local, state, or federal jails, where they were kept shackled and held in secret, their families left in the dark as to their whereabouts and status. Others were actually picked up in of the middle of the night

*Some of those deported had been admitted to the U.S. under political asylum provisions, because the INS had determined that they faced persecution at home.

by INS agents who would break into apartments and homes and drag off people suspected of having some link to terrorists. All too often these people were held without charge, abused in jail, and then deported.

That's what happened to Ehab Elmaghraby, an Egyptian resident living in New York, who was picked up in the post-9/11 roundup of allegedly suspicious Arab males. After being deported by the INS to Egypt, Elmaghraby returned to the United States under a special court order that allows him to file suit against the Justice Department for his abuse while in detention. The thirty-seven-year-old man, who owned a small deli-restaurant in Times Square, had been held by federal authorities in the New York Metropolitan Detention Center, where he was kept in solitary without charge for almost a year before being shipped off to Egypt. That was bad enough, but Elmaghraby alleges that during that whole period he was kept from seeing an attorney, was regularly beaten, was accused of being a terrorist, was left outside for hours in the rainy detention center yard on cold days, was denied medical care, was strip-searched in front of female guards, was kept in ankle shackles, and was regularly pushed to the ground so that his face was injured and his teeth broken. "I was in life and I went to hell," he said. Elmaghraby was termed a "person of high interest" by the Justice Department, but it appears there was no reason for this other than random, unverified calls from tipsters who had claimed he "looked suspicious."[24]

In February 2006, the government settled out of court a federal lawsuit filed by Elmaghraby, awarding him $300,000 in damages. No charges were ever made against him.

A Justice Department inspector general's report has confirmed that the brutal treatment meted out to detainees like Elmaghraby, far from being the rogue actions of some sadistic guards, were more or less standard for the Muslims who were rounded up by the government. The report documented the regular physical abuse of detainees, as well as the fact that virtually none of them had any terrorism links. It stated dryly: "We found significant problems in the way the detainees were handled."[25]

In some ways the current roundup of Muslims in America has been worse than the Japanese internments, because at least all those World War II–era internees were publicly identified. Their fates were known, their friends and families on the outside knew how to reach them, and they were not silenced. Nor did they face deportation.* By contrast, the latest internees have more often than not "disappeared," to use a terrifying term parlanced in Latin American dictatorships.

The USA PATRIOT Act, pushed through Congress by the administration a month after the 9/11 attacks, helped initiate this domestic reign of terror visited on the U.S. immigrant community by authorizing the INS to detain immigrants without charge for up to seven days. But as a belated report by the Justice Department's inspector general revealed, many captives were in fact held illegally without charge for as long as eight months, denied access to attorneys, and then, after secret hearings, deported.

Perhaps the most terrifying fact about these mass roundups is that almost every single person detained thus far has proven to be wholly innocent. But the government secrecy and climate of fear fostered by the Bush administration has caused Americans to permit this mistreatment to happen. According to that official report, released in 2004, although then Attorney General Ashcroft and President Bush initially touted the roundups as evidence of an aggressive administration's "war on terror," *only one* of those thousands of immigrants picked up in the sweeps was ultimately convicted of terrorism, and that was on a charge not of "terrorism," but of "supporting terrorism."**

The whole sorry process has been, and remains, completely unconstitutional. As David Cole, a professor of law at Georgetown University and an attorney with the Center for Constitutional Rights, points out in his book *Enemy Aliens,* the protections afforded by the Bill of Rights against illegal search and seizure, against arrest and detention without charge, and against discrimination based upon race and religion, among other things, refer to "persons," not "citizens." That is, everyone in the United States, whether here as a tourist or as an illegal alien, is covered. The use

*Decades later, Congress officially voted out a resolution of apology for the World War II detentions and also established a token compensation fund.
**Under new PATRIOT Act and other post 9/11 laws, people can be (and have been) convicted of "supporting terrorism" even if they gave money to a charity that unbeknownst to them was providing funds to some other organization identified by the government as terrorist-linked.

of that word, "person" was hardly accidental, since the authors of the Constitution were careful to use the term "citizen" in other places, for example, in defining the eligibility to serve in federal elective office.

Those good citizens who do not find the abuse of aliens by federal police to be a matter of great concern should recall the fates of Jose Padilla and Yaser Hamdi, who as we saw were stripped of their citizenship rights by the president. As Cole notes, Americans need to pay special attention to the way the government treats immigrants, for history has shown that the way law enforcement authorities treat resident foreigners can frequently be a harbinger of how they will later treat citizens:

> The line between citizen and foreigner, so natural during wartime, is not only easy to exploit when restrictive measures are introduced, but also easy to breach when the government later finds it convenient to do so. The transition from denying the rights of enemy aliens to infringing those of American citizens was unusually swift with Hamdi and Padilla; more often, the transition takes years to complete. But history suggests that the transition is virtually inevitable, and that therefore in the long term, the rights of all of us are in the balance when the government selectively sacrifices foreign nationals' liberties.[26]

Combine the government's unconstitutional and draconian treatment of Arab and other Islamic immigrants and the president's assertion of both a right to spy at will on anyone, and to declare anyone to be an "enemy combatant." Now strip away all constitutional rights so that someone so accused has no recourse to the courts, and you get a terrifying picture of government run amok. This is a constitutional crisis crying out for the remedy of impeachment. Anyone who believes he or she is immune from such treatment has little understanding of history. Imagine this nightmare: An overeager NSA Internet monitor detects an unsolicited e-mail to your computer from a suspected terrorist-linked organization. This is reported to the FBI. Agents have you declared an "enemy combatant" and you're packed off, without your family's knowledge, to a military base in a remote state, or perhaps to Guantanamo. You're not permitted to call your lawyer. You're not even allowed your "one phone call." There you could sit indefinitely, without knowledge of the charge against you, while you are subjected to presidentially approved "extreme methods" of interrogation aimed at finding out who you know and how you're linked to international terror organizations.

Is this what Americans voted for in 2000 and 2004? Clearly the answer is no. Equally clearly, the president's authorization of unconstitutional actions by the nation's federal law enforcement authorities is an impeachable act.

* * * * * * * * * * * * *

# EIGHT

* * * * * * * * * * * *

## *Vengeance and Betrayal*

ARTICLE IV: In his conduct of the office of President of the United States, George W. Bush, contrary to his oath faithfully to execute the office of the President of the United States, and to the best of his ability preserve, protect, and defend the Constitution of the United States, and in violation of his constitutional duty to take care that the laws be faithfully executed, allowed the disclosure of the name of a CIA undercover operative in violation of both the Intelligence Identities Protection Act of 1982 and the Espionage Act of 1917, lied to the American people about the president's role in the disclosure, obstructed justice by hiding his personal knowledge of the deliberate leaking of the identity of an undercover operative to the press, and engaged in a conspiracy to cover up the White House's and particularly the Vice President's office's roles in the public disclosure.

I have nothing but contempt and anger for those who be-
tray the trust by exposing the name of our sources. They
are, in my view, the most insidious of traitors.
*—Former President George H. W. Bush, in a speech at CIA
headquarters in Langley, Virginia, on April 26, 1999*

PRESIDENT BUSH'S direct personal culpability in the illegal exposure of the identity of a CIA operative may not be known until the results of further investigation by either special counsel Patrick Fitzgerald,
a congressional committee, or enterprising journalists, yet it seems clear
already that even if he did not directly order the outing of an agent, the
president was involved in protecting those in the White House who
handled the dirty work. Such an effort to interfere with a federal criminal investigation would be obstruction of justice—an impeachable
crime. It seems even clearer that the president was not telling the truth
to the American people when he promised back in 2003 and again in
2004 to get to the bottom of the scandal and to fire anyone found to
have been involved in the crime. Lying to the American people, as President Nixon learned, is also an impeachable offense.

If the story of the Bush administration's scandals were made into a
movie, Valerie Plame Wilson would have a good shot at a starring role,
playing herself. Glamorous wife of a heroic, handsome career diplomat
and strikingly good-looking herself, Plame was living the kind of im-
probable double life that authors of spy thrillers try to conjure up to
make their plots more fantastic. A CIA undercover operative posing as a
suburban working mom, Plame's specific area of expertise was to monitor and to help deter the spread of weapons of mass destruction—
especially nuclear weapons.

Why do we know this?

Because, in 2003, several key people in the White House, acting in
concert and clearly under instructions from the highest levels, deliberately slipped Plame's identity to several prominent members of the media, blowing her cover and her career. This campaign, aimed at

undermining claims by Plame's husband that the administration's story that Hussein had tried to buy a necessary component of a nuclear weapon from Niger was bogus, potentially placed many of Plame's overseas contacts at deadly risk, or at a minimum ended their usefulness as sources on an issue of urgent concern to the nation and the world.

What was done to Plame must be established to have been a federal crime. Indeed, it could have been several federal crimes at once—possibly violating both the Covert Agent Identity Protection Act of 1982 and the Intelligence Identities Protection Act of 1947, as well as the Espionage Act of 1917. Why it was committed goes to the heart of the whole Iraq War deception. Whether those crimes are impeachable ones, or perhaps lead to the indictment of the vice president, depends on whether the responsibility for ordering their commission can be traced up to the offices of the vice president and the president. By early 2006, with the indictment of Vice President Cheney's chief of staff I. Lewis "Scooter" Libby, and the continuing investigation of Bush's key political strategist Karl Rove, the trail already has reached the upper levels of the White House hierarchy, with no reason to think the buck stops there. Indeed, in his defense Libby has admitted his knowledge about Plame came directly from Vice President Cheney. As Prosecutor Fitzgerald reported, "Mr. Libby testified that he was authorized to disclose information about the National Intelligence Estimate (Plame's identity) to the press by his superiors."

## Conjuring Up a Yellow-Cake Shipment and a "Mushroom Cloud"

It should be clear at this point that the Bush-Cheney administration, which had its sights set on Baghdad and "regime change" from the day it took office, was by 2002 well on the way to invading Iraq, and was only looking for ways, to borrow from the Downing Street memo, to "fix the facts" so as to win public support for war. The game plan was to make Saddam Hussein look scary to Americans, and what better way to scare people than to say that this bloody dictator was trying to get The Bomb?

Thus ensued a campaign of deceit and fabrication of evidence designed to make it look as though Iraq was only months away from having a nuclear device, when in fact, as UN inspectors had concluded based upon careful research, there was no nuclear program at all.

And thus we had the story of the aluminum tube shipments—tubes that the administration insisted were "only suitable" for use in gas centrifuges designed for separating bomb-grade U-235 from the more common, nonfissionable U-238 isotope of uranium. In reality, the pipes were too short, and were in other ways unsuited for that purpose, but were ideally suited for other legal uses, such as fuselages for small battlefield rockets.

And we had the story of Iraq's supposed efforts to buy refined uranium ore—"yellow cake" in industry parlance—from Niger, an impoverished, landlocked nation in the center of northern Africa.*

The Niger yellow-cake story reportedly dates back to 1999, when the French, who have control over the uranium mining in Niger, suspected possible smuggling from some abandoned mines. An investigation found no evidence of smuggling, but the speculation may have led some people in Italy with connections to Italian intelligence and to the Niger embassy in Rome to smell easy money.

According to an investigation by the widely respected Italian newspaper *La Repubblica,* on January 2, 2001, a former officer of Italy's intelligence service, the Servizio per le Informazioni e la Sicurezza

*It was always a measure of the weak case for Iraq's posing a nuclear threat that the best the administration could come up with was highly questionable evidence of centrifuges and uranium ore purchases, since these are only preliminary steps in the making of a bomb. For example yellow cake, a raw form of uranium oxide, is just one step out of the mine. To become a bomb the ore must first be refined into pure uranium. Then it must be vaporized into a gas and put into an extremely high-tech centrifuge, where the lighter and fissionable U-235 isotope—which represents only a tiny fraction of naturally occurring uranium—must be separated from the heavier and much more common, but not fissionable, U-238. And that is only the start of the process of making a bomb. Then comes the design and construction of a device that will actually detonate. Even if it were true that Iraq was trying to get yellow cake, most experts agree it would have been years from a bomb, even without factoring in the difficulties posed by an embargo.

Militare (SISMI), together with a woman who had worked in the Niger embassy, broke into the Niger embassy. Suspiciously, the only things stolen were letterhead stationery and a government seal. A second burglary occurred on January 31 at the home of Niger's ambassador to Italy.

Documents were then forged using the stolen papers and seal, and were handed over to French intelligence—which immediately recognized them as crude forgeries and promptly junked them. As a French official told the *La Repubblica* reporters investigating the story,

> Niger is a French-speaking place and we know how they do things there. But no one would have mistaken one minister for another in they way they did in that useless parcel of garbage.[1]

That might have been the end of the story, but for the Bush administration's need to create a powerful and dangerous Iraq. Never mind that the Niger documents were fakes (see appendix B—Niger Forgeries), and that there was no attempt by Iraq as late as 1999 or 2001 to purchase yellow cake in Niger or anywhere else in the world. The documents provided a good story line for the people working at the White House and in the Pentagon's Office of Special Plans trying to build a case for war. Shortly after the attacks on the Pentagon and World Trade Center, SISMI, under a new director appointed by Italian Prime Minister S. Berlusconi, passed the dodgy documents to Britain's MI6.

The conservative Berlusconi, eager to develop close relations with the new U.S. president, visited the White House in October 2001, and handed over the dossier on Iraq's alleged efforts to buy uranium from Niger. The dossier, which the U.S. State Department described as "highly suspect," was essentially the same set of forged documents which French intelligence had rejected. Among the obvious mistakes in the documents was that they had been signed by a Niger official who had already left office by the date in question. The package reportedly included some earlier records of an actual attempt by Hussein to buy yellow cake from Niger in the mid-1980s, clumsily passing that aborted deal off as occurring some fifteen years later.

By this point, Vice President Cheney and his top lieutenant Libby were making regular visits to the CIA to pressure agency analysts into building a case for invading Iraq by skewing the evidence to show that Iraq possessed weapons of mass destruction and had an advanced nuclear weapons development program. The Niger document fit nicely with this plan, forgery or not. But with both the CIA and the State Department raising serious questions about the document's authenticity, a new approach was needed.

In late December a meeting was held in Rome. The attendees reportedly included Michael Ledeen, an associate of Defense Department Undersecretary Secretary for Policy Douglas Feith and a key figure in the current Bush administration's war propaganda program. Also reportedly there were Larry Franklin, a top Defense Intelligence Agency Middle East analyst who later pleaded guilty to passing classified information to two employees of the America Israel Public Affairs Committee, convicted bank swindler Ahmed Chalabi, then head of the Iraqi National Congress, and Harold Rhode, of the Defense Department's Office of Special Plans. On the Italian side were the heads of SISMI and the Italian Defense Department.[2]

According to Carlo Bonini, an investigative reporter with the Italian newspaper *La Repubblica*, it was probably at this high-powered meeting that the plan to recycle the Niger documents through British intelligence was hatched.[3] Indeed, this was a theory proposed by an Italian parliamentary committee investigating the forged documents, which in early 2005 investigated the activities of Ledeen. (A copy of that committee report has reportedly been provided to special counsel Fitzgerald.)

Ledeen, a fellow at the American Enterprise Institute, a right-wing think tank in Washington, D.C., denies that he was involved in the Niger affair. In an e-mail to Larisa Alexandrovna, an editor of the online journal *The Raw Story*, the man who played a crucial middleman role in the Reagan-era Iran arms-for-hostage scandal, says "I've said repeatedly, I have no involvement of any sort with the Niger story, and I have no knowledge of it aside from what has appeared in the press. I have not discussed it with any government person in any country."[4]

Bonini and fellow journalist Giuseppi d'Avannzo, in *La Repubblica*, also link Steven Hadley to the Niger forgeries, noting that then Deputy

National Security Adviser Hadley met in Washington on September 9, 2002, with SISMI chief Nicolo Pollari just a month before the yellow-cake story was made public by the White House.[5] (Hadley was promoted to National Security Adviser after his boss, Condoleezza Rice, was bumped up to Secretary of State in 2005.)

Meanwhile, the CIA, unwilling to just go along with the program, wanted better evidence. Enter Valerie Plame, who worked in the Agency's counter-proliferation division. Although there is some dispute exactly who first came up with the idea, in February 2002 Plame suggested to the CIA director of operations that her husband, Joseph Wilson—who had "good relations" with Niger's prime minister and the minister of mines and with the French who ran the mining—be sent to check out the story. Wilson, a career diplomat and former NSC staffer who as ambassador to Iraq had heroically shepherded Americans out of the country before the first Gulf War, was dispatched to Niger, and returned to say the yellow-cake story was hokum.

As Seymour Hersh wrote in *The New Yorker* magazine:

[Wilson] learned that any memorandum of understanding to sell yellow cake would have required the signatures of Niger's Prime Minister, Foreign Minister, and Minister of Mines. "I saw everybody out there," Wilson said, and no one had signed such a document. "If a document purporting to be about the sale contained those signatures, it would not be authentic." Wilson also learned that there was no uranium available to sell: it had all been pre-sold to Niger's Japanese and European consortium partners.[6]

This clearly was not the news the White House and Pentagon wanted to hear, so it was ignored. Over the next months White House and Pentagon references to alleged recent Iraqi efforts to buy yellow cake continued unabated. This disinformation continued to receive coverage thanks to the help of cooperative reporters like *The New York Times'* Judith Miller, who was later publicly reprimanded and taken off the story by the paper for her "credulous" and poorly documented reporting on Iraq's nonexistent WMDs.

Beginning in August 2002, Cheney began referring to Iraq's alleged nuclear program as a "mortal threat" to America. By the fall of 2002, both National Security Adviser Rice and Bush himself began referring to a "mushroom cloud" from Hussein threatening America.[7] The latter reference coincided with the creation of the White House Iraq Group (WHIG) by Bush Chief of Staff Andrew Card and Bush political strategist Rove. WHIG's stated goal was "educating" the American public about the threat posed by Saddam Hussein. Typical of its work was a statement by Rice made in an interview on CNN's *Late Edition* on September 8, 2002, that "there will always be some uncertainty about how quickly he can acquire nuclear weapons, but we don't want the smoking gun to be a mushroom cloud."

To back up these unsupportable but frightening claims, the administration began citing "documents" in the hands of British intelligence, which turn out to have been the same forged materials from Rome that had been rejected by French and U.S. intelligence services. Recycled, they were presented to Congress and the public as new and credible British evidence. This deception culminated in President Bush's famous "sixteen words" spoken during his January 28, 2003, State of the Union address, as the final touches were being put on the administration's Iraq invasion plan. "The British government has learned that Saddam Hussein recently sought significant quantities of uranium from Africa," the president told the nation.[8] This statement, made in an official, constitutionally mandated report to the Congress and to the American people, was a lie. It is inconceivable that the president did not know that it was a lie, as similar words had been removed from a speech he'd made three months earlier. Therefore, it is grounds for impeachment.

Over the ensuing months, after the invasion and overthrow of Hussein, as casualties mounted and efforts to find the tyrant's alleged WMDs produced absolutely nothing, the administration continued to repeat the Niger yellow-cake story mantra, in an effort to deflect growing domestic criticism of the war. All this hyping of a nonexistent threat shocked Wilson, who assumed his report had been heeded. Though he had initially supported the overthrow of Saddam Hussein, this manifest fraud increasingly angered the normally diplomatic and bureaucratically correct ambassador. During late spring, he began privately leaking information about his trip and his findings to members of the media. On

May 6, Nicholas Kristof, a columnist for *The New York Times,* first mentioned Wilson's report in an article. Without identifying the source, he wrote that a central claim for Bush's war rationale had been investigated and rejected by a "former ambassador to an African country." Wilson later went to *The Washington Post* with his story. He also talked to two congressional committees. Finally, deciding to go public, he wrote an opinion piece in *The New York Times.* In it he said:

> Did the Bush administration manipulate intelligence about Saddam Hussein's weapons programs to justify an invasion of Iraq?
>
> Based on my experience with the administration in the months leading up to the war, I have little choice but to conclude that some of the intelligence related to Iraq's nuclear weapons program was twisted to exaggerate the Iraqi threat.

Wilson was even more specific in condemning the Bush statement in his State of the Union address concerning the alleged Iraqi attempt to purchase yellow-cake ore in Niger. He writes:

> In late February 2002, I arrived in Niger's capital, Niamey, where I had been a diplomat in the mid-70s and visited as a National Security Council official in the late 90s . . .
>
> I spent the next eight days drinking sweet mint tea and meeting with dozens of people: current government officials, former government officials, people associated with the country's uranium business. It did not take long to conclude that it was highly doubtful that any such transaction had ever taken place.
>
> Given the structure of the consortiums that operated the mines, it would be exceedingly difficult for Niger to transfer uranium to Iraq. Niger's uranium business consists of two mines, Somair and Cominak, which are run by French, Spanish, Japanese, German, and Nigerian interests. If the government wanted to remove uranium from a mine, it would have to notify the consortium, which in turn is strictly monitored by the International Atomic Energy Agency. Moreover, because the two mines are closely regulated, quasi-governmental entities, selling uranium would require the approval of the minister of mines, the prime

minister and probably the president. In short, there's simply too much oversight over too small an industry for a sale to have transpired.[9]

## *White House Attack*

Even before Wilson went public with his story, a worried White House began looking for ways to counter his seriously damaging critique. On May 23, 2003, Senator Pat Roberts (R-KS) and Senator Jay Rockefeller (D-WV), the ranking members of the Senate Intelligence Committee, had jointly requested the State Department inspector general and CIA inspector general each to review the issue of the Niger documents. Less than a week later, on May 29, Lewis Libby, Cheney's chief of staff, asked both Undersecretary of State for Arms Control John Bolton, and Marc Grossman, Undersecretary of State for Political Affairs, for information about the CIA mission to Niger. Grossman reportedly obtained a classified report from the State Department's intelligence bureau, and briefed Libby on its contents. Meanwhile, Frederick Fleitz, Bolton's chief of staff, obtained Plame's identity and her relationship to Wilson, and passed that information to his boss. Bolton informed Libby, who then requested a full report from Bolton on Wilson's trip. With Rockefeller upping the ante by calling for a joint Senate Intelligence Committee/Armed Services Committee investigation into the Niger forgeries, Libby ordered up all CIA documents on Wilson's trip.

By June 11 Libby had established that Wilson's wife worked for the CIA and was at least in part a factor in his being sent to Niger, although it cannot be confirmed that he knew at that point she was an undercover operative. However, as explained in the Libby indictment drawn up by Special Counsel Fitzgerald, the following day, June 12, Cheney informed Libby that Plame worked in the CIA's counterintelligence division.[10] During that period in early June, the indictment alleges that there were discussions in the vice president's office, which reportedly included Cheney, Libby, Cheney's chief counsel David Addington, senior national security aide John Hannah, Cheney press secretary Catherine Martin, and other White House officials, about going to the press with the Wilson/Plame connection. Three days later, Libby was at the CIA discussing Plame and Wilson.

On June 23, the first leak to the press came, with Libby meeting *New York Times* reporter Judith Miller. Miller's notes, subpoenaed by Prosecutor Fitzgerald, say Libby told her about "Wilson's activities" and at the same time sought to place the "blame for intelligence failures on the CIA." One day after the publication of Wilson's opinion piece in the *Times*, Libby told White House Press Secretary Ari Fleischer (who resigned his post shortly afterward) that it was "not widely known" that Wilson's wife worked for the CIA.

The following day the White House acknowledged that the Niger documents were forgeries, with CIA Director George Tenet taking the blame and saying that the claim about an Iraqi attempt to buy uranium in Africa should have been deleted from the president's State of the Union address. There has, since that time, been an effort by the White House to shift the blame for the inclusion of those sixteen words to bureaucratic bungling, but this excuse doesn't hold up. The yellow-cake reference was first included in a speech given by the president three months earlier in Ohio. At that time, the CIA had challenged the evidence and it had been removed. Its inclusion in the January State of the Union address was a deliberate ignoring of the CIA's objections and other evidence that had been presented showing that the claim was bogus.

During this period, Karl Rove, the president's chief strategist and closest political confidante, began talking to the press about Wilson, beginning with *Time* magazine reporter Matthew Cooper and, probably, conservative CNN political commentator Robert Novak.[11] According to a *Washington Post* report, White House sources leaked this information about Plame's identity to as many as six reporters—and these sources reportedly included Libby, probably Rove, and possibly others including the vice president. Finally Novak, on July 14, revealed Plame's identity in his syndicated column. A supporter of the administration, Novak questioned Wilson's motives for going public with his information about his Niger fact-finding trip. Citing "two senior administration officials" as his sources, Novak outed Plame as Wilson's wife and as a CIA agent. In his column he suggested that "nepotism" was the motive behind the CIA's choice of Wilson for the Niger assignment.

On July 30, the CIA notified the Justice Department of a possible offense under federal law "concerning the unauthorized disclosure of classified information," and several days later completed an eleven-question damage assessment, as required in such cases. A justice department investigation was subsequently opened into the leak, though under Attorney General John Ashcroft's watchful eye.

By this point, the administration was scrambling to cover itself. Appearing on NBC's *Meet the Press* on September 14, Cheney claimed he didn't know Wilson was sent to Niger. Asserting that he didn't even know Wilson had a wife, he said, "He never submitted a report that I ever saw when he came back. I don't know Mr. Wilson." Later testimony in the government's Plame outing investigation shows that Cheney was lying. Because of the vice president's unique position as the second-highest elected official in the land, this lie to the American people itself, while not a crime, could constitute grounds for impeachment.

In October 2003, Karl Rove reportedly called *Hardball* host Chris Matthews to say that Plame was "fair game," making it clear that for the White House, targeting her was a legitimate means to undermine Wilson, and with him his statements regarding the Niger documents. This type of personal attack had been standard operating procedure for Rove throughout his career. At the same time, White House Press Secretary Scott McClellan was telling inquiring Washington reporters that it was "totally ridiculous" for them to suspect Rove of having a role in Plame's outing.

On October 7, Bush himself weighed in on the Plame outing story. Claiming he wanted to know who had outed her, he said flatly that he would fire anyone in his administration who had exposed an agent. He claimed he had no idea who had leaked the story to Novak, saying "I don't know if we're going to find out the senior administration official. Now, this is a large administration, and there's [sic] a lot of senior officials." A day later, Rove was interviewed by the FBI. He reportedly told the agents he had only identified Plame after Novak's column had revealed her identity—a claim he had to go back on just before Fitzgerald's announcement of indictments against Libby, when Rove's attorney rushed forward with "corrected" information that, in fact, Rove had met earlier with *Time* magazine's Cooper. Rove's sudden "recall" of the Cooper meeting came only after Cooper dropped his refusal to speak to

Fitzgerald, agreed to be questioned, and turned over his notes to investigators. In other words, after his lie had been revealed to Fitzgerald. (Memories in this case seem to get jogged whenever Fitzgerald comes up with new evidence. According to a Justice Department source, Libby has even hired a memory expert as part of his defense team.)

Asked directly by reporters at a press conference on October 10 whether Rove or other key White House aides had been the source of the Plame leak, press secretary McClellan said he had spoken with Rove, Libby, and Elliott Abrams, "and those individuals assured me they were not involved in this." More lies, although no one knows if Rove and Libby had lied to McClellan or if McClellan was being less than truthful.

On December 30, after protests from the FBI and federal prosecutors, Attorney General Ashcroft recused himself from the Plame investigation, which up to that point he had reportedly insisted on monitoring on a daily basis. Career prosecutor Fitzgerald was named special counsel to pursue the case and a grand jury was impaneled in Washington, D.C.

Over the course of 2004, Fitzgerald's grand jury quietly met and interviewed Libby several times. The grand jury also heard from Rove and other figures in the Plame outing case. Rove, in fact, was called before the grand jury at least four times. Fitzgerald's case was seriously impeded by the lack of cooperation of several key journalists, notably Miller and Cooper, who both fought subpoenas ordering them to testify and turn over their notes of conversations with figures under investigation, including Libby and Rove. Miller ultimately went to jail for eighty-five days for contempt before finally agreeing to cooperate with Fitzgerald.

## *Duck and Cover*

Miller's and Cooper's notes and testimony gave Fitzgerald the evidence he needed to gain a grand jury indictment of Cheney's chief of staff I. Lewis "Scooter" Libby on five counts of perjury, false statements, and obstruction of justice. The charges, all felonies, carry a potential penalty of up to thirty years in prison and $1.25 million in fines. The indictment alleges that Libby lied to agents of the FBI and to the grand jury multiple times by implying that he had learned of Plame's identity and relationship to Wilson from reporters, when in fact it was the other way around, that he had revealed her identity to reporters, and that he obstructed prosecutorial efforts to get to the truth of the story. The indictment also alludes to an "official A," widely believed to be Karl Rove, who told Libby he had spoken to Novak about Plame's identity and that Novak would be reporting the story.

With Fitzgerald's investigation still underway before a newly impaneled second grand jury, and with Libby's trial scheduled to be held in 2007, it is difficult to know where things will go and who else may be drawn into the scandal. But the Libby indictment makes it clear that the vice president was involved in discussions about Wilson and Plame, and that Cheney had provided Libby with information regarding Plame's undercover identity, contrary to what he had stated publicly about his knowledge of Wilson and Plame. In a letter to the federal court, Prosecutor Fitzgerald says that Libby told the Grand Jury that he had been instructed to leak highly classified information to the press by his "superiors." Libby worked directly under Vice President Cheney. Investigative journalist Murry Waas, writing in *The National Journal*, has reported that unidentified sources close to the Libby case informed him that it was Cheney himself who authorized Libby's leak of a National Security Estimate.

As Waas writes:

Beyond what was stated in the court paper, say people with firsthand knowledge of the matter, Libby also indicated what he will offer as a broad defense during his upcoming criminal trial: that Vice President Cheney and other senior Bush administration officials had earlier encouraged and authorized him to share classified information with journalists to build public support for going to war. Later, after the war began in 2003, Cheney authorized Libby to release additional classified information, including details of the NIE [National Intelligence Estimate], to defend the administration's use of prewar intelligence in making the case for war.

Waas adds that Libby's claim regarding the Vice President

significantly adds to a mounting body of information that Cheney played a central and personal role in directing efforts to counter claims by Wilson and other administration critics that the Bush administration had misused intelligence information to go to war with Iraq.[12]

In a development reminiscent of the belated discovery about President Nixon's Oval Office tapes, it was learned in early March 2006 that some 250 allegedly "missing" e-mails requested three years earlier from the White House by prosecutor Fitzgerald had turned up. In late February, court records show the White House turned over 250 e-mails, which Libby's attorney said he was informed were "from the office of the vice president." It remains to be seen what is on those additional e-mails, which the White House had earlier claimed had not been properly preserved. A record of their existence had reportedly been initially discovered by Fitzgerald's investigators on computers confiscated from the office of the vice president.[13]

As for President Bush, it is difficult to imagine that he is telling the truth about what he knew at the time of the outing, and what he knows now. Novak himself, the reporter who blew Plame's cover, has said that he believes Bush knew the identity of Novak's "two senior administration official" sources from the beginning, despite the president's feigning of ignorance. "I'm confident the president knows who the source is," he told a luncheon audience at the John Locke Foundation in Raleigh, North Carolina, "so I say, 'Don't bug me. Don't bug Bob Woodward. Bug the president as to whether he should reveal who the source is.' "[14]

It is important to note here that Bush, in early June 2004, acknowledged that he had consulted with a criminal attorney in the Plame outing case, saying, "This is a criminal matter, it's a serious matter."[15]

Former Nixon White House attorney John Dean, commenting on the disclosure, which he called a "stunning and extraordinary development," writes:

It is possible that Bush is consulting Sharp only out of an excess of caution—despite the fact that he knows nothing of the leak, or of any possible coverup of the leak. But that's not likely.

On this subject, I spoke with an experienced former federal prosecutor who works in Washington, specializing in white collar criminal defense (but who does not know Sharp). That attorney told me that he is baffled by Bush's move—unless Bush has knowledge of the leak. "It would not seem that the President needs to consult personal counsel, thereby preserving the attorney-client privilege, if he has no knowledge about the leak," he told me.[16]

Further evidence that Bush knew about the outing of Plame and who was involved comes in an article in the New York *Daily News*, which reports:

> An angry President Bush rebuked chief political guru Karl Rove two years ago for his role in the Valerie Plame affair, sources told the *Daily News*.
> "He made his displeasure known to Karl," a presidential counselor told *The News*. "He made his life miserable about this."
> . . . Other sources confirmed . . . that Bush was initially furious with Rove in 2003 when his deputy chief of staff conceded he had talked to the press about the Plame leak.[17]

As Rep. John Conyers (D-MI), the ranking Democrat on the House Judiciary Committee and the man who would chair that committee if Democrats were to regain control of the House in November 2006, put it immediately after the announcement of Libby's indictment:

> The indictment details a flurry of activity in the Administration to discredit Wilson and, within the Administration, the wildfire-like spread of information about his wife's occupation. The Administration's defenders would have us believe that this all transpired without the awareness or assent of the President or the Vice President.
> Scooter Libby was apparently lying and obstructing justice. What was he trying to hide?
> The truisms of Watergate are the same: it is not the crime, it is the cover-up and, when there is a cover up, there is a crime.
> And the questions are the same: What did the President and Vice President know and when did they know it?[18]

The outing of Valerie Plame's identity as an undercover CIA agent could prove to be a felony, violating two federal statutes. An agent who was deeply involved in the crucial work of monitoring attempts to surreptitiously spread nuclear weapons around the world (and specifically in Iran) was unmasked, thereby destroying her effectiveness. Plus, her politically motivated unmasking quite possibly jeopardized the lives or careers of her overseas contacts. This was an example of the administration's engagement in a crime simply out of political expedience. The White House was willing to violate the law to cover up its warmongering lies. The impeachable violations involved in the Plame case are legion. If, as it seems increasingly likely, the vice president was directly involved in plans to out Plame, the conspiracy would be impeachable. If either executive participated in the actual leak, it would be impeachable. And if the president is found to have been part of any cover-up of these crimes, as Richard Nixon learned decades ago, it would be an impeachable case of conspiracy and obstruction of justice.

★ ★ ★ ★ ★ ★ ★ ★ ★ ★ ★ ★ ★

# NINE

★ ★ ★ ★ ★ ★ ★ ★ ★ ★ ★ ★ ★

## *Breaking Things: Bush's Way of War*

ARTICLE V: In his conduct of the office of President of the United States and in his role as Commander in Chief, George W. Bush, contrary to his oath faithfully to execute the office of the President of the United States, and to the best of his ability preserve, protect, and defend the Constitution of the United States, and in violation of his constitutional duty to take care that the laws be faithfully executed, did repeatedly violate International Law, the Nuremberg Tribunal Charter and the Geneva Conventions on the Conduct of War, to which the United States is a signatory, and which thus carry the force of U.S. law under the Constitution. These high crimes committed by the President include the official sanctioning and application of torture, the "renditioning" of captives to other nations known to practice torture, and the illegal invasion of another country that posed no imminent threat.

No physical or mental torture, nor any other form of coercion, may be inflicted on prisoners of war to secure from them information of any kind whatever. Prisoners of war who refuse to answer may not be threatened, insulted, or exposed to any unpleasant or disadvantageous treatment of any kind.
> —*Third Geneva Convention Relating to the Treatment of Prisoners of War*

I'm a war president. I make decisions here in the Oval Office in foreign-policy matters with war on my mind.
> —*President George W. Bush, speaking on NBC's* Meet the Press, *February 8, 2004*

IT WOULD be impossible to overstate the shock and horror felt in the United States and throughout the world when photographs began appearing showing Iraqi prisoners being tortured. These photographs, taken by both whistleblowing troops and by the torturers themselves, gloating over their handiwork, showed naked prisoners leashed like dogs, being taunted by female guards, or piled upon each other or set upon by German Shepherds. One photograph showed a hooded man balanced on a small box, connected to electrical wires which he'd been told would electrocute him if he moved. Another photo showed the battered and bruised body of a captured Iraqi general, dead after having been kicked and suffocated in a sleeping bag, allegedly the result of torture gone awry. Other sets of photographs, shown to members of Congress who began holding hearings into the abuses, were deemed to be so revolting, ranging from rapes in progress, to body parts, to soldiers posing with decapitated heads, that they have never been released by the government. All the victims were prisoners of war* who, under the terms of the Third Geneva

---

*In fact, the military has admitted that many of those captives, at Abu Ghraib, in Afghanistan, and even in Guantanamo, were not enemy fighters or terrorists

Convention, had basic rights which the United States was bound to honor. It did not. (See appendix C—Taguba Report.)

More shocking than the photos and the acts of torture themselves—which never led to any senior military or civilian officials being punished—was the discovery that torture, under Commander in Chief George W. Bush, Attorneys General John Ashcroft and Alberto Gonzales, and Secretary of Defense Donald Rumsfeld, had become official American policy. The administration has gone to great lengths to make specious and cynical legal arguments defending this president's right to define away torture, and to define captives as "terrorists" or "enemy combatants" instead of as prisoners of war protected by the Geneva Conventions to which the United States is a founding signatory.

All of this legal posturing is a major scandal in and of itself. And given that the Nuremberg Charter makes it clear that failure by leaders to prevent torture and abuse of POWs is itself a crime, all the legal dodging, the covering up, and the failure to punish those who gave the orders to torture could constitute an impeachable crime by the commander in chief.

The Geneva Conventions are crystal clear on the subject of torture: Any soldier captured during a war—and the war in Afghanistan and the war in Iraq are both unarguably wars—is required to be treated in accordance with the Third Convention Regarding the Treatment of Prisoners of war. Moreover, that convention states:

> Should any doubt arise as to whether persons, having committed a belligerent act and having fallen into the hands of the enemy, belong to any of the categories enumerated in Article 4, such persons shall enjoy the protection of the present Convention until such time as their status has been determined by a competent tribunal.[1]

There has been a vast amount of incontrovertible evidence of torture and abuse at the Pentagon's detention center in Guantanamo Bay,

---

at all, but were wrongful arrests—people who had been turned in to U.S. forces by personal enemies seeking revenge, or just caught up in a U.S. raid because they were in the wrong place at the wrong time.

where the government as of March 2006 was still holding about five hundred captives whom the president insists are not prisoners of war. Indeed, in mid-February of 2006 the United Nations Human Rights Commission, after an eighteen-month investigation by five of the world's leading human rights experts, declared that the detention center at Guantanamo Bay, Cuba, is little more than a torture center. In a scathing indictment of the United States, the five Special U.N. Human Rights Rapporteurs called for the immediate shutdown of the Guantanamo facility, access to courts in the United States or in other countries for all those detained there, and an end to United States efforts to get around international proscriptions against torture by redefining the term.[2]

Most of those held at Guantanamo were captured in the course of a few months of war in Afghanistan. The war there between the United States and the Taliban government, which began on October 7, 2001, ended with the fall of the Taliban's last stronghold at Tora Bora in March 2002, or, by some accounts, in October 2002, when a new government was formed in Kabul. Whichever date it was, at the end of hostilities, under international law, POWs are to be released, and, if they have been removed from their country, repatriated. Yet, it wasn't until mid-2004—after most of the captives had been locked up illegally at Guantanamo for more than two years—that any semblance of a tribunal was even held to determine who was a POW and who was not. Those so-called tribunals that were held then claimed to have established that 93 percent of the captives were *not* POWs entitled to protection. But a federal district judge subsequently ruled that the "tribunals," which did not provide captives with legal counsel or access to the evidence used against them, but which, ironically, permitted the use of evidence obtained under torture, were fundamentally flawed and illegal.[3] The UN Human Rights report asserts that what the United States called tribunals were not legitimate proceedings. The Center for Constitutional Rights asserts that all requests for witnesses by captives at these proceedings were summarily rejected as "unreasonable" by the very officers assigned to act as "representatives" for the captives.

To make matters worse, it appears that most of those held at Guantanamo are not terrorists or even people who fought against U.S. forces. A study of available Pentagon data on the over five hundred captives held at Guantanamo conducted by the law school at Seton Hall University concluded that most of the prisoners being held had simply been turned over to U.S. forces by people who wanted the bounty being paid for captives. A summary of the study reports that:

1. Fifty-five percent (55 percent) of the detainees are not determined to have committed any hostile acts against the United States or its coalition allies.

2. Only 8 percent of the detainees were characterized as Al Qaeda fighters. Of the remaining detainees, 40 percent have no definitive connection with Al Qaeda at all and 18 percent have no definitive affiliation with either Al Qaeda or the Taliban.

3. The Government has detained numerous persons based on mere affiliations with a large number of groups that in fact, are not on the Department of Homeland Security terrorist watchlist. Moreover, the nexus between such a detainee and such organizations varies considerably. Eight percent are detained because they are deemed "fighters for;" 30 percent considered "members of;" a large majority—60 percent—are detained merely because they are "associated with" a group or groups the Government asserts are terrorist organizations. For 2 percent of the prisoners their nexus to any terrorist group is unidentified.

4. Only 5 percent of the detainees were captured by United States forces; 86 percent of the detainees were arrested by either Pakistan or the Northern Alliance and turned over to United States custody. This 86 percent of the detainees captured by Pakistan or the Northern Alliance were handed over to the United States at a time in which the United States offered large bounties for capture of suspected enemies.

5. Finally, the population of persons deemed not to be enemy combatants—mostly Uighers—are in fact accused of more serious allegations than a great many persons still deemed to be enemy combatants.[4]

The Third Geneva Convention on POWs mandates that all captives receive humane treatment, bars the segregating of prisoners in individual cells, and prohibits all forms of torture, including treatment that is "degrading or humiliating." All of these requirements have been violated, not just in Guantanamo, but at Abu Ghraib prison and other sites around Iraq, in Afghanistan at Bagram Airbase, and reportedly at various other secret locations around the world to which captives have been illegally transferred or "renditioned," to use the government's ominous terminology. The government has admitted, and photographs and testimony by soldiers and FBI agents have shown, that prisoners in Iraq, Afghanistan, and at Guantanamo have been kept isolated in individual cells—a direct violation of the convention. The government has also argued that interrogation techniques, which include lengthy periods of being forced to remain in painful "stress" positions, periods of enforced sleeplessness, being left in the cold or in extreme heat, and even more severe measures, are not cases of "torture." All of this abuse is manifestly a violation of the Third Geneva Convention, which states unambiguously that war prisoners held captive may not be isolated from their companions, and that they may not be subjected to "physical or mental torture, nor any other form of coercion" or "threatened, insulted, or exposed to any unpleasant or disadvantageous treatment of any kind." (See appendix D—ICRC report.)

The Bush administration has claimed that the wave of violations of this convention by U.S. military forces, by CIA agents, and by other government agencies, was not policy but rather the work of a few "bad apples" in the lower ranks. Their own documented record shows the untruthfulness of this dodge, though. In fact, the policy of torture that has so poisoned America's image around the globe, and which has inflamed passions in Iraq, Afghanistan, and across the Arab and Muslim world, is the direct result of policies approving torture endorsed by President Bush, Vice President Cheney, two attorney generals, and Secretary of Defense Donald Rumsfeld.

## *Approval of Torture Came Right After 9/11*

The first inkling that the U.S. policy on handling captives might take a nightmarish turn came in 2001, within days of the 9/11 attacks, when Vice President Dick Cheney told NBC's Tim Russert:

> We also have to work, though, sort of the dark side, if you will. We've got to spend time in the shadows in the intelligence world. A lot of what needs to be done here will have to be done quietly, without any discussion, using sources and methods that are available to our intelligence agencies, if we're going to be successful. That's the world these folks operate in, and so it's going to be vital for us to use any means at our disposal, basically, to achieve our objective.[5]

As we will see, the policy permitting torture was soon instituted in Afghanistan. Evidence of this came in a memo to the president from his White House legal counsel, Alberto Gonzales, who warned his boss that the American treatment of detainees captured in that conflict might be criminally prosecutable under the War Crimes Act, a measure passed in 1996, which made violation of the Third Geneva Convention punishable as a violation not just of international law, but of U.S. law. At that point, the president had two options: he could have ordered all mistreatment and torture of captured fighters to cease, or he could ignore the law and the abuses. Bush chose the latter option, attempting to keep the policy quiet, and issuing an executive order on torture. (See appendix E—FBI Report.) This secret document "opted the U.S. out" of the Geneva Conventions, in hopes of shielding American soldiers (and, Gonzales hoped, the president himself) from prosecution, and simultaneously authorized the continued use of internationally banned tactics. Indeed, in a memo to the president in January 2002, Gonzales actually advised the president that "high officials," the president included, could eventually be prosecuted for war crimes, and suggested that by declaring torture victims not to be POWs, he might insulate himself and subordinates from such an eventuality. With that presidential decision, according to Elizabeth Holtzman, a former member of Congress from

New York who sat on the House Judiciary Committee that voted out bills for Nixon's impeachment, "He himself may have violated the War Crimes Act, along with those who actually inflicted the abuse."[6]

If so, that violation was an impeachable act.

A few months after that, in February 2002, President Bush issued another secret executive order stating that Al Qaeda captives would not be considered to be prisoners of war under the Geneva Conventions, and thus would not be protected by the Third Geneva Convention prohibition against torture, which the convention defines as "any act by which severe pain or suffering, whether physical or mental, is intentionally inflicted on a person."

On August 1, 2002, Gonzales sought and received from the Justice Department a memo opening the door to a wide array of forms of torture. Ignoring the Geneva Convention definition of the term "torture," the so-called "Gonzales memo," actually written by Jay Bybee, declared:

> We conclude that for an act to constitute torture . . . it must inflict pain that is difficult to endure. Physical pain amounting to torture must be equivalent in intensity to the pain accompanying severe physical injury, such as organ failure, impairment of bodily function, or even death.[7]

Three years later Bush appointed Gonzales attorney general of the United States. Bybee, meanwhile, after writing his torture-justifying memo, was nominated by Bush to a seat on the Ninth Circuit Court of Appeals. His role in authorizing torture only came out later.

It's hard to see how anyone could reconcile this definition with the Geneva Conventions, particularly since the same Third Geneva Convention goes on to say that prisoners "may not be threatened, insulted, or exposed to any unpleasant or disadvantageous treatment of any kind."

Since there are myriad tortures that have been devised by the minds of men that fall short of the Gonzales memo's narrow definition, this memo was basically construed by Bush and the Pentagon hierarchy to mean that torture of a lesser nature, such as what was later employed at Abu Ghraib, was okay. But the same memo went on to suggest that the new definition of a kind of "torture lite," which could be legally used against Al Qaeda captives, might also be useable against other captives—

even prisoners of war like the Taliban, and later, Iraqi fighters. ("Torture lite," it should be noted, could be quite nasty, including such things as being shackled for forty-eight hours to a pin on the floor in ovenlike heat.) This opinion was based upon a new and highly controversial concept popular with Bush and Cheney—a president's special authority as commander in chief in time of war. As the Gonzales memo explained:

> As Commander-in-Chief, the President has the constitutional authority to order interrogations of enemy combatants to gain intelligence information concerning military plans of the enemy. The demands of the Commander-in-Chief power are especially pronounced in the middle of a war in which the nation has already suffered a direct attack. In such a case, the information gained from interrogations may prevent future attacks by foreign enemies. Any effort to apply [the law against torture] in a manner that interferes with the President's direction of such core war matters as the detention and interrogation of enemy combatants thus would be unconstitutional.[8]

It turns out that, for a brief period, the torture at Guantanamo that the Gonzales memo and the ensuing presidential authorization for torture led to was halted, thanks to the objections of a top Pentagon lawyer. In February 2006, it was revealed that Alberto Mora, a Republican political appointee to post of general counsel to the Department of the Navy, in December 2002 had spoken out against the new coercive techniques for use at Guantanamo, which Defense Secretary Rumsfeld had approved on December 2. Mora had been alerted to the new policy on coercive techniques by David L. Brandt, who at the time was director of the Naval Criminal Investigative Service. Mora warned senior defense department officials that the new policy verged on torture, and could lead to the possibility of senior officials being prosecuted. Mora had asked at the time, "Have we jettisoned our human rights policies?" His protest and warning reportedly led to a temporary retraction of Rumsfeld's orders. However, such is the administration's obsession with getting past the concerns about Geneva Conventions and international law that a few months later, in April 2003, new orders from Rumsfeld, authorizing similar coercive interrogation techniques, were issued—this time without Pentagon lawyers like Mora being notified.[9]

When word of the Gonzales memo leaked out in the media—something which happened just after the first stories about the atrocities at Abu Ghraib were breaking—the country, and the entire world, was outraged. The White House immediately backed off its position, with the Justice Department issuing a new opinion that torture causing "severe" pain, not just "extreme" pain, would be prohibited. That second memo left torture permissible, however, if the pain caused was not "severe"—and still endorsed abuse that the Geneva Convention specifically bans. Additionally, the Justice Department left the power to decide on the permissibility of torture up to the president.

In such a permissive environment, it is little wonder that torture became rampant in the American battle zones of Afghanistan and Iraq. As Major General Antonio Taguba reported in his official investigation into the conditions at Abu Ghraib, referring to just that one most publicly known torture facility, the abuses he found included:

> Breaking chemical lights and pouring the phosphoric liquid on detainees; Threatening detainees with a charged 9mm pistol; Pouring cold water on naked detainees; beating detainees with a broom handle and a chair; threatening male detainees with rape; allowing a military police guard to stitch the wound of a detainee who was injured after being slammed against the wall in his cell; sodomizing a detainee with a chemical light and perhaps a broom stick; using military working dogs to frighten and intimidate detainees with threats of attack, and in one instance actually biting a detainee.[10]

It may well be that many of the instances of torture at Abu Ghraib and elsewhere went beyond what the White House, the Justice Department, and the Pentagon were specifically authorizing in memos and verbal instructions. But clearly the soldiers tasked with running detention facilities or conducting interrogations in Afghanistan, Iraq, Guantanamo, and elsewhere, who made no attempt to hide what they were doing from superiors, felt that they were doing what they were supposed to be doing. The reason for this belief can be traced directly to the permissive attitude—and even the encouragement to turn to the "dark side"—that they were getting from the very top of the chain of command, namely the president and vice president of the United States.

As reports of torture, in Afghanistan, at Abu Ghraib, and at other sites around Iraq, in Guantanamo, and elsewhere began to surface, including a number of cases in which the victims reportedly had died after being tortured, Congress attempted to take action. Sen. John McCain (R-AZ), himself a former POW who had suffered torture at the hands of his Vietnamese captors, was outraged at reports the U.S. forces were torturing prisoners. McCain put forward a bill that would ban the practice outright, whether by the military or by the CIA. The measure, passed by a 90–9 margin in the Senate and attached to a military appropriations bill, also passed in the House by a veto-proof margin. President Bush showed his obsession with keeping torture as an approved policy when he repeatedly sent his vice president to the Hill in an unsuccessful attempt to kill the bill, or to render it toothless.

McCain stood his ground, though, and in January 2006 the measure passed.* But when the president signed it, he also signed something called a "signing statement," stating that he would not be bound by the provisions of the bill in his role as chief executive and commander in chief (another impeachable action which will be discussed in the next chapter). In other words, even in the face of global, public, and congressional approbation, George Bush continues to insist that he has the power to authorize torture of American captives. This brazen violation of the Third Geneva Convention Regarding the Treatment of Prisoners of War, a criminal offense of the highest order, and a violation of international law, is an impeachable offence. (Likewise impeachable, as an abuse of power, is the president's willful refusal to be bound by an act of Congress flatly outlawing torture, but more on that in chapter 10.)

---

*The larger Detainee Treatment Act of which it was a part actually rendered the McCain amendment relatively useless as a protection against torture, as it included language precluding captives from using habeas corpus proceedings and specifically barring those captives at Guantanamo from any legal actions.

## *Administration Hides First Evidence of Torture*

The history of America's illegal torture policies dates back to the earliest days of the Afghanistan invasion. One of its first victims, in fact, was an American, John Walker Lindh, who became known to his countrymen in late 2001 as "The American Taliban." The story of how his torture and abuse was covered up by the administration says much about the White House's own awareness of the heinousness of its criminal torture policy.

As a young man of nineteen, Lindh, a child of privilege from Marin County, California, who had turned to Islam while in high school, decided to travel to Pakistan to study his chosen religion more deeply. Attending a Pakistani religious school, he learned of the raging battle in Afghanistan by the ultrafundamentalist Taliban to rid the country of the last remnants of the country's former occupier, Russia. Inspired by that story, Lindh traveled to Afghanistan and signed on to be a fighter for the faith. That was in August 2001. At that time, the United States and the new Bush administration were on semifriendly terms with the Taliban government. The United States had even provided that Taliban government with funds to curb poppy cultivation in hopes of curtailing heroin traffic. The United States was also involved, in conjunction with the oil company Conoco, in negotiations with the Taliban government concerning the construction of an oil pipeline through Afghanistan.

A few weeks after Lindh's fateful and adventurous decision, while he was in the Afghan desert training to be a fighter, America was attacked and went to war against the Taliban. Caught by this change of sides, Lindh was in no position to lay down his rifle and just walk away.

Before long, Lindh was captured by the Northern Alliance forces of General Rashid Dostum, along with hundreds of Taliban and Al Qaeda fighters, and taken to the Qala-I-Jangi, a fort belonging to Gen. Dostum near Mazar-I-Sharif where American forces were based. When his captors learned that Lindh was an American, two tough CIA officers were called in to question him. They did so, reportedly rather brutally, in an open courtyard, as Lindh's Taliban and Al Qaeda comrades-in-arms looked on. At some point his treatment sparked a riot, the fort was taken over by the prisoners, and one of the CIA agents, Michael Spann, was killed. The uprising, which lasted several days, was ultimately put down, and Lindh was recaptured.

Brought to Bagram Airbase, the main U.S. base in Afghanistan, Lindh, who was dehydrated, starving, and suffering from a festering bullet wound in his leg, found himself duct-taped to a gurney, blindfolded with tape, and left in a dark, sealed, unheated metal shipping container—a fate suffered by many of America's captives in that war. He was removed, still on the gurney, once a day to be fed and interrogated. His leg was left untreated for days. Allegedly tortured physically and mentally, he was repeatedly threatened with death and mockingly reminded, when he asked for a lawyer, that "nobody knows you're here." As Seymour Hersh notes in his book *Chain of Command* on the administration's torture scandal, so confident were American troops in Afghanistan in the fall of 2001 about their ability to abuse captives like Lindh that

> his American interrogators stripped him, gagged him, strapped him to a board, and exhibited him to the press and to any soldier who wished to see him.[11]

Eventually, after he cracked and signed a written confession in which he admitted being a traitor, Lindh was brought back to the United States, where a gloating Attorney General John Ashcroft hailed the capture of an "American Taliban," and talked of having him tried on the capital charge of treason. With Lindh's confession in hand, the hard-line Ashcroft had what looked like an open-and-shut case—his first big win in the government's so-far bumbling war on terror.

A trial was scheduled—it was timed nicely to coincide with the first anniversary of 9/11 in Virginia's Fourth Circuit—but it never happened. Lindh's family had hired a crack trial lawyer, James Brosnahan, who had decided to challenge the confession letter. Lindh claimed he had signed it under torture and wanted it tossed out. After a flurry of legal motions, the judge agreed that Lindh should be able to call soldiers from Bagram and captives being held at Guantanamo as witnesses to his torture at a hearing on a motion to suppress the letter.

A hearing, sure to be explosive in its revelations about torture of POWs in American custody, was set for Monday, June 15, 2002.

The Friday before that hearing, the government came to Brosnahan with an offer of a deal. The heavy charges against Lindh of terrorism, attempted murder, and conspiracy to kill Americans would be dropped if he would plead guilty to just a charge of providing assistance to a banned country (really a civil violation aimed at corporations that do business with countries like Cuba or North Korea) and to carrying a weapon. Another part of the deal was that Lindh would have to sign a letter saying he had "never been mistreated" by his American captors. There was one more condition: the deal had to be agreed to that Friday. If the suppression hearing took place Monday, all bets were off.

Lindh agreed to the deal. He was sentenced to twenty years in jail on the reduced charges. To ensure his silence the Justice Department sought and obtained an extraordinary gag order barring him from talking about his experience in U.S. military custody for the duration of his sentence.

Why did the government offer Lindh this deal? Why did prosecutors demand he sign the letter denying he had been tortured? And why did they insist on a gag order?

Clearly, in June 2002 the U.S. government did not want anyone learning that torture had become official policy for American forces in Afghanistan. Yet, we've subsequently learned that the torture policies approved for Afghanistan POWs and tested on Lindh "migrated" from there to Guantanamo, along with the Afghan POWs themselves, and then "migrated" from Gitmo to Abu Ghraib Prison and other holding facilities in Iraq, where their exposure did incalculable damage to the American effort to win over Iraqis.

And, by the way, the man who negotiated the deal that silenced Lindh was Michael Chertoff, then head of the Justice Department's criminal division, and now secretary of the new Homeland Security Department.[12]

The high level of official involvement in this case (Ashcroft and Chertoff and perhaps others) suggests that the White House was behind the attempt to bury early evidence of official torture in Afghanistan. Certainly, there is nothing unusual about plea bargains; the overwhelming majority of federal criminal cases are settled without a trial. But this was a plea bargain that the administration clearly was desperate to get because it didn't want that suppression hearing to be held. If it were to turn out that the administration was deliberately trying to cover up evidence of an official policy of torture through its silencing of Lindh, this could be an impeachable offense.

## Getting by Torture Constraints
## (With a Little Help from Our Friends)

In cases where even the minimal constraints on torture have prevented the CIA or the Pentagon from getting the information they wanted from captives, the White House has turned to another tactic, reportedly long used by the Agency, but never so prolifically: renditions. Renditioning, or rendering, is the official euphemism used to describe the kidnapping of someone and transporting him to another country where rules on torture don't exist. We only know about this practice because a few of those who were "renditioned" managed to get home and tell their stories. One of those was Maher Arar, a Canadian citizen who, during a stopover at Kennedy International Airport in on his way home to his family in Ottawa, was grabbed by U.S. agents, held nine days in the Metropolitan House of Detention in New York (where he was denied food, prevented from sleeping, and endlessly interrogated). He was then rendered by CIA jet first to Jordan, where he was badly beaten, and then to Syria, where he was subjected to brutal torture for ten months in "a grave-like cell." When the Canadian government finally won his release, the Syrians, who had beaten him repeatedly with electrical cables all over his body, said upon his release that they had never had any interest in him, but had held him only "as a show of good will" toward the United States. Arar was never charged with any crime.[13]

Another rendition victim we know about was Khaled El-Masri, a German national who was kidnapped on a holiday trip to Macedonia by a gang of seven or eight men wearing ski masks and renditioned to Afghanistan's Bagram airbase, where he claims he was repeatedly tortured before the German government discovered his plight and convinced the United States that they'd picked up the wrong man. In a legal brief filed as part of his subsequent lawsuit against the CIA, El-Masri says that even before he was taken to Afghanistan, he was beaten severely, his clothes were sliced off him, he was thrown to the floor, his hands pulled back, and a boot was then placed on his back. At that point, something hard was jabbed up his anus. He was then put into a diaper and marched to the plane, his feet in shackles, then thrown face down on the deck, spread-eagled, with his arms and legs fastened to the plane's sides. Finally he was given two injections, which rendered him unconscious.

After that ordeal, El-Masri reports that he was held in a one-man cell for four months, with nothing to read, and no contact with others, and that he was constantly reminded that he was "in a country with no laws and that no one knew where he was." There was further abuse during his detention until he was abruptly flown to Albania and released, alone, on a mountain road. His case had turned out to be a matter of mistaken identity, though he was held even after his passport checked out and proved the error. Only intervention by the German government won his release from this private hell.[14]

There are reports of hundreds of secret CIA flights from the United States and other locations to a "gulag" of secret prisons allegedly being used for the purpose of torturing suspects like El-Masri—ironically, many of these places were formerly the infamous gulag prisons of the Soviet Union and its eastern European satellite states, most notably Poland and Rumania.

Guantanamo Bay, where more than one thousand captives, mostly from the Afghanistan invasion, were brought, and have been held indefinitely as prisoners in the War on Terror, or until tried by military tribunals, is a terminus for many victims of the rendition policy. Some of the captives, who have been there for nearly five years, are alleged Al Qaeda fighters captured in Afghanistan or Pakistan. Some are alleged Afghan fighters from the Taliban army, whose claim to POW status should be unquestioned. But many of those in detention at the base are simply innocent bystanders, picked up in the heat of battle, or "reported" to U.S. military authorities by personal enemies anxious to be rid of them, or to get the reward money the United States was offering in fliers rained down from the sky all over the country.[15] Some who were rendered to Guantanamo weren't even teenagers at the time of their capture. As of January 2006, only nine of the hundreds of captives at the base had even been charged with any offense, although according to testimony from FBI agents who visited the base, and to an Amnesty International report, many of them have been subjected to torture. As was discussed previously, the administration's position—absurd to the point of Alice in Wonderland—is that the Guantanamo Bay navy base is not technically U.S. soil, because it is on Cuban territory leased by the United States from the government of Cuba. What happens there, the White House argues, is not subject to the jurisdiction of U.S. courts. As the Amnesty International report on Guantanamo put it, "The detention facility at Guantánamo Bay has become the gulag of our times."[16]

Even as the domestic and international outcry over the abuses at Guantanamo was crescendoing, with mounting calls for the detention camp's closure and a settling of all the cases being held there, there has come word of another camp of equal size—this one inside Afghanistan—which has been holding upward of five hundred "enemy combatants" for as long as three or four years without giving them access to lawyers. Located at Bagram Airbase, near the capital city of Kabul (where Lindh and other early captives in the war against the Taliban were initially held and apparently tortured), this "son of Gitmo," as critics are calling it, reportedly boasts even worse conditions than Guantanamo.

As *The New York Times* reported in its article breaking the story:

> From the accounts of former detainees, military officials and soldiers who served there, a picture emerges of a place that is in many ways rougher and more bleak than its U.S. counterpart on Cuba.
>
> Men are held by the dozen in large wire cages, the detainees and military sources said, sleeping on the floor on foam mats and, until about a year ago, often using plastic buckets for toilets. Before recent renovations, they rarely saw daylight except for brief visits to a small exercise yard.
>
> "Bagram was never meant to be a long-term facility, and now it's a long-term facility without the money or resources," said one Defense Department official who has toured the detention center.
>
> Comparing the prison to Guantánamo, the official said, "Anyone who has been to Bagram would tell you it's worse.[17]

David Cole, an attorney and constitutional law specialist at Georgetown University, commented on the news, saying

The Bagram story raises serious questions about the Bush administration's unwillingness to be bound by law. The administration chose Guantánamo in the first place because it thought it was a law-free zone. Now that the Supreme Court has said that the administration is actually accountable to legal limits at Guantánamo, it is turning to other avenues to avoid accountability. The only real solution is to conform its conduct to the law, not to continue to evade legal responsibility for its actions.[18]

All this vicious activity has done immense and immeasurable damage to America's reputation in the world as a model of justice and freedom. And all of it is patently illegal. If the "war" on terror really is a war, as President Bush and Vice President Cheney claim it is, in justifying the president's claim to be a permanent commander in chief who can make his own rules, then the captives of that war must be considered POWs under the Geneva Conventions, not "enemy combatants" as the president has declared them, and therefore outside the protection of the conventions. If we are at war, then rendition is just as illegal as is torture. If the "war" is not a war, and the captives are not POWs, then they are, by default, common criminals, and in U.S. custody criminals are protected against torture and rendition by the U.S. Constitution.

As the Geneva Convention on POWs states:

> Prisoners of war may only be transferred by the Detaining Power to a Power which is a party to the Convention and after the Detaining Power has satisfied itself of the willingness and ability of such transferee Power to apply the Convention. When prisoners of war are transferred under such circumstances, responsibility for the application of the Convention rests on the Power accepting them while they are in its custody.
>
> Nevertheless if that Power fails to carry out the provisions of the Convention in any important respect, the Power by whom the prisoners of war were transferred shall, upon being notified by the Protecting Power, take effective measures to correct the situation or shall request the return of the prisoners of war. Such requests must be complied with.[19]

Bush's policy of torture and his approval of the use of "rendition" to try to shift the act of torture into the hands of other states, as well as his creation of torture gulags around the world, chief among them Guantanamo, are all grotesque violations of international law and of the U.S. Constitution, and constitute grounds for his impeachment.

## Presidential Culpability and a Crime Against Peace

War crimes typically are not prosecuted against the leaders or generals of nations that have been victorious in war, and for the obvious reason: who's going to do it? The Nuremberg Tribunals, which prosecuted Nazi war criminals, the postwar tribunals of Japanese military leaders, and the more recent prosecutions of war criminals from Bosnia, Yugoslavia, and elsewhere before the International Court in The Hague, have all involved leaders who lost their respective conflicts. That does not mean that the leader of a nation who orders or commits war crimes, yet remains in power, should be allowed to escape accountability, only that the indictment and prosecution must be the responsibility of that leader's own people. Significantly, war crimes, as violations of international law, are not merely obscure technical transgressions. Because the Geneva Conventions—very much a goal and product of U.S. postwar diplomacy—were signed and ratified by the U.S. Congress, under the Constitution they become an integral part of U.S. law. In other words, a war crime committed by an American citizen, whether an Army private or the commander in chief, is equally a serious violation of federal law. When the president breaks the law, and the crime causes harm to the nation, it is grounds for impeachment.

The invasion of Iraq itself is the greatest of war crimes. The Nuremberg Tribunal Charter, drawn up at the end of World War II by the United States and the other victorious allies, established that an unprovoked war of aggression against a nation that poses no imminent threat to the aggressor is a special category of war crime: a "crime against peace." As the Charter states:

Principle VI: The crimes hereinafter set out are punishable as crimes under international law:

*(a) Crimes against peace:*

(i) Planning, preparation, initiation or waging of a war of aggression or a war in violation of international treaties.[20]

As we saw in chapter 5, the Bush-Cheney administration went to great lengths of deception and misrepresentation—targeting Congress, the media, and the United Nations—all in an attempt to make the case that Iraq did in fact pose an imminent threat, and did so knowing that this was a lie. That propaganda campaign, which included lying, distortion, and manipulation, all aimed toward gaining support from the American public for an unprovoked and illegal war of aggression, is a second violation of the Nuremberg Charter, which defines the crime as:

(ii) Participation in a common plan or conspiracy for the accomplishment of any of the acts mentioned under (i).

The all-out effort to convince the United Nations Security Council that Iraq posed an urgent threat to world peace and security—made by Secretary of State Colin Powell shortly before the already arrayed U.S. invasion force began its assault—failed.* Had the United Nation endorsed an invasion, the United States would have had the legal sanction to invade Iraq—which of course is why the administration made the attempt. Instead, however, Security Council members chose to believe the reports of UN weapons inspectors and International Atomic Energy Agency inspectors who concluded that Iraq no longer had WMDs, or even a nuclear weapons development program. All of this was known before the invasion of Iraq even began. This means that whether or not Congress can be considered to have provided the president with some

---

*Some of the "bad intelligence" that was being pushed at the U.N. was so transparently false and fabricated that Secretary of State Colin Powell, who was to make the formal presentation of the case for war to the Security Council, simply refused to present it, saying he was "not going to say this bullshit." Even so, he ended up presenting "evidence" that turned out to have been fake.

kind of token authorization to go to war back in October 2002, the invasion itself on March 20, 2003, was, to put it simply, unjustified and illegal under international law, and thus under U.S. law.

For this gravest of international crimes, which has resulted in the destruction of a country and the deaths of tens of thousands of innocent civilians, among them uncounted thousands of women and children, as well as thousands of American soldiers, the president, who has repeatedly insisted that the decision to go to war was his and his alone, should be impeached.

# TEN

## *Abuse of Power, Criminal Negligence, and Other Crimes*

Article VI: In his conduct of the office of President of the United States and in his role as Commander in Chief, George W. Bush, contrary to his oath faithfully to execute the office of the President of the United States, and to the best of his ability preserve, protect, and defend the Constitution of the United States, and in violation of his constitutional duty to take care that the laws be faithfully executed, has both abused his power, violating the constitutional limits placed upon the executive branch, and acted in criminally negligent fashion, ignoring environmental protection laws, election, and various other laws. He has also, in criminally negligent fashion, failed to act in a timely fashion to protect the lives and property of the public during a national emergency, and in the face of clear evidence of potentially disastrous global warming.

IT IS one of the more bizarre peculiarities of the Bush-Cheney administration that, as aggressive as it has been at seeking to expand the power of
the executive branch and the president at the expense of the other
branches of the federal government, the president himself has displayed a
stunning contempt for the actual job of governing—as have many of his
appointees to top administrative posts. Even as the Bush administration
tries to expropriate or usurp, it has repeatedly failed to make use of executive powers it clearly does have when the health, safety, and welfare of
the public are at stake. On the one hand, President Bush has declared it
his unfettered prerogative to strip Americans of their citizenship rights at
his own whim, to declare war at a time and place of his own choosing, to
violate international laws banning torture, and even to interpret acts of
Congress as he sees fit. On the other hand, this self-styled imperial leader
has allowed American soldiers to go to war inadequately armed and without body armor. He ignored the plight of a storm-hammered city for
many critical days, in fact, even after he had been informed the New Orleans levees had broken he went golfing, resulting in needless death and
suffering, and the near loss of a great metropolis. Perhaps most inexcus-
ably of all, the president has failed to take any significant action to combat the threat to life on the planet posed by accelerating global warming,
despite near unanimity among the scientific community that it is almost
too late. Indeed, he and his administration have actively obstructed efforts domestically and globally to combat climate change.

Let's look first at the issue of abuse of power.

## *A New Imperial Presidency*

Shortly after the U.S. Supreme Court had declared him president,
President-"elect" George W. Bush, expressing frustration at the com-
plexities of pulling together his new administration, remarked, "If this
were a dictatorship, it'd be a heck of a lot easier, just so long as I'm the
dictator."[1] The statement may have been made in jest, but the ensuing
months and years have made it apparent that this president (along with
his vice president) is not content to operate within the constraints of a
more than two-centuries-old system of checks and balances, and in-

stead wants to run a presidency that pretty much does whatever it wants, when it wants. And that is not a joke.

In the early days of his first term, the initial power grab came in the form of refusals to accept or even to go through the motions of complying with congressional oversight. As we've discussed earlier, the White House early on refused congressional requests for information about the makeup of an energy policy task force set up under the vice president, forcing Congress to go to court. Information requested by Congress concerning the true costs of an administration-proposed Medicare drug program was not provided, and, in fact, when information was given, it was knowingly false, grossly understating the true cost of the program. Over time, though, the president advanced from stonewalling and lying to Congress, to simply bypassing the legislative branch altogether.

There was also, early in the president's first term, the beginning of a Nixon-like program of domestic spying. As James Risen has written in his book, *State of War*, the NSA's campaign of monitoring Americans' domestic electronic communications began shortly after 9/11. The president justified this willful violation of federal law by making a claim of an implied congressional authorization (see chapter 7), and by the equally dubious assertion that as commander in chief in wartime, he had the power to ignore federal law. It is an assertion that if accepted would, as the dean of Yale Law School observed, just as easily empower the president to reintroduce slavery and summary execution.

Without question, however, the president's boldest and most unconstitutional usurpation of power is seen in an action that came to light during the debate over the administration's authorization of the use of torture. Stunned and outraged by the mushrooming torture scandals and the damage they were doing to America's image abroad and to the war efforts in Iraq and Afghanistan, both houses of Congress, in late 2005, passed, by wide, veto-proof margins, a measure banning the use of torture by any American agency, including the CIA.

The president, realizing he couldn't block passage of the bill, signed it into law, but while doing it, also issued a letter called a "signing document," which stated: "The executive branch shall construe [the law] in a manner consistent with the constitutional authority of the President . . . as Commander in Chief."[2]

This was immediately explained by White House staffers as meaning that if the president felt he needed to ignore this law, or any law, he would be legally free to do so. It turns out that Bush had, by that point in his five years as president, quietly issued over five hundred such "signing statements" while putting his signature to bills approved by Congress. In each of those cases, he was asserting a claim as the nation's president and commander in chief, to interpret, execute, and enforce the law in question in his own way, and not necessarily in the manner Congress intended. This is an astonishing assertion of presidential primacy.* It is based upon an obscure, far-right, and highly controversial political concept called the Unitary Executive Theory, under which the presidency is seen as incorporating both legislative and judicial authority, as well as executive authority.** But as Elizabeth de la Vega, a veteran federal prosecutor, now retired, puts it:

> Not having heard of this concept, and thinking perhaps that I had missed something in Constitutional Law, I decided to survey a random sampling of attorneys about it. The group included civil practitioners, prosecutors, a federal judge, a former federal prosecutor who has a PhD as well as a J.D., defense attorneys, and a U.S. magistrate.

*It must be noted that Bush is not the first president to issue signing statements. President Clinton before him, and others back to President Franklin Roosevelt and even earlier, have done the same, usually when they felt that a portion of a law passed by Congress would be unconstitutional, or when they felt it would unconstitutionally restrict presidential authority. But in the entire history of the presidency before Bush, only several dozen such signing statements have been issued. The sheer scale of the Bush use of such documents represents a qualitative difference—a true affront and challenge to Congressional authority and to the Constitution's assignment of powers to the three branches of the federal government.

**The term "unitary executive," almost unknown in the literature on the presidency, appears in a number of presidential signing letters. It is also a concept endorsed by the latest Bush appointment to the Supreme Court, Sam Alito, who initially proposed the idea of signing letters to President Reagan, as a junior attorney in the Reagan White House.

The precise question was, "When did you first hear about the Unitary Executive Theory of the Presidency?" Most said, "The past few weeks," but my favorite was, "A few seconds ago, when you asked about it." All agreed that the term does not appear in the U.S. Constitution and that, the last time they checked, we still had three branches of government.[3]

De la Vega is right, of course. The Constitution is quite clear on the point. Regarding the power of the president, Article II, Section 1 states:

The executive power shall be vested in a President of the United States of America.

Article II goes on to enumerate that power in full, stating:

The President shall be commander in chief of the Army and Navy of the United States, and of the militia of the several states, when called into the actual service of the United States; he may require the opinion, in writing, of the principal officer in each of the executive departments, upon any subject relating to the duties of their respective offices, and he shall have power to grant reprieves and pardons for offenses against the United States, except in cases of impeachment.

He shall have power, by and with the advice and consent of the Senate, to make treaties, provided two thirds of the Senators present concur; and he shall nominate, and by and with the advice and consent of the Senate, shall appoint ambassadors, other public ministers and consuls, judges of the Supreme Court, and all other officers of the United States, whose appointments are not herein otherwise provided for, and which shall be established by law: but the Congress may by law vest the appointment of such inferior officers, as they think proper, in the President alone, in the courts of law, or in the heads of departments.

The President shall have power to fill up all vacancies that may happen during the recess of the Senate, by granting commissions which shall expire at the end of their next session.

That's it. Nowhere does the Constitution give to the president the power to interpret laws passed by Congress. Nor does it say that as commander in chief he has any powers reaching beyond control over the military. Indeed, the Constitution is quite clear on who has legislative power—the Congress. As Article I states:

> All legislative powers herein granted shall be vested in a Congress of the United States, which shall consist of a Senate and House of Representatives.

The key word there is "all." Furthermore, Article I states that Congress shall have the power:

> To make all laws which shall be necessary and proper for carrying into execution the foregoing powers, and all other powers vested by this Constitution in the government of the United States, or in any department or officer thereof.

Finally, the Constitution makes it clear what branch of government gets to determine issues of "law and equality." As Article III states, it is the judiciary, not the executive branch:

> The judicial power shall extend to all cases, in law and equity, arising under this Constitution, the laws of the United States, and treaties made, or which shall be made, under their authority;—to all cases affecting ambassadors, other public ministers, and consuls;—to all cases of admiralty and maritime jurisdiction;—to controversies to which the United States shall be a party;—to controversies between two or more states;—between a state and the citizens of another state;—between citizens of the same state claiming lands under grants of different states, and between a state, or the citizens thereof, and foreign states, citizens, or subjects.

Political analysts have frequently pointed out that during the first five years of the Bush presidency he has never used a veto. Not once. And he is the only president since James Garfield (who held office for only six months in 1881 before being assassinated)* to accept every single bill sent to him by Congress. We now can understand why. Instead of vetoing bills he doesn't like, this president just issues a "signing document" saying he isn't going to obey or enforce the bill in question, or some portion of that bill, and Congress be damned.**

This, of course, is not the way the Founding Fathers envisioned the executive branch operating. Indeed, the president's repeated, deliberate overriding and ignoring of acts of Congress is nothing short of a direct violation of his oath of office, in which he swore to "preserve, protect, and defend the Constitution of the United States." As such, those actions constitute the very gravest of impeachable offenses. As former congresswoman Liz Holtzman wrote in *The Nation* magazine:

> A President, any President, who maintains that he is above the law—and repeatedly violates the law—thereby commits high crimes and misdemeanors, the constitutional standard for impeachment and removal from office . . .
>
> The framers of our Constitution feared executive power run amok and provided the remedy of impeachment to protect against it. While impeachment is a last resort, and must never be lightly undertaken (a principle ignored during the proceedings against President Bill Clinton), neither can Congress shirk its responsibility to use that tool to safeguard our democracy. No President can be permitted to commit high crimes and misdemeanors with impunity.

Referring to Bush's claim that he has the inherent right to ignore the FISA law passed by Congress, and order warrantless spying on Americans by the NSA, Holtzman wrote:

*Not counting Garfield, who hardly had time to veto a bill, one has to go back to Millard Fillmore, who was president from 1850 to 1853, to find a president who never vetoed a bill.

**The proof that this is an outrageous and unconstitutional usurpation of legislative and judicial power is that for years presidents have sought "line item" veto power to delete just parts of congressional acts with which they disagreed. That power to legislate or alter a law has always been denied to them by a Congress jealous of its power to write the laws.

If the President is permitted to break the law on wiretapping on his own say-so, then a President can break any other law on his own say-so—a formula for dictatorship. This is not a theoretical danger.[4]

The same might equally be said about permitting the president to decide which laws he will obey and which he will ignore. The willful breaking of a federal law by the president is a felony, and, since he cannot be indicted, calls for his impeachment. The willful decision to ignore or overrule hundreds of laws passed by Congress is an appalling abuse of power and a violation of the president's oath of office. It poses a threat to the very foundation of constitutional government. It cries out for impeachment.

## *Gross Negligence as a Leader: Katrina*

Even as President Bush and his vice president have been laying claim to executive powers more appropriately belonging to an absolute monarchy, for more than five years they have demonstrated an astonishing disinterest in the actual business of governing the country. Bush has famously spent much of his time away from Washington "clearing brush" on his ranch in Crawford, Texas, and was there, in fact, vacationing in Crawford and making political run-outs to fundraising functions in the southwest, as Katrina, the worst hurricane in a century, bore down on the city of New Orleans. The president remained on vacation for critical days after the city's inadequate and underfunded levee system was breached, and the city flooded, stranding tens of thousands of its poorer residents in their homes or on their roofs, or in the Superdome and the convention center. Millions of Americans watched in horror as hundreds of people died of disease, starvation, and drowning while waiting for the federal government to respond to a disaster of such epic proportions that no local government in America could have had the capability of meeting it. Instead of taking charge, the president, however, stuck to his vacation.

Consider the timeline of this national catastrophe.

On Friday, August 26, 2005, after watching the steady march of

Katrina across the Gulf of Mexico, Louisiana Gov. Kathleen Blanco declared a state of emergency, convinced by hurricane experts that the city was likely to face a direct hit by an unusually severe hurricane. By early morning on August 27, Katrina was upgraded to a Category 3 storm, and Blanco asked President Bush, then at his ranch in West Texas, to declare a federal state of emergency in Louisiana, which would free up federal assistance to the area. At the time, Governor Blanco said:

> I have determined that this incident is of such severity and magnitude that effective response is beyond the capabilities of the State and affected local governments, and that supplementary Federal assistance is necessary to save lives, protect property, public health and safety, or to lessen or avert the threat of a disaster.[5]

The White House responded by declaring a national emergency in the state—a fairly routine procedure in the case of hurricanes—and by handing the responsibility for managing the response to the Federal Emergency Management Agency (FEMA).

Over the course of the following night, Katrina was progressively upgraded, as predicted, to a Category 4 and then, by early morning on August 28, to a Category 5 hurricane, a storm capable of causing cataclysmic danger. That morning, with the storm's eye still about twenty-four hours away from landfall and packing 160-mph winds, a local daily, *The Lafayette Daily Advertiser*, published a lead story quoting the National Hurricane Center forecasters as predicting that the city's levee system would collapse under Katrina's onslaught, inundating the sub-sea-level city of New Orleans:

> "Coastal storm surge flooding of 18 to 22 feet above normal tide levels, locally as high as 28 feet, along with large and dangerous battering waves can be expected near and to the east of where the center makes landfall," according to National Hurricane Center forecaster Richard Pasch.
>
> "Some levees in the Greater New Orleans area could be overtopped," he said.[6]

That morning, New Orleans Mayor Ray Nagin ordered the first mandatory evacuation of the city in history, admitting, "We're facing the storm most of us have feared. This is going to be an unprecedented event." Bush, as well as Homeland Security Secretary Michael Chertoff and FEMA Director Michael Brown, were all directly warned about the likelihood of a levee failure that day by Max Mayfield, director of the National Hurricane Center.[7] That afternoon, the National Weather Service warned of a looming crisis, even without a levee breach, saying:

> Most of the area will be uninhabitable for weeks, perhaps longer. . . . At least one-half of well-constructed homes will have roof and wall failure. All gabled roofs will fail, leaving those homes severely damaged or destroyed. . . . Power outages will last for weeks. . . . Water shortages will make human suffering incredible by modern standards.[8]

On the morning of September 11, 2001, the president, after a few minutes of vacant staring when informed of the attacks, sprang into action and was quick to visit the sites of destruction. Not this time. This time, despite dire warnings of a greater threat—the destruction of an entire American city—Bush stayed in vacation mode at his ranch. As president, Bush could have taken charge, whipping the Homeland Security and FEMA bureaucracy into action. As commander in chief, he could have federalized the nation's state-by-state National Guard Units and ordered them to the region. He could have marshaled the active duty forces of the military to be ready for action. It could have been the moment he truly became the "man of action" character he had played so glibly on the deck of the aircraft carrier USS *Abraham Lincoln* when he proclaimed about Iraq, "Mission accomplished."

Instead, he again proved to be a master of inaction. By late that evening journalists were reporting that the river water was topping city levees. There was also the first evidence that the federal disaster response was falling short. Residents without cars had been unable to leave the city. Thirty thousand were crowding into the city's Superdome, which had only thirty-six hours' worth of food and water supplies. A

Louisiana National Guard request to FEMA for seven hundred buses had produced only one hundred.[9]

At 7 A.M. on August 29, Katrina hit New Orleans. By 8 A.M. Mayor Nagin was reporting that the levees had breeched and the city faced "significant flooding." The president was on the phone with Secretary Chertoff, but, astonishingly, the topic of their conversation wasn't Katrina and New Orleans; it was immigration.[10] Late that afternoon, the president celebrated Senator John McCain's birthday in Phoenix and then flew to California for a meeting with seniors to promote his Medicare drug plan.[11] At 8 P.M., with the city flooded, Governor Blanco repeated a desperate plea to the president for aid, saying, "Mr. President, we need your help. We need everything you've got." The president reportedly went to bed early, without acting on her request.[12] The following day, August 30, with reports pouring in on the news of a flooded city, with people reportedly trapped in their attics or on rooftops, and with other reports of mass looting and anarchy in the city, the president, seemingly more concerned with avoiding a meeting with anti-war protester Cindy Sheehan, who was camped out near Crawford, than with the Louisiana disaster, continued with business as usual. He spoke at a naval base, attended a California fundraiser, and played guitar in a photo-op with country singer Mark Willis, before finally returning to Crawford, Texas, to finish his scheduled vacation. It was not until August 31, more than forty-eight hours after the hurricane had struck, four days after receiving warnings that the city faced disaster, that President Bush flew back to Washington, saying he would begin work creating a task force to deal with the New Orleans crisis.

At 4 P.M. on August 31, two days after Katrina, the president gave his first address on New Orleans. *The New York Times* reported that

> nothing about the president's demeanor—which seemed casual to the point of carelessness—suggested that he understood the depth of the current crisis."[13]

Indeed, there were later reports that during the early days of the disaster the president had not even bothered to watch the news, so that ultimately his staff had to compile a CD of television stories about the unfolding disaster to impress upon him the scale of the crisis.[14] At that point, with a reported 80,000 New Orleans residents stranded in the flooded city without food or water, and with federal help for the city still nowhere in sight, Bush was pronouncing himself pleased with FEMA's efforts. Homeland Security chief Chertoff, too, was saying he was "extremely pleased" with the government's response.

A day later, on September 1, the Homeland Security regional director Terry Ebbert declared that the federal response to the crisis was "a national disgrace."[15] By September 2, the White House was in a Rove-designed spin mode, attempting to blame the deadly failures in New Orleans on state and local officials.[16] In fact, Bush traveled to Alabama, which was also suffering the wrath of Katrina, where he lavished praise upon Michael Brown, his appointed FEMA Director. "Brownie," he told him, "you've done a heck of a job."

Comedians joked that with just a little less effort Brown might have earned the same Presidential Medal of Freedom given to CIA Director Tenet after the disastrous intelligence failures over predicting 9/11.

But the truth is that it was really the president who was doing "a heck of a job." On February 28, 2006, the Associated Press broke a story about a video recording it had obtained from the administration through a Freedom of Information Act request. That video, made on August 28, a day *before* the storm made landfall, showed the president and his Homeland Security chief, Chertoff, being repeatedly warned by FEMA officials and hurricane watchers that the New Orleans levees could be breached, that the sports center was not equipped to handle refugees and might not even survive a Category 5 storm, and that rescue teams and resources were inadequate for the looming disaster. Incredibly, the president in the video asks not one single question, but simply asserts that "We are fully prepared."[17]

Even the much-criticized Brown comes off better than the president in the video, warning the president that

> I'm concerned about . . . their ability to respond to a catastrophe within a catastrophe.

The video and other documents obtained by the Associated Press make it even more difficult to understand the president's bizarre failure to focus on the growing disaster in New Orleans, and his insistence on "staying the course" of his Crawford vacation program. The records also bring into question the administration's claims that the poor federal response to the New Orleans disaster had been the result of poor information and confusing signals. As the AP journalists write:

> Some of the footage and transcripts from briefings Aug. 25–31 conflicts with the defenses that federal, state and local officials have made in trying to deflect blame and minimize the political fallout from the failed Katrina response:
>
> - Homeland Security officials have said the "fog of war" blinded them early on to the magnitude of the disaster. But the video and transcripts show federal and local officials discussed threats clearly, reviewed long-made plans and understood Katrina would wreak devastation of historic proportions. "I'm sure it will be the top 10 or 15 when all is said and done," National Hurricane Center's Max Mayfield warned the day Katrina lashed the Gulf Coast.
>     "I don't buy the 'fog of war' defense," Brown told the AP in an interview Wednesday. "It was a fog of bureaucracy."
> - Bush declared four days after the storm, "I don't think anybody anticipated the breach of the levees" that gushed deadly flood waters into New Orleans. He later clarified, saying officials believed, wrongly, after the storm passed that the levees had survived. But the transcripts and video show there was plenty of talk about that possibility even before the storm— and Bush was worried too.[18]

While there is certainly plenty of blame to go around in the collective failure to protect the residents of New Orleans from the storm and the flooding (Mayor Nagin, for example, should have realized that many of the city's residents, poor and without cars, could not hope to comply with his evacuation order), it was clearly the inexcusable inattention by federal authorities, beginning with the president, to the looming crisis and the early reports of disaster that was the major contributor to the unnecessary deaths and suffering that occurred following the predicted levee failures. This ineptitude and inattention, which crossed the line into the realm of criminal negligence, deserves to be considered as possible grounds for impeachment.

The failure of early rescue efforts was also compounded by the depleted condition of the Louisiana National Guard, a third of whose members had to watch in despair on TVs and computers in Iraq and elsewhere in the Middle East, where they had been shipped on presidential orders, and were unable to help rescue their families or save their homes. To make matters worse, almost all of the Louisiana Guard's amphibious vehicles had been shipped over to Iraq for use by occupation forces, leaving the forces remaining in the state unable to reach people in those large stretches of the city where the water was more than nine feet deep. For sending the National Guard to fight halfway around the world in a war of choice and leaving the nation itself undefended, the president should be impeached either on a charge of treason or of gross negligence.

The Founding Fathers pointedly rejected a proposal by George Washington himself that maladministration be included as a ground for impeachment, understandably fearing that almost every president might end up being harassed by such charges at some point. But as Elizabeth Holtzman explains in an article in *The Nation* magazine, President Bush's failure to govern on many issues (as in the case of his nonresponse to Hurricane Katrina's vicious assault on the city of New Orleans), takes maladministration to a whole new level. As she puts it:

> Upon assuming the presidency, Bush took an oath of office in which he swore to take care that the laws would be faithfully executed. Impeachment cannot be used to remove a President for maladministration, as the debates on ratifying the Constitution show. But President Bush has been guilty of such gross incompetence or reckless indifference to his obligation to execute the laws faithfully as to call into question whether he takes his oath seriously or is capable of doing so.[19]

## No Plan, No Armor, No Leadership

But gross presidential negligence began much earlier than 2005.

No American president has ever dared send the military into a large-scale war with so little planning—particularly with regard to what to do after the initial objective of conquest has been met. The White House advance men did a magnificent job of getting a banner saying "Mission Accomplished" hung across the superstructure of the aircraft carrier *Abraham Lincoln,* but Bush as commander in chief, and his team of desk warriors, headed by Vice President Dick Cheney and Secretary of Defense Donald Rumsfeld, had done less than nothing to prepare for running the country they had conquered so quickly. Plans and predictions that had previously been drawn up by the State Department in anticipation of an invasion of Iraq, plans that had been made by top military strategists, were ignored and ridiculed. Indeed, even when then Army Chief of Staff Gen. Eric Shinseki predicted, a month before the U.S. invasion, that the Pentagon would need to put several hundred thousand troops in Iraq to conduct a successful occupation and reconstruction of the soon to be war-torn land, he was publicly denounced by Rumsfeld and by Paul Wolfowitz, the second-ranking civilian in the Defense Department, and drummed out of office by the White House. The president and his advisers wanted a war on the cheap, and they didn't want anyone questioning them about their plan, such as it was, even one of their top generals.[20]

Later news reports have made it evident that Shinseki was right, though. Moreover, the administration consistently ignored and kept private the repeated urgings of top generals in Iraq and recommendations by the head of the Provisional Authority, L. Paul Bremer, that more troops be added to the occupation force. The result, most military experts agree, has been higher U.S. and Iraqi casualties than otherwise would have occurred. If this was gross negligence on the part of the president, Holtzman and others think it may be impeachable. (It might also be considered an impeachable political offense if the president deliberately kept troop deployments too low for fear of a voter backlash in November 2004, should the war appear to be too big and too costly. Particularly if, as some military experts claim, having too few men on the ground was allowing the insurgency to grow and was producing higher U.S. casualties.)

The same lack of planning occurred in the ability of the military to provide sufficient armor for American troops or for their vehicles. Even as it became deadly evident after the initial invasion that an insurrection was developing in Iraq, and that the favored weapon of these terrorists were IEDs (improvised explosive devices), as these buried bombs were called, thanks to a lack of planning American soldiers were forced to travel around Iraq in lightly armored Humvees, vehicles which were extremely vulnerable to IEDs, as well as to the rocket-propelled grenades and AK47 rounds favored by Iraqi fighters. Even more astoundingly, although the military had developed advanced body armor that could protect troops against the shrapnel from IEDs and from most light arms fire, most troops who wanted body armor had to purchase it for themselves or have their families buy it on the private market and send it to them. Troops were also trying to armor their Humvees themselves, using scrap metal and plywood scrounged up in Iraq's dumps. The situation has persisted throughout the war. In an astonishing report in February 2006, it was revealed that soldiers were actually being billed for their protective armor, which was bloodied or destroyed when they were wounded in combat. Even Republicans in Congress have blasted the White House and the Pentagon for this lack of adequate armor for American troops and their vehicles, shortages that continued as the war approached its third anniversary.[21]

Elizabeth Holtzman is scathing in her indictment of the president for these deadly lapses. Noting that there was no particular urgency for invading Iraq when the president issued his command to commence the war, she says:

> The President's failure as Commander in Chief to protect the troops by arming them properly, and his failure to plan for the occupation, cost dearly in lives and taxpayer dollars. This was not mere negligence or oversight—in other words, maladministration—but reflected a reckless and grotesque disregard for the welfare of the troops and an utter indifference to the need for proper governance of a country after occupation. As such, these failures violated the requirements of the

President's oath of office. If they are proven to be the product of political objectives, they could constitute impeachable offenses on those grounds alone.[22]

If the United States had been under attack, or had been threatened with an imminent attack, sending troops into battle under these less than ideal conditions would have been justified, but that was not the situation. Even if Iraq had possessed WMDs of various sorts, even if Saddam Hussein had been trying to develop a nuclear weapon, and even if the tales of his buying centrifuge parts and trying to buy uranium ore had been fact instead of lies, the country was years away from posing a threat to the United States. In addition to not having those weapons, they had no means of delivering them. The only real threat that Bush faced was growing sentiment in America that the war was not necessary. So his decision to go to war when he did was purely political. As such, it was his responsibility as president and as commander in chief to ensure that his forces were ready. Instead, he fired or ignored those military officers who said they weren't, and then went ahead with an invasion, putting American GIs needlessly at risk.

For this he should be impeached.

## *Weather to Impeach*

Viewed simply in terms of the size and enormity of the impact of presidential failure to govern and to act in response to a crisis threatening the nation, the president's greatest failure has to be his handling or nonhandling of the global warming crisis. There is little question among the world's scientific community concerning the basic reality of global warming—the earth is getting hotter at a frightening and record pace, the Arctic icecap is disappearing at an accelerating rate, and even the huge Antarctic ice sheet is beginning to hasten its slide to the sea. Sea levels are already rising measurably, weather patterns are changing in the United States and around the globe, storms are becoming more powerful, deserts are expanding, and the rain forests, crucial to the earth's ability to absorb excess carbon dioxide, are dying off or being harvested or burned off. While there are responsible scientists who question whether what is happening is a man-caused phenomenon, their numbers are extremely few, and more often than not, their corporate connections make their opinions suspect. Overwhelmingly, the conclusion of scientific experts is that human activity, and especially industrial activity and the combustion engine, are causing climatic changes that threaten life on earth.

Prior to Bush's taking office, the nations of the world met and negotiated the Kyoto Accord, which was designed to get all countries to begin tempering and ultimately to start reducing their production of greenhouse gasses. It is these greenhouse gasses that seem to be at least partially responsible for rising temperatures on earth. The United States was a key negotiator in those talks, as it should have been, given that the United States is the largest single producer of greenhouse gasses. President Clinton never sent the Accord to the Senate for ratification, fearing it wouldn't pass, but he said the United States would seek to meet greenhouse gas reduction targets.

On taking office, the Bush administration almost immediately pulled out of the Kyoto Accord, and made no attempt to comply with its requirements for limiting the production and release into the atmosphere of greenhouse gasses. Though the president had promised during his campaign to seek a limit on carbon dioxide released by power plants, the major contributor to global warming, once in office he dropped all talk of such regulatory efforts.

Despite the best efforts of Tony Blair, Great Britain's prime minister, a friend of the president's, and Bush's closest ally in the war on Iraq, President Bush has walked away from all international efforts to combat global warming, even to the point of playing an obstructionist role in negotiations. His administration has even on several occasions sought to alter reports on the state of the environment from its own agencies in an effort to diminish any concerns among the public about global warming. For example, in 2003 the White House forced the Environmental Protection Administration to delete from its annual report on the state of the environment a statement that "climate change has global consequences for human health and the environment," and also a conclusion that recent global warming has been "likely mostly due to human activities."[23] More recently, in December 2005 and January 2006, the administration sought to silence NASA's chief climate scientist, James Hansen, who has been warning loudly that time is running out for the world to act to prevent a global warming catastrophe, and that a "tipping point" may be reached after which nothing can be done to stop the trend.[24]

The issue, however, could not be more serious. James Lovelock, a leading environmental scientist and the man who developed the now widely accepted concept of the earth as a planetary control system of mutually interrelated processes which include life itself—a concept called *Gaia*—warns that unless the United States, together with the emerging economies of China and India, quickly act to make major reductions in their industrial emissions of $CO_2$, the main cause of global warming, it will be too late to fix the problem, which he warns could doom the world to 100,000 years of oven-like heat.[25]

Not all environmental and weather scientists are as alarmist as Lovelock, but the consensus opinion is that the earth will be warming by as much as 4 to 8 degrees over the course of this century, which would result in sea levels rising significantly and flooding coastal areas, crop yields falling, and species of all sorts dying off. Even the Pentagon views the impacts of global warming as a major threat to the national security of the United States, with a study made public in 2004 warning that by 2025 global warming could cost millions of lives, and plunge most of Europe into a "Siberian climate." That study asserted that the threat of rapid climate change to global stability would "vastly eclipse" the president's worry about terrorism, leading to possible megadroughts, famine, and widespread rioting, with the competition for diminishing resources setting the stage for nuclear conflicts.[26]

In the face of all this, once again the president of the United States has done less than nothing—assuming nothing would be simply maintaining the status quo—and in fact has actively obstructed domestic and international efforts to combat the warming trend. Using trade threats and other bullying tactics abroad while spreading disinformation domestically, as he has done for five years in office, his actions border on the criminal. Obviously, presidents have a right and duty to make policy, and on one level, how to deal with the threat of global warming can be seen as simply a policy matter. But when nearly every former Environmental Protection Agency director from the presidency of Richard Nixon through Bush's own first-term EPA director Christine Whitman meet and agree that so-called "market solutions" alone are not going to prevent disaster, as happened in January 2006, and the president still fails to act, arguably we have moved into the realm of criminal negligence—and perhaps even conspiracy.

Who can fathom why this president is so congenitally unwilling to confront the challenge of global warming? Perhaps it is a matter of his catering to the parochial interests of the oil industry, which so heavily funded his two presidential campaigns, and to which his vice president remains financially linked. Or maybe he sees the looming disaster as the realization of some fundamentalist vision of Armageddon. Whatever his reasons, the very survival of the nation and world may be threatened by his inaction and obstruction. Surely such willful behavior on a matter of such life-and-death concern represents a failure to live up to his oath of office, and should at least be considered as a ground for impeachment.

## *Corruption: Case in the Making*

As this book went to press, stories were just beginning to come out linking Republican megalobbyist Jack Abramoff to the White House and to President Bush. After Abramoff pleaded guilty to federal felony fraud and bribery conspiracy charges he turned state's evidence and produced a list of more than sixty Republican members of Congress to whom he had given significant amounts of money on behalf of his corporate clients. Initially, President Bush claimed complete ignorance. The president did not know Abramoff personally, the White House said. But at the same time, the White House stonewalled requests for information regarding any contacts between Abramoff and the president or his staff. Gradually, however, word began leaking out that the initial story was not correct. *Time* magazine reported having five photographs of the president with Abramoff, and the president and his wife prominently donated six thousand dollars' worth of Abramoff campaign contributions to one of the charities the lobbyist represented. The White House claimed that those photographs were taken at large social events, during which numerous people get to have their picture taken with the president. But subsequently it was reported that Abramoff charged clients $25,000 for "face time" with the president, and the first photograph to be published in which both Abramoff and the President appeared showed Bush shaking hands with Abramoff client, Kickapo Traditional Tribe of Texas Chairman Juan Garza Jr., while the lobbyist is seen smiling broadly in the background.

While the scandal has so far impacted mainly the Congress, where some sixty Republican members are linked to Abramoff, it has already reached far deeper into the White House than just one small donation to the president's campaign war chest. In September 2005, David H. Safavian, the head of procurement for the White House and a man with close ties to Abramoff, resigned his post after being arrested by the FBI and charged with lying and obstructing the federal investigation into Abramoff. Safavian had been appointed by President Bush to be the top administrator at the federal procurement office in the White House Office of Management and Budget, where he set purchasing policy for the entire U.S. government. Earlier in Bush's term, Safavian, who has pleaded not guilty to the federal charges, had been chief of staff of the General Services Administration.[27]

Where all this will go over time is anyone's guess, but with pundits calling the Abramoff case the biggest political corruption scandal in decades, and with links to the White House that are far closer than any thus far admitted by the administration, it is not hard to imagine that bribery could eventually come to be another impeachable charge.

The other area where corruption charges ought to be considered as possible grounds for impeachment is the massive signing of no-bid contracts with politically well-connected firms during the war in Iraq and the "reconstruction" period that followed. Congressional investigators conducting an impeachment inquiry into presidential corruption might want, for example, to examine the initial group of companies selected by the White House and Pentagon to bid on a $900-million initial reconstruction contract in Iraq back in early March 2003, before the *actual* invasion even began. Those firms, which included Bechtel, Flour, Halliburton subsidiary Kellogg, Brown

& Root, Louis Berger Group, Parsons Corporation, and Washington Group International, Inc., collectively contributed $3.5 million in the prior two election cycles, 66 percent of it going to Republican candidates, including the president. Halliburton alone, which was headed by Vice President Cheney until 2000, and which is still paying him deferred compensation while he is vice president, gave $17,677 to the Bush/Cheney campaign in 2000.[28] Bechtel, with close ties to Rumsfeld and to the Bush family, won a $680-million Iraq reconstruction contract in March 2003—a nice return on its $1.3 million in campaign "investments," 77 percent of which went to Republican candidates, including Bush-Cheney.

In the case of these contracts, as in the case of most of the contracts signed while Iraq was being run by the Paul Bremer's Coalition Provisional Authority, the government strictly limited bidding or assigned contracts on a no-bid basis* to a select few preselected American firms. Not surprisingly, nearly all of these firms tended to be heavy contributors to Republicans and to the Bush-Cheney presidential ticket. Halliburton, famously, the Cheney-linked construction and oil services conglomerate, was a big winner of no-bid contracts for reconstruction and for providing services to the U.S. military.

The Bush administration acknowledged that bidding for the early reconstruction and service contracts in Iraq was being restricted to a few select U.S. firms. According to administration officials this was done for "security reasons," as though some U.S.-based firms couldn't be trusted. What made that explanation ring a little hollow was that even respected companies from America's staunchest ally, the United Kingdom, whose men were also dying in battle in the sands and alleyways of Iraq, were barred from the profitable contracts, to the great vexation of the British Parliament. Firms based in other NATO countries, presumably key U.S. allies even if they were not members of the Iraq war "Coalition of the Willing," were also barred from bidding, raising suspicions

---

*Something that also happened in the early days of the New Orleans post-Katrina rebuilding effort, until howls of protest from Congress led the administration to back off and put contracts to bid.

that this may have been more a matter of paying back generous campaign contributors than of exercising prudent caution about security concerns.*

A study released in January 2006 suggests that in addition to political corruption there may have been other reasons for this policy: an effort to hide the administration's predetermination to go to war. That report, by the special inspector general for Iraq reconstruction, concludes that early reconstruction contracts worth $1.9 billion were awarded to Cheney's old firm, Halliburton (actually its subsidiary KB&R) in November 2002, four months *before* the U.S. invasion, but were kept secret "to avoid the impression that the U.S. government had already decided on intervention." (Remember, at that time, November 2002, the administration was still telling Congress and the American public that it was pursuing a diplomatic solution to Iraq's alleged WMD threat, and had no plans to go to war.) The report says that this secret contracting for postinvasion Iraq was the rule through January 2003, and that the early no-bid process "cast a long shadow" over the later procurement orders, by putting a no-bid and apparently corrupt and politically linked system in place.[29]

Evidence that the White House was carefully doing advance planning about the money-making aspect of postwar Iraq is especially ironic, given the Bush administration's near-total failure to do any political, social, or military planning for the occupation and reconstruction period.

Now, even though investigations have only begun digging into the incredible cesspool of corruption in Iraq, where over nine billion taxpayer dollars designated for reconstruction have simply gone missing, proving bribery in a court of law will be a tough challenge. But in the case of impeachment, the standards are not as strict as "proof beyond a reasonable doubt." Certainly, with the lives of American troops in the

---

*German Firms were barred, even though Germany hosts an airbase that is the primary hospital site for evacuated U.S. casualties, and even though German intelligence services provided key information about Iraq's invasion defense plans to the Pentagon.

balance, the mere appearance of war profiteering being abetted or covered up by a president or by key members of his administration deserves to be carefully examined. A House Judiciary impeachment panel would be the appropriate venue to do that.

# ELEVEN

## *Impeaching Other Bush Administration Officials*

THE PRESIDENT of the United States is the only person who is protected, while in office, from being indicted and arrested in a criminal case, so bringing a president to justice requires the arduous and politically challenging process of impeachment. Other officers, such as the vice president and members of the president's cabinet have no such protection from prosecution and can simply be indicted for crimes while in office—as happened most recently to Nixon's vice president, Spiro Agnew.

Nonetheless, the Constitution also pointedly extends the process of impeachment to "all civil officials," and over the course of history, the process has been used—primarily against federal judges. The reason to have impeachment available for government officials other than the president is that assaults on the Constitution are often not crimes, as is commonly understood, and might never meet the standard for a criminal indictment. Many offenses are purely political, such as lying to the American people or abuse of power. For that reason we need to also consider the impeachable acts of others in the Bush administration, notably Vice President Dick Cheney, Secretary of Defense Donald Rumsfeld, National Security Adviser and later Secretary of State Condoleezza

Rice, and White House Counsel and subsequently Attorney General Alberto Gonzales.

## *Vice President Dick Cheney*

Vice President Dick Cheney, surely the most powerful vice president in the history of the United States, has clearly played a central role in most of the crimes and abuses of the Bush administration. It was Cheney who, in a series of furtive but well documented visits to CIA headquarters during the run-up to the Iraq invasion, pressured CIA bureaucrats and lower level analysts to make Iraq appear as dangerous as possible, and to present a trumped-up argument that Iraq was developing and stockpiling weapons of mass destruction. Cheney, at least as much as the president, lied to the American people about Iraq's alleged nuclear threat. It is Cheney, too, who has constantly pushed the idea of an imperial presidency, unanswerable to Congress or to the courts. Cheney has also been a principal advocate of torture, even limping on his cane (he'd just had knee surgery) over to Congress repeatedly to lobby against a measure introduced by Republican Senator John McCain of Arizona to outlaw torture. Indeed, Lawrence Wilkerson, who was former Secretary of State Colin Powell's chief of staff during Bush's first term, has said the authorization and even encouragement to torture captives came from Cheney. As Wilkerson puts it:

> It was clear to me there that there was a visible audit trail from the vice president's office through the secretary of defense down to the commanders in the field.[1]

It would take unusual and uncharacteristic courage for Congress to impeach a high U.S. political figure like Cheney for a war crime like torture.* It's a charge that, while extremely serious, is typically brought

---

*Technically, of course, since the United States is a signer of the Geneva Convention on the treatment of prisoners of war, torture is also a federal, not just an international, crime.

against the losers in a war. But torture in this context is a bit different, and there is good reason for patriotic Americans to consider impeaching its primary advocates. The scandal of America's campaign of torture of captives in the "War on Terror" has been graphically displayed in photographs from Abu Ghraib, and graphically described in accounts from Afghanistan's Bagram Air Base, from Guantanamo Bay, and from victims who were renditioned to various secret CIA-run gulag prisons around the world. These crimes, sanctioned and indeed promoted by the administration, and particularly by the vice president, have served as a prime recruiting tool for insurgents in both Afghanistan and Iraq. Without a doubt, America's torturing of captives has also helped swell the ranks of terror recruits across the Islamic world. Patriotic Americans and troops in the field alike should be anxious to restore this nation's soiled honor by eradicating this stain from both the military and from the civil government, and by punishing those who spread it. Wilkerson, who in addition to serving in Powell's state department, also was a colonel in the army, says that in his view Cheney's "advocacy of terror" was a violation of U.S. law, and he adds, "I would suspect that it is, for whatever it's worth, an international war crime as well."[2]

It may well be that Cheney should be impeached not just on torture charges, but on many of the same counts that have been proposed against the president in this book. But there are also some charges that belong uniquely to the vice president. One of these should probably be the outing of Valerie Plame Wilson. If only because it is possible that underlings like Karl Rove and Andrew Card may have deliberately kept the president in the dark—giving him "plausible deniability," as Washington scandal jargon puts it—Bush may not have been involved in the actual conspiracy to expose Plame's undercover CIA identity to the media. While the president may be guilty only of obstructing the inquiry into who in the White House outed the agent in violation of federal law, Cheney seems to have been more actively involved in the conspiracy to out Plame, and in the outing itself.* The federal indictment of Cheney's top aide, I. Lewis "Scooter" Libby, includes references to Cheney's having

---

*Certainly he lied on national television when he denied even knowing Joseph Wilson.

provided information about Plame's job and her relationship to Wilson to Libby, and possibly others.[3] (See appendix G—Libby indictment). With special council Patrick Fitzgerald still investigating and calling witnesses before a second grand jury in the Plame case in February 2006, it remains possible that Cheney will be indicted along with his chief of staff. But even if it turns out that Fitzgerald does not have sufficient evidence to justify such an indictment, an impeachment panel might arrive at a different conclusion regarding Cheney's role in the case.

Cheney also is much more directly linked to the widespread corruption and alleged war profiteering in Iraq. The vice president, who was CEO of Halliburton until he became a candidate for vice president in 2000, has never really cut his ties with that quintessentially Republican oil services and construction conglomerate. Ordinarily, when a person assumes federal office, she or he is required to sever any commercial or financial relationships, particularly with companies that could stand to gain from the person's position in government. Cheney chose not to do that, however, setting, as the number two man in government, a stunningly low bar for financial integrity in the Bush administration. As the Congressional Research Office reported in 2003, the vice president was at that time, two years into office, holding 433,000 Halliburton stock options and receiving an average of about $175,000 a year in "deferred compensation" from the company. The options alone, by late 2005, were worth $9.2 million. Halliburton was the single largest beneficiary of early no-bid contracts awarded by the Pentagon before and after the Iraq invasion and is the largest private contractor in Iraq. By the beginning of 2006 they had received almost $11 *billion* in contracts from the Bush-Cheney administration. The company also received controversial no-bid cleanup and reconstruction contracts after Hurricane Katrina devastated New Orleans. The vice president's obvious ability to influence the steering of contracts to his former company, and the clear financial interest he would have in doing so because of his continued ties, constitute a *prima facie* case of not just garden variety corruption, but, in the case of Iraq reconstruction contracts, of war profiteering.

Making this even worse, Halliburton has been mired in scandals involving some of those contracts. Halliburton and its subsidiary, Kellogg, Brown & Root, have been accused of generating several hundred million dollars in overcharges on no-bid contracts in Iraq. One such scandal involved alleged overcharges on a contract for providing food and supplies in Iraq to coalition troops in Kuwait. In that case, Halliburton admitted one and possibly two employees took $6.3 million in kickbacks to use a particular politically well-connected subcontractor in Kuwait. A day after that disclosure, despite the company's dismal reputation and dismal performance record, the Pentagon awarded Halliburton another $1.2-billion contract for rebuilding Iraq's southern oilfields—a clear indication of the company's beyond-reproach standing with the Bush-Cheney White House.[4]

When American troops are fighting and dying, it is simply shameless and inexcusable for the second-highest elected official in the nation to refuse to divest himself of holdings and financial ties that at the very least present the appearance of a huge financial conflict of interest. As the Congressional Research Service report put it, quoting from federal conflict-of-interest guidelines, Cheney's deferred compensation and options holdings must be

> considered among the "ties" retained in or "linkages to former employers" that may "represent a continuing financial interest" in those employers which makes them potential conflicts of interest.[5]

The vice president seems strangely more concerned with the tax consequences of taking his compensation in a lump sum, and with maximizing his gain on his options holdings, than with maintaining an appearance of financial independence and probity as a national leader. He has denied that his owning of Halliburton options and receipt of compensation from the firm are in any way unethical, whatever the CRS might say. The week that the CRS issued its report, Cheney told NBC television:

> I've severed all my ties with the company, gotten rid of all my financial interest. I have no financial interest in Halliburton of any kind and haven't had, now, for over three years.[6]

This, of course, was an outright lie. Cheney aides explained the apparent discrepancy between Cheney's public statement and the fact of his op-

tions and compensation by claiming the vice president's financial arrange-
ments with his former employer didn't constitute "financial ties." They
note that Cheney claims to have promised to give any after-tax profits
from his options holdings to charity—although this lack of financial
"ties" might have been made clearer simply by giving the options *themselves* to charity, rather than an unenforceable promise of future profits.

The contrast between Cheney and another famous vice president
from an earlier day is instructive. Harry Truman caught President
Franklin Roosevelt's eye as a vice presidential prospect in large part because of his role as an aggressive, no-nonsense prosecutor of war profiteering during World War II. Now we have a wartime vice president
who is directly profiting from war-related contracts awarded by an administration in which he has extraordinary control to a company he led
until becoming vice president. Even if his motives in clinging to his
Halliburton assets were wholly innocent, he has set a standard at the
top of the administration that is clearly contributing to the unseemly "gold
rush" mentality among U.S. contractors in Iraq, where billions of dollars
in U.S. aid has simply vanished without a trace, even as American soldiers
are still dying, and where contract after contract has been awarded to corporations with a track record of ladling cash into Republican coffers.

Cheney's blatant cronyism is clearly a situation where a federal
prosecutor might feel there wasn't enough of a case to bring an indictment for corruption, but where a House impeachment panel might well
come to a different conclusion.

### *Secretary of Defense Donald Rumsfeld*

Donald Rumsfeld, who is both the oldest and youngest man to serve as
Secretary of Defense, is a key figure in the Bush administration. As Defense Secretary under Gerald Ford, Rumsfeld was Dick Cheney's men-
tor. Currently, Bush, Cheney, and Rumsfeld form a tight triumvirate in
the area of military and international affairs. The defense secretary,
however, has a curious relationship to Iraq. In fact, he has had a curious
relationship with several of America's stated enemies and geopolitical
rivals. In the 1980s, Rumsfeld, as President Ronald Reagan's special en-

voy to the Middle East, was "the main conduit for crucial American intelligence, hardware, and strategic advice" to Saddam Hussein, who at the time was in a bitter war with his neighbor, Iran. Indeed, he visited Hussein shortly after the dictator's notorious use of poison gas on some of Iraq's own citizens and offered not a word of criticism. During the 1990s, with a Democrat in the White House, Rumsfeld was in private industry, serving as a $190,000-a-year member of the board of directors of ABB, a Swiss-based engineering firm, which in those years supplied North Korea with not one but two light-water nuclear reactors—reactors which North Korea later used to manufacture the plutonium for its nuclear bombs. Those people who assume this might have been done without Rumsfeld's knowledge would be completely wrong. ABB has stated that all its board members were specifically informed of the nuclear reactor deals with North Korea, which were highly controversial at the time.[7] Rumsfeld, whose career has been as much in the business world as in politics, was also a partner in a company that sold specialty spyware to China—software designed to protect Chinese government computers from spying and sabotage.[8] He sold his holdings in Chengwei Ventures Fund I, valued at between $250,000 and $500,000, upon taking his job with the Bush administration.

While such past corporate relationships might raise some eyebrows and questions, Rumsfeld's relationship to torture is anything but ambiguous. While it was White House and Justice Department lawyers who wrote the memos that justified torture of captives in Afghanistan and Iraq, and at the Guantanamo Camp prison compound, Secretary of Defense Donald Rumsfeld, as the top civilian in the Pentagon, and as the man ultimately in charge of day-to-day running of the U.S. military, was torture's chief apologist and promoter. While President Bush may have privately authorized torture (all the while publicly denying that the U.S. tortures), and Vice President Cheney may have encouraged its application, Rumsfeld was the official who handled the nuts and bolts of getting the racks and the waterboards constructed and put to use. As Col. Janis Karpinski, the demoted brigadier general who took the rap for the torture scandal at Abu Ghraib, explains, Rumsfeld transferred Gen. Geoffrey Miller, who had been commander in charge of the inmates at Guantanamo, to Baghdad with instructions to help interrogators in Iraq "enhance" their interrogation techniques. Karpinski, who had been in charge of the Abu Ghraib prison, says Gen. Miller, who outranked her by a star, informed her he was going to "Gitmo-ize" the prison at Abu Ghraib. She also says that on touring the prison compound subsequent to Miller's arrival, she found that at various locations photocopies of a December 2, 2002, memo written by Secretary Rumsfeld were posted—a memo which described authorized forms of torture, including, "stress positions, noise and light discipline, the use of music, disrupting sleep patterns, those kind of techniques."[9]

Karpinski adds that there was a handwritten note on the margin of those posted Rumsfeld memos, which "appeared to be in the same handwriting" as Rumsfeld's signature at the bottom of the page, saying, "Make sure this happens." Rumsfeld has been sued by the ACLU and a group called Human Rights First over his role in allowing prisoners in U.S. military custody to be tortured. Says Lucas Guttentag, lead counsel in that case:

> Secretary Rumsfeld bears direct and ultimate responsibility for this descent into horror by personally authorizing unlawful interrogation techniques and by abdicating his legal duty to stop torture.[10]

Seymour Hersh, one of the journalists who broke the My Lai war crime scandal during the Vietnam War, states that Rumsfeld's "disdain" for the Geneva Conventions on treatment of prisoners was widely known and openly expressed. It was also opposed within the military establishment. Hersh reports that by mid-2003

> Rumsfeld's apparent disregard for the requirements of the Geneva Conventions while carrying out the war on terror had led a group of senior military legal officers from the Judge Advocate General's (JAG) Corps to pay two surprise visits within five months to Scott Horton, who was then chairman of the New York City Bar Association's Committee on International Human Rights. "They wanted us to challenge the Bush Administration about its standards for detentions and interrogation," Horton told me in May 2004. "They were urging us to get involved and speak in a very loud voice. It came pretty much

out of the blue. The message was that conditions are ripe for abuse, and it's going to occur . . . They told him that, with the war on terror, a fifty-year history of exemplary application of the Geneva Conventions had come to an end.[11]

When the Abu Ghraib scandal first broke, there was a widespread expectation that Rumsfeld would resign, if only to take responsibility for the abuses and shield the president from blame. There were calls from members of Congress for him to resign, and he claims that he did offer to do so, but President Bush did not ask him to leave. Rumsfeld did express "regret" for the tortures of prisoners held at Abu Ghraib during his testimony to Congress, following the global, domestic outcry that followed publication of photos of the abuse. But he did not accept responsibility, blaming the instances of torture instead, as did the president, on low-ranking troops, rather than on his own and other government and military memos and instructions. Under both U.S. and international law, however, torture of POWs is a serious crime, and so is any failure to prevent it by senior officers and civilian authorities. And Rumsfeld, documents show, did not just ignore evidence of torture, he actively encouraged torture. (See appendix H—Rumsfeld instructions.) Obviously he was aware of the consequences of that policy, as initially, when evidence of the abuses at Abu Ghraib was first brought to his attention he, along with the White House, sought to hide it from the American public and the rest of the world. If the Justice Department is not willing to indict the secretary of defense for his role in authorizing this crime, he should be impeached for it.

But torture of prisoners is only the most egregious and obvious of Secretary Rumsfeld's impeachable transgressions.

Certainly, if President Bush is to be considered culpable for the criminally negligent act of sending American troops into Iraq and Afghanistan with inadequate body armor, then Secretary Rumsfeld is equally impeachable on the same grounds. Rumsfeld has compounded the felony, too, by his display of glacial aloofness when the issue was raised by a National Guard infantryman bound for the front during a public Q&A with the secretary in Kuwait. Asked by these troops about the lack of adequate armor for their bodies and for the Humvees and trucks they would have to drive in Iraq, Rumsfeld angrily and callously retorted, "You go to war with the army you have."[12] Of course, it was because Rumsfeld, along with the president, vice president, and national security adviser, were pushing for an invasion of Iraq on a rushed timetable that the "army we have" was not fully equipped in the first place. Besides, the invasion by that point had already happened two years before. Even in early 2006, as the war was entering its fourth year, there are shortages of armor, and not all Humvees and trucks are armored.

As secretary of defense, Rumsfeld was also intimately involved in the deceitful and duplicitous work of the Department of Defense's notorious Office of Special Plans, which essentially provided him and the White House with an alternative "analysis unit" that, through 2002 and early 2003 would churn out ready-made "evidence" of Iraqi WMDs. As we saw in chapter 4, the OSP was central to the White House campaign to undermine more realistic and honest State Department and CIA reports in order to mislead Congress, the media, and the American public about the alleged imminent threat posed by Saddam Hussein's Iraq. This campaign of deception, which resulted in a thoroughly unnecessary and unjustified war, and in the deaths of thousands of Americans, is an impeachable offense.

As secretary of defense, Rumsfeld also oversaw the Pentagon's own illegal incursions into domestic surveillance. This is a repeat of the illegal domestic spying the DOD engaged in during the Johnson and Nixon administrations, when the Defense Intelligence Agency collected dossiers on more than ten thousand Americans. While the NSA domestic spying authorized by Bush has dominated headlines in 2006, about the same time that news of that scandal broke there came word that the Pentagon was also back in the domestic spying business in a major way. One group, the Counter Intelligence Field Activity group, was established to spy on groups that were considered "threats" to military bases in the United States. Instead of looking for terrorists, however, it turns out that CIFA has spent most of its time spying on perfectly peaceful and legal anti-war protesters. For example, on April 5, 2005, CIFA agents spied on a group of UC Santa Cruz students protesting the presence of military recruiters on campus.[13] This was one of some fifteen hundred "incidents," which were recorded in a dossier compiled by spies working for CIFA that were in a four-hundred-page secret file obtained by NBC in December 2005.

The program allegedly began in 2003 on the orders of Deputy Secretary of Defense (and now World Bank head) Paul Wolfowitz, who authorized a program called TALON, for Threat and Local Observation Notice, a program of gathering local "raw information" on "suspicious incidents."[14] The intelligence gathering, by undercover military, quickly moved from looking for terrorists (if that was ever its real goal) to monitoring antiwar and antimilitary groups—everything from student protest organizations to Quaker meetings. "I think Americans should be concerned that the military, in fact, has reached too far," says NBC News military analyst Bill Arkin.[15]

This kind of domestic spying violates not just the First Amendment of the Constitution, which protects free speech and assembly, and the right peaceably to redress grievances, but also violates the Posse Comitatus Act, which for a century and a half has barred military activity within the domestic United States except in a state of declared martial law. As the head of the Department of Defense, Rumsfeld should be impeached for this major constitutional violation.

As head of the Department of Defense, and the man with ultimate responsibility for the conduct of the twin wars in Iraq and Afghanistan, Rumsfeld is also responsible for the war crimes of which the U.S. military is guilty—crimes that go beyond just torture and abuse of captives.

Under the Geneva Conventions, it is illegal for military forces to deliberately target civilians or to bar noncombatants from leaving the scene of battle. It is illegal to attack cities or civilian groups as retribution for the acts of enemy forces, even if those forces may have come from a particular city. As well, certain weapons, like napalm, are illegal, while others, like antipersonnel weapons, are banned for use in populated areas or, as in the case of phosphorus, are banned for use against people. The U.S. military is guilty of all of these violations.

A number of these war crimes were perpetrated during the assault on and destruction of Fallujah in late 2004. As 10,000 heavily armed U.S. Marines and other troops cordoned off this city in western Iraq in preparation for a massive assault that would level a historic city of 300,000, thousands of refugees streamed out, seeking to escape the inevitable carnage and destruction. According to a reporter with *The New York Times* who was embedded with American forces, not everyone who wanted to leave was allowed to escape, however. Dexter Filkins reported on a group of several hundred refugees from the doomed city who had been detained by the encircling American troops. Women and small children, he wrote, were allowed to leave. Men and boys, though—even young boys—had their hands tested for traces of gunpowder, but then they were turned back into the soon-to-be-devastated city to fend for themselves, even those completely innocent Iraqis who had tested negative. Filkins reported that the military *policy* apparently was that all those "of fighting age" were being presumed to be the enemy, and the Pentagon's goal of the attack on Fallujah—the largest campaign in the war except for the initial drive on Baghdad—was to trap and kill as many of the "enemy" as possible. It is a story that has been repeated all over Iraq, as U.S. troops have treated all "men and boys of fighting age" as potential enemies, subject to bombing, shooting, and arrest. It is also a war crime. Under the Fourth Geneva Convention—part of a set of four international treaties signed by approximately 115 nations including the United States back in 1949, in the wake of the atrocities of World War II, all intended to make war less brutal for both soldiers and civilians—civilians have the absolute right to flee a scene of combat. (And under these rules children *under the age of fifteen* are to be treated with special care.)

In fact, the very U.S. assault on Fallujah, which led to as many as six thousand civilian deaths and probably many more,\* was itself among the grossest of Geneva Convention violations. The original assault on Fallujah, which had been mounted earlier in the year in the wake of the brutal killing, burning, and dismemberment of four "civilian contractors"—mercenaries working for the U.S. military who are not subject to U.S. legal jurisdiction or the military code—had been quite expressly in retribution for that ugly incident. After the "Blackhawk Down" incident in Somalia which resulted in severe criticism of the Clinton administration, the Bush administration could not let such visible

---

\*The five to six thousand figure was reported by the Iraqi government based upon its own investigation. The U.S. military has not provided any official tallies of civilian deaths in the Iraq war.

brutality against Americans go publicly unpunished, so this large scale and mostly unnecessary assault had been given the go ahead. That initial assault had been called off, largely for political reasons, because of the slow pace of advance into the city and what the White House considered to be politically unacceptable U.S. casualties. So a second, larger assault in November was presented to the American public, which had been inflamed by the mercenary slayings, as a continuation of that earlier aborted assault. It, too, in other words, was an act of retribution. But while Fallujah was unarguably a hotbed of insurgent activity, the leveling of the city was a grotesque overreaction, akin to how the Wehrmacht used to destroy villages when its troops were struck by partisans in France or eastern Europe. The Geneva Conventions expressly outlaw "collective punishment," and specifically the retributive destruction of cities in response to enemy actions.

Rumsfeld's direct role in the criminal ordering of Fallujah's destruction may not be clear at this point, but under the precedent established in the Nuremberg Trials and also by the prosecution and eventual execution for war crimes of General Tomoyuki Yamashita, the head of Japanese forces in World War II, the senior commander of military forces is responsible for war crimes if he is found to have failed to properly instruct, or to restrain his troops, allowing war crimes to occur. Moreover, there is good reason to believe that the assault on Fallujah was a focus of attention and planning at the highest levels of the DOD. It was long planned, and politics played a key role in its timing: it was delayed past the November presidential election reportedly because of administration fears about the political impact of possible high levels of American casualties.* Furthermore, as constitutional lawyer Francis Boyle puts it:

> According to basic principles of international criminal law, all high-level civilian officials and military officers in the U.S. government who

---

*The political delay of the invasion, after the military was already in place and ready to move in, may have actually been the reason behind the decision to bar males from leaving the city. In fact, the real insurgents in Fallujah, with plenty of warning of what was coming, mostly managed to slip out of the city, leaving only a limited number of 'martyrs' to exact a toll on the U.S. invaders.

either knew or should have known that soldiers or civilians under their control committed or were about to commit international crimes, and failed to take the measures necessary to stop them, or to punish them, or both, are likewise personally responsible for the commission of international crimes. This category of officialdom who actually knew or at least should have known of the commission of such substantive or inchoate international crimes under their jurisdiction and failed to do anything about it typically includes the Secretary of Defense, Secretary of State, Director of Central Intelligence, the National Security Adviser, the Attorney General, the Pentagon's Joint Chiefs of Staff, and regional CINCs, and presumably the President and Vice President. These U.S. government officials and their immediate subordinates, among others, were personally responsible for the commission or at least complicity in the commission of crimes against peace, crimes against humanity, and war crimes as specified by the Nuremberg Charter, Judgment, and Principles—at a minimum. In international legal terms, the Bush Jr. administration itself should be viewed as constituting an ongoing criminal conspiracy under international criminal law.[16]

The city of Fallujah was the scene of other intentional war crimes, too, with belated acknowledgement by the Pentagon that prohibited weapons were used, including a napalm-like weapon and phosphorus.* The latter material, legal for use as a night flare or for producing a smoke screen, is specifically banned not just under international law but in the U.S. military code itself, as a weapon against people, whether civilian or military, and yet is was used repeatedly and in large quantities during the Fallujah campaign.

The charge that phosphorus was used against civilians was first

---

*The Pentagon has denied that it used napalm, which since 1987 has been banned for use against people, by making the technical argument that the substance it used, MK77, is chemically different, being made from kerosene instead of naphtha. In fact, in function and in the nature of its horrific impact on the human body, where it sticks, burns, and literally melts the flesh, the two products are indistinguishable.

made in a documentary film by an independent Italian journalism team[17] and broadcast on Italy's RAI-TV, and initially it was vehemently denied by the Pentagon, the State Department, and the White House. But subsequent reporting disclosed that the weapon, so common it has a GI nickname, "Willie Pete," or "WP," was heavily used to devastating effect in Fallujah in a technique called "shake and bake." As an official after-action report published in the March–April 2005 edition of the Army's *Field Artillery* Magazine, an official military publication, put it, quoting officers who fought in Fallujah:

> "WP proved to be an effective and versatile munition. . . . We used it for screening missions at two breeches and, later in the fight, as a potent psychological weapon against the insurgents in trench lines and spider holes when we could not get effects on them with HE (high explosive)" munitions.
>
> "We fired 'shake and bake' missions at the insurgents, using WP to flush them out and HE to take them out."[18]

Phosphorus weapons are particularly obscene, burning on contact with skin, and going right down to the bone. Pentagon claims that this use of phosphorus was permissible because it was "not used against civilians," are specious. Firstly, the military's own officer training manual[19] clearly states: "It is against the law of land warfare to employ WP against personnel targets." Secondly, the military's demonstrated policy, throughout Iraq, of considering "all males of fighting age" to be potential enemies assures that noncombatants will be targeted along with fighters, particularly in the case of a weapon like this that is dropped scattershot with the intention to spread it over a wide area.

It is, of course, possible that the decision to illegally use phosphorus weapons in Fallujah, like the illegal decision to prevent civilians and even young boys from leaving the scene of a future assault, was made locally, not in the White House or the Pentagon. However, the abject failure of the secretary of defense to see that these clear violations of the laws of war be investigated and prosecuted makes Secretary Rumsfeld himself a party to the crime under the Nuremberg Charter, and thus warrants his impeachment. (Interestingly, a poll of active duty soldiers and Marines in Iraq conducted by Zogby International in early 2006 found that four out of five opposed the use of napalm and phosphorus weapons.)[20]

Finally, Rumsfeld should be impeached on the same issue of corruption and war profiteering in Iraq as Vice President Cheney. Rumsfeld, as head of the DOD, is the prime overseer of the vast, corrupt, and ineptly managed U.S. occupation of Iraq. The hugely lucrative contracts to supply the U.S. military machine and rebuild Iraq after the war have all fallen under Rumsfeld's purview. The fact that so many of those contracts have gone to Republican-linked companies, often under no-bid terms, that so many billions of dollars have disappeared and that the government has continued to award contracts to companies like Halliburton, even after they have been involved in scandal there, raise questions that only an impeachment inquiry can properly answer.

## Secretary of State Condoleezza Rice

The woman who served for four years as George Bush's national security adviser, and who is now the nation's secretary of state, played a crucial role in the administration's campaigns of lies and distortions about the need to go to war in Iraq. As a charter member of the White House Iraq Group (WHIG), she was a key figure in the spread of misinformation to the media and to Congress about alleged WMDs in Iraq. It was Rice who first issued the deliberately panic-inducing warning that the smoking gun could be a "mushroom cloud" coming from Iraq.

With the administration facing reports from a former UN weapons inspector that its case against Iraq on WMDs was "overblown," Rice was sent out to stir up public fears. Although CIA analysts and UN inspectors were reporting that there was no evidence of an active Iraqi nuclear weapons program, and though experts had debunked claims that aluminum tubes purchased by Iraq were for a uranium-refining centrifuge, in an interview on CNN in early September 2002 the president's national security adviser offered up a number of lies:

- Rice asserted that at that point the administration had not decided to go to war against Iraq, although as we saw in

chapter 4, equipment and troops were already being diverted
from Afghanistan for that purpose and, as the so-called
Downing Street memo to British Prime Minister Tony Blair
made it clear, the policy of going to war had already been
set.

- Rice claimed that the aluminum tubes purchased by Iraq
  "are only really suited for nuclear weapons programs, centrifuge programs." In fact, the administration knew that the
  nuclear experts had said the tubes in question were cut too
  short to be used for that purpose, and that in fact they were
  suitable only for use as fuselages for small battlefield rockets.

- While acknowledging that "there will always be some uncertainty" in predicting how close Iraq might be to developing
  a nuclear bomb, Rice famously warned, "We don't want the
  smoking gun to be a mushroom cloud."[21]

Coming a year after the terror of 9/11, these statements by Rice—all
false and all manipulatively designed to scare—played a crucial role in
the Bush scheme to win public support, and a congressional authorization for his already-planned invasion of Iraq. Rice's reference to the aluminum tubes was particularly disingenuous and was part of an elaborate
WHIG disinformation campaign which involved reporter Judith Miller
and *The New York Times*. WHIG, of which Rice was a member, reportedly leaked the story that Iraq had purchased the tubes to Miller,[22] who
accommodatingly published that information in the *Times*. (Miller's reporting was later criticized by the paper's own editors as "credulous"
and thinly sourced.) Rice and Vice President Cheney then turned around
and cited Miller and the *Times* as their source in making their bogus
claims that Saddam Hussein was attempting to develop a nuclear bomb.

For her active role in this elaborate deception, Rice should be impeached.

Rice should also be impeached for her role as secretary of state in
covering up the U.S. role in illegally "renditioning"—and even kidnapping on foreign soil—suspected terrorists and captives from Iraq and
Afghanistan. During a European tour designed to tamp down public
outcry among NATO allies over U.S. torture and rendition policies,

Rice reportedly apologized to German officials for the kidnapping and torture in Afghanistan of a German citizen wrongfully suspected of being a terrorist. (Actually, Germany's newly elected Prime Minister Angela Merkel said Rice had apologized for the incident, but Rice later claimed to U.S. reporters that she'd done no such thing.) During a speech on that same trip the new secretary of state stated that "the United States does not permit, tolerate or condone torture under any circumstances." She also said, "The United States does not transport, and has not transported, detainees from one country to another for the purpose of interrogation using torture. The United States does not use the airspace or the airports of any country for the purpose of transporting a detainee to a country where he or she will be tortured."[23]

The only way any of those statements can be said to be anything but bald-faced lies would be if Rice is defining the term torture to mean something worse than what was being done to people like the German Khaled El-Masri or the several other victims of U.S. torture and rendition whose stories have come to light.

For these lies, which have seriously harmed U.S. international relations with its allies, and which inevitably come home and deceive the American people as well, Rice should be impeached.

## Alberto Gonzales

Gonzales served as President Bush's chief White House counsel during his first term, and replaced John Ashcroft as attorney general in Bush's second, and has had his career closely tied to the younger George Bush's political history. Bush named the Texas native his general counsel when he became governor of Texas in 1994. Three years later, Bush nominated Gonzales to be Texas Secretary of State, a position he held until 1999, when Bush nominated him to a seat on the Texas Supreme Court. Gonzales has provided legal cover for Bush almost from the beginning of the president's political career. In 1996, he kept the future president from being called to jury duty in a drunk-driving case. The prosecutor in the case later charged that he had been "deceived" by Gonzales and Bush because, in his jury questionnaire, the governor had illegally failed to note that he himself had pleaded guilty to misdemeanor drunk driving in 1976.[24]

During his tenure as the governor's counsel in Texas, Gonzales also displayed a predisposition to give short shrift to legal niceties, even where it was a matter of life and death. As Governor Bush's lawyer, Gonzales had the job of reviewing Texas death row inmates' petitions for clemency. Critics have accused him of paying only minimum attention to those petitions, every one of which he recommended that the governor should deny. Texas, under Governor Bush, and with Gonzales's endorsement, executed more people than any other governor in history.[25]

As President Bush's White House counsel, Gonzales crafted a remarkable and shocking memo on January 25, 2002 (see appendix F—Gonzales memo), which advised the president that he need not apply the Geneva Conventions for Treatment of Prisoners of War to captives in the war in Afghanistan—either Taliban or Al Qaeda. The Justice Department, under the leadership of Attorney General Ashcroft, had issued a memorandum on July 18, making that same argument, and the president had concurred, making that determination. This had led to an unusual protest from Secretary of State Colin Powell, a former armed forces chief of staff who was reportedly "outraged" at the Justice Department's advice. Gonzales, in his memo, backed the Justice Department view and argued against the secretary of state's view. He wrote in his memo to the president:

> As an initial matter, I note that you have the constitutional authority to make the determination you made on January 18 that the GPW [Geneva Convention III on the Treatment of Prisoners of War] does not apply to the conflict with al Qaeda. I also advised you that the DOJ's opinion concludes that there are reasonable grounds for you to conclude that the GPW does not apply with respect to the conflict with the Taliban. I understand that you decided that GPW does not apply and, accordingly, that al Qaeda and Taliban detainees are not prisoners of war under the GPW.

He went on to advise the president that as commander in chief he had the power to in effect ignore international law at will. As he wrote:

As an initial matter, I note that you have the constitutional authority to make the determination you made on January 18 that the GPW does not apply to al Qaeda and the Taliban.

In a bit of legal sleight-of-hand, Gonzales argued that because the Taliban didn't control all of the territory of Afghanistan, it thus did not constitute a government, but was simply a "militant, terrorist-like group." Never mind that the U.S. government, prior to 9/11, had been dealing with that very Taliban government, providing money for a program aimed at reducing opium poppy farming in the country, and discussing a possible pipeline through the country. But when the United States began battling Taliban fighters, in Gonzales's view the government that had ruled much of Afghanistan from the capital of Kabul was no longer a government, and its army was no longer an army. As a consequence of that theory, any captives in that war would not enjoy the protections of the Geneva Conventions. The significance of this finding on Gonzales's part was that:

> In my judgment, this new paradigm renders obsolete Geneva's strict limitations on questions of enemy prisoners and renders quaint some of its provisions . . .

Later in his memo, Gonzales discussed the issue of possible future prosecution of the president for war crimes because of U.S. treatment of captives. He advised the president that by accepting his attorney's and the Justice Department's recommendation that the Geneva Conventions not apply to Taliban and Al Qaeda captives, the president would have legal cover from future prosecution. Such a decision by the president, he said,

> substantially reduces the threat of domestic criminal prosecution under the War Crimes Act.

That 1996 act, he noted,

> prohibits the commission of a 'war crime' by or against a U.S. person, including U.S. officials. "War crimes" for these purposes is de-

fined to include any grave breach of GPW or any violation of common Article 3 thereof (such as "outrages against personal dignity"). Some of these provisions apply (if the GPW applies) regardless of whether the individual being detained qualifies as a POW. Punishments for violations of Section 2441 include the death penalty. A determination that the GPW does not apply would mean that Section 2441 would not apply to actions taken with respect to the Taliban.

Gonzales was clearly worried that the "gloves off" treatment of captives that the president was authorizing could later lead to prosecution. As he warned in the memo:

> It is difficult to predict the motives of prosecutors and independent counsels who may in the future decide to pursue unwarranted charges based on Section 2441. Your determination [that the Geneva Conventions would not apply to Taliban and Al Qaeda captives] would create a reasonable basis in law that Section 2441 does not apply, which would provide a solid defense to any future prosecutions.[26]

It is evident that the president's counsel was creating a shameless legal dodge for the president so that Bush could authorize others to engage in what the rest of the world would call war crimes, while creating a paper trail that would allow Bush to duck possible prosecution as a war criminal at some future time. For this bit of legal skullduggery, more appropriate to a mob lawyer than a presidential legal counsel, Gonzales, now the nation's top justice officer, should be impeached.

Attorney General Gonzales should also be impeached for violating his oath of office. On taking his new position, Gonzales had to swear an oath pledging to

> support and defend the Constitution of the United States against all enemies, foreign and domestic; that I will bear true faith and allegiance to the same; that I take this obligation freely without any mental reservation or purpose of evasion; and that I will well and faithfully discharge the duties of the office on which I am about to enter.

Instead of doing that, Attorney General Gonzales has played the role of presidential apologist and defender in trying to justify to Congress the president's ultimate power grab—his use of so-called "signing statements" to overrule or negate parts of acts of Congress even as he signs them into law. For example, Bush relied on such a statement when he signed the McCain torture ban measure in the 2006 military spending authorization bill, and, reportedly, in signing over five hundred other bills passed by the Congress, as well as his blatantly illegal authorization for the National Security Agency to monitor the private electronic communications of American citizens without bothering to obtain a warrant as required under the Foreign Intelligence Surveillance Act. Amazingly, in a forty-two-page "white paper" sent to Congress in January 2006, Gonzales essentially defined the president's powers during time of war as limitless.

Gonzales's two principle arguments in that White Paper were that as commander in chief in time of war, the president has virtually unfettered power on any matter relating to war, foreign affairs and "protecting America from attack," and that Congress, when it passed the Authorization for Use of Military Force a week after the 9/11 attacks, gave the president authority both overseas and domestically which put him at "the zenith of his powers."

As Gonzales put it:

The President has the chief responsibility under the Constitution to protect America from attack, and the Constitution gives the President the authority necessary to fulfill that solemn responsibility. The President has made clear that he will exercise all authority available to him, consistent with the Constitution, to protect the people of the United States.[27]

Regarding the Authorization for the Use of Military Force, Gonzales wrote:

AUMF indicates Congress's endorsement of the President's use of his constitutional war powers. This authorization transforms the struggle against al Qaeda and related terrorist organizations from what Justice

Jackson [in the Truman-era *Youngstown Steel* case] called "a zone of twilight," in which the President and the Congress may have concurrent powers whose "distribution is uncertain,"[28] . . . into a situation in which the President's authority is at its maximum because "it includes all that he possesses in his own right plus all that Congress can delegate."[29] With regard to these fundamental tools of warfare—and, as demonstrated below, warrantless electronic surveillance against the declared enemy is one such tool—the AUMF places the President's authority at its zenith.

Conveniently ignored by Gonzales is the fact that the White House specifically attempted to get Congress, in the AUMF, to include domestic operations within the purview of its authorization, and it was rebuffed. Also ignored by Gonzales in his argument is the fact that the warrantless searches are in direct conflict with the FISA law passed by Congress in 1978. Furthermore, it is clear that the NSA spying in question was not directed solely, or even perhaps principally against foreign agents but against American citizens, and not even against citizens suspected of spying or of having links with terrorists.

The most frightening part of Gonzales's argument is that because the United States is supposedly engaged in a "War on Terror"—a war that presumably has no boundaries or front lines or theaters of war—the president's extraordinary powers as commander in chief, which in the Constitution expressly apply to only the military, apply everywhere, including in the domestic United States. As Gonzales puts it:

> . . . the extent of the President's Commander in Chief authority necessarily depends on where the enemy is found and where the battle is waged . . . [30]

This is a blanket authorization for unchecked presidential power within the United States—power to spy without a warrant, power to arrest and take into custody, indeed power to conduct any and all operations having to do with conducting a "War on Terror." As *The New York Times* commented, in a half-page editorial on the NSA warrantless spying campaign:

The Constitution does suggest expanded presidential powers in a time of war. But the men who wrote it had in mind wars with a beginning and an end. The war Mr. Bush and Mr. Cheney keep trying to sell Americans goes on forever and excuses everything.

. . . Mr. Gonzales [in his White Paper to Congress] claimed historic precedent for a president to authorize warrantless surveillance. He mentioned George Washington, Woodrow Wilson, and Franklin D. Roosevelt. These precedents have no bearing on the current situation, and Mr. Gonzales' timeline conveniently ended with F.D.R. rather than including Richard Nixon, whose surveillance of antiwar groups and other political opponents inspired FISA in the first place.[31]

The *Times* editorial writers are absolutely correct. The situation in America today, with the country functionally at peace (the Afghanistan war supposedly ended with the establishment of a new government in that country, and despite all the fighting in Iraq, technically the United States is not at war; it is providing an Iraq occupation force at the invitation of that country's newly elected government), is fundamentally different from the situations faced by Washington during the Revolutionary War, Wilson during World War I, or Roosevelt during World War II. To argue, as Gonzales does, that the so-called "War on Terror," a police action that could last a generation or longer, justifies the president exercising the same kind of far-reaching and wide-ranging "temporary" war powers that presidents enjoyed during those earlier conflicts "for the duration," is tantamount to saying the country should just scrap the Constitution.

For providing that kind of enabling legal advice to the president, and for thus abetting unconstitutional abuse of power and violation of the First and Fourth Amendments of the Constitution by the president, instead of upholding his oath of office to "support and defend" the Constitution, Attorney General Alberto Gonzales should be impeached.

In his role as "mob attorney" for the White House, Gonzales has apparently also not been above lying for his boss. Sen. Russ Feingold (D-WI), in late January 2006, recalled that a year earlier, when he had asked Gonzales during the latter's confirmation hearing testimony before the Senate Judiciary committee (which was under oath), about whether he thought the president's authority could extend to approving warrantless eavesdropping on Americans, Gonzales had lied, dismissing the question as "hypothetical." According to a report in *The Washington Post*, at that hearing Gonzales went on to tell Feingold and the rest of the committee that

> it was "not the policy or the agenda of this president" to authorize actions that conflict with existing law. He added that he would hope to alert Congress if the president ever chose to authorize warrantless surveillance, according to a transcript of the hearing.[32]

In a prepared statement, Senator Feingold said, "It now appears that the Attorney General was not being straight with the Judiciary Committee and he has some explaining to do." The senator was being too gentle. In truth, it appears to be substantially more than that. President Clinton was impeached for lying under oath to a grand jury asking him if he had had sex with an intern. Surely, if that petty lie was grounds for impeachment, then so is a major lie under oath by a nominee for Attorney General of the United States made before the U.S. Senate during his confirmation hearing. The attorney general, after all, is the top enforcer of the nation's laws and should be setting an unassailable standard for respect for the law and for the sanctity of an oath to tell the truth.

## Following the Trail

It is worth recalling that the transgression that really finished off the criminal presidency of Richard Nixon—the discovery of his secret Oval Office recordings, and the discovery of incriminating statements on those tapes that implicated him directly in the attempted cover-up of the Watergate scandal—were the result of the impeachment-related hearings underway in the Congress. Without those hearings, and the sworn testimony that they elicited from key White House and Republican campaign officials, the tape recording system might have remained a secret, the impeachment votes in the House Judiciary Committee might never have happened, and the president might have been able to continue with his criminal administration, his secret spying programs, and his imperial presidency.

Just so, it is quite possible that an impeachment hearing involving Vice President Cheney, Defense Secretary Rumsfeld, Secretary of State Rice, or Attorney General Gonzales—or even a select committee to investigate possible impeachable actions, as proposed by Rep. John Conyers—would bring to light evidence linking President Bush to the transgressions under investigation. This is particularly likely with respect to such issues as the government's campaign of sanctioned torture of war captives, the outing of Valerie Plame Wilson, the campaign of deceit leading up to the invasion of Iraq, and possibly the criminal conduct of the war as well.

This likelihood makes it all the more important that impeachment efforts be brought by the Congress against these four key members of the Bush administration.

# EPILOGUE

## *The Case for Impeachment*

**It takes a lot of degeneration before a country falls into dictatorship, but we should avoid these ends by avoiding these beginnings.**

*—Sandra Day O'Connor*

**FIVE YEARS** into the Bush administration, America faces a crisis.

The danger this time is not the disintegration of the country, but rather the disintegration of a revolutionary and brilliant form of government based upon the concept of protecting liberty by keeping power divided and limited.

The Founding Fathers of this nation, who had experienced life under the thumb of a monarch and a foreign parliament in which they had no representation or power, were profoundly concerned about the threat that a new tyrant could arise in their midst during troubled times. They attempted to minimize the danger by dividing government among three separate branches—the Presidency, the Congress, and the Judiciary. Aware of how a document, the Magna Carta in the mother country of Great Britain, had helped to protect the power of Parliament against encroachments by the King, they also created something new—a document setting out the rules by which the new government would operate. To this they almost immediately added a set of amendments, the Bill of Rights, which defined the rights that belonged as a birthright to all people living in the United States of America.

Over the centuries since the founding of the United States and the ratification of the Constitution, there have been threats to both. By waging war in 1812, the British sought unsuccessfully to undo the revolution of just a generation earlier. In 1860 half the country sought to secede. Through the decades there have been additional threats to the Constitution and the Bill of Rights, among them the Alien and Sedition Acts, the Red Scare, the attempt by President Franklin Roosevelt to pack the U.S. Supreme Court, the political repression of the McCarthy period, and COINTELPRO. Largely unscathed, the Constitution, tripartite government and the liberties of the American people have survived. There have been defeats, such as the gradual erosion of the Constitution's unambiguous stipulation that only Congress can declare war (today presidents too often have sent troops into battle and informed Congress later). But in many important ways, such as with the abolition of slavery, the extension of the vote to women, and the enactment of the Civil Rights Act, the protections of the Constitution have expanded.

But with the administration of George Bush, all that progress and that tradition is now at grave risk.

The Bush administration, to a degree that is unprecedented and frightening, is asserting a right to unfettered presidential power. As we have seen, Bush is claiming the authority to decide upon setting the country at war—not just a police action but an all-out war to topple a government and occupy a country. He is claiming the right to take the basic constitutional rights of citizenship from an American on his own authority—to lock up, detain indefinitely, and perhaps even execute that citizen, denying him the right to a lawyer, to a trial, or even to know what he is charged with. He is claiming the right to ignore laws passed by the Congress, the right to decide on his own what those laws mean and to act according to his own interpretation, and even the right to ignore court orders. He is claiming that as commander in chief he has powers that are outside the normal constraints of the Constitution: the power to spy on Americans without a court order, the power to ignore international law and treaties approved by Congress and signed by former presidents, the power to ignore requests from Congress for information about government activities.

The president makes these outrageous assertions based upon the self-serving argument that the nation is at war and that he is therefore not just president, but commander in chief. It is true that in certain circumstances with the nation at war, a president, as commander in chief over the military, has certain added powers and responsibilities, but this "war" he is referring to is not really a war. The so-called "War on Terror" is a police action against stateless terrorists—and as such it has no beginning and no end. If we were to accept the president's claim that it is a war, and that this justifies making him a de-facto dictator and Congress and the Courts vestigial, we are permanently revoking the Constitution and all the rights and the checks and balances that the Founders so carefully put in place.

The president is dead wrong.

The Constitution was not just conceived as a document for the good times. It was meant to guide the nation through times of conflict, trouble, and stress as well.

Part of the problem is that with both houses of Congress in the hands of the president's party, and with the courts increasingly filled with appointees of this president and other Republican presidents before him—and with the Democratic opposition party still weak and divided itself—there is little will in the two other branches to oppose this unprecedented power grab by a chief executive.

Part of the problem, too, is an inattentive and complicit mass media. Conglomerized into giant entertainment enterprises, the media are more concerned with winning licensing deals and gaining approval for further mergers and less regulation, than with playing their constitutional role as a Fourth Estate monitoring and exposing government abuse.

That leaves it up to *the People* to defend the Constitution.

The means is there to end this crisis: impeachment.

As we have demonstrated, there is no shortage of impeachable crimes that have been committed by this president and this administration. There is only a shortage of courage in the Congress to hold the president accountable.

*We the People* of the United States, who for too long have been negligent about the obligations of citizenship, must stand up and demand action from our elected representatives to defend the Constitution, to defend the Bill of Rights, and to defend the tradition of separation of powers that has sustained this nation for over two centuries from attack by a power-mad president who has broken his oath of office. If our representatives won't do their job, they should be held accountable on Election Day, 2006.

We must stop listening to the president and his supporters as they pour scare stories in our ears and ask for more dictatorial power to "keep Americans safe." America was not built by a flock of cowering sheep.

If we fail to stand up for the Constitution now, it may only be a piece of paper by the end of President Bush's second term. Then it will be time to be afraid.

# APPENDICES

## *Appendix A*
### *The Downing Street Memo*

The so-called Downing Street Memo, first disclosed in a May 1 article published by the *Sunday Times* of London, was written by a top foreign policy aide to British Prime Minister Tony Blair, Matthew Rycroft, on July 23, 2002. It reports on a visit to Washington by "C," the code name for Sir Richard Dearlove, head of Britain's equivalent of the CIA, called MI6. Dearlove had met with senior leaders in the United States, including his counterpart, CIA Director George Tenet. The memo makes it clear that the Bush administration, contrary to its public statements, had already decided to invade Iraq, and that it would "fix the facts" to justify the war. (Note: This is not an image of the actual Downing Street memo, as that document was never made public by the reporter at the *Times* to whom it was provided, out of concern that the original could help British officials trace the source of the leak.)

**SECRET AND STRICTLY PERSONAL—UK EYES ONLY**

DAVID MANNING
From: Matthew Rycroft
Date: 23 July 2002
S 195 /02

cc: Defence Secretary, Foreign Secretary, Attorney-General, Sir Richard Wilson, John Scarlett, Francis Richards, CDS, C, Jonathan Powell, Sally Morgan, Alastair Campbell

## IRAQ: PRIME MINISTER'S MEETING, 23 JULY

Copy addressees and you met the Prime Minister on 23 July to discuss Iraq.

This record is extremely sensitive. No further copies should be made. It should be shown only to those with a genuine need to know its contents.

John Scarlett summarised the intelligence and latest JIC assessment. Saddam's regime was tough and based on extreme fear. The only way to overthrow it was likely to be by massive military action. Saddam was worried and expected an attack, probably by air and land, but he was not convinced that it would be immediate or overwhelming. His regime expected their neighbours to line up with the US. Saddam knew that regular army morale was poor. Real support for Saddam among the public was probably narrowly based.

C reported on his recent talks in Washington. There was a perceptible shift in attitude. Military action was now seen as inevitable. Bush wanted to remove Saddam, through military action, justified by the conjunction of terrorism and WMD. But the intelligence and facts were being fixed around the policy. The NSC had no patience with the UN route, and no enthusiasm for publishing material on the Iraqi regime's record. There was little discussion in Washington of the aftermath after military action.

CDS said that military planners would brief CENTCOM on 1-2 August, Rumsfeld on 3 August and Bush on 4 August.

The two broad US options were:

(a) Generated Start. A slow build-up of 250,000 US troops, a short (72 hour) air campaign, then a move up to Baghdad from the south. Lead time of 90 days (30 days preparation plus 60 days deployment to Kuwait).

(b) Running Start. Use forces already in theatre (3 x 6,000), continuous air campaign, initiated by an Iraqi casus belli. Total lead time of 60 days with the air campaign beginning even earlier. A hazardous option.

The US saw the UK (and Kuwait) as essential, with basing in Diego Garcia and Cyprus critical for either option. Turkey and other Gulf states were also important, but less vital. The three main options for UK involvement were:

(i) Basing in Diego Garcia and Cyprus, plus three SF squadrons.
(ii) As above, with maritime and air assets in addition.
(iii) As above, plus a land contribution of up to 40,000, perhaps with a discrete role in Northern Iraq entering from Turkey, tying down two Iraqi divisions.

The Defence Secretary said that the US had already begun "spikes of activity" to put pressure on the regime. No decisions had been taken, but he thought the most likely timing in US minds for military action to begin was January, with the timeline beginning 30 days before the US Congressional elections.

The Foreign Secretary said he would discuss this with Colin Powell this week. It seemed clear that Bush had made up his mind to take military action, even if the timing was not yet decided.

But the case was thin. Saddam was not threatening his neighbours, and his WMD capability was less than that of Libya, North Korea or Iran. We should work up a plan for an ultimatum to Saddam to allow back in the UN weapons inspectors. This would also help with the legal justification for the use of force.

The Attorney-General said that the desire for regime change was not a legal base for military action. There were three possible legal bases: self-defence, humanitarian intervention, or UNSC authorisation. The first and second could not be the base in this case. Relying on UNSCR 1205 of three years ago would be difficult. The situation might of course change.

The Prime Minister said that it would make a big difference politically and legally if Saddam refused to allow in the UN inspectors. Regime change and WMD were linked in the sense that it was the regime that was producing the WMD. There were different strategies for dealing with Libya and Iran. If the political context were right, people would support regime change. The two key issues were whether the military plan worked and whether we had the political strategy to give the military plan the space to work.

On the first, CDS said that we did not know yet if the US battleplan was workable. The military were continuing to ask lots of questions.

For instance, what were the consequences, if Saddam used WMD on day one, or if Baghdad did not collapse and urban warfighting began? You said that Saddam could also use his WMD on Kuwait. Or on Israel, added the Defence Secretary.

The Foreign Secretary thought the US would not go ahead with a military plan unless convinced that it was a winning strategy. On this, US and UK interests converged. But on the political strategy, there could be US/UK differences. Despite US resistance, we should explore discreetly the ultimatum. Saddam would continue to play hard-ball with the UN.

John Scarlett assessed that Saddam would allow the inspectors back in only when he thought the threat of military action was real.

The Defence Secretary said that if the Prime Minister wanted UK military involvement, he would need to decide this early. He cautioned that many in the US did not think it worth going down the ultimatum route. It would be important for the Prime Minister to set out the political context to Bush.

Conclusions:

(a) We should work on the assumption that the UK would take part in any military action. But we needed a fuller picture of US planning before we could take any firm decisions. CDS should tell the US military that we were considering a range of options.

(b) The Prime Minister would revert on the question of whether funds could be spent in preparation for this operation.

(c) CDS would send the Prime Minister full details of the proposed military campaign and possible UK contributions by the end of the week.

(d) The Foreign Secretary would send the Prime Minister the

background on the UN inspectors, and discreetly work up the ultimatum to Saddam.

He would also send the Prime Minister advice on the positions of countries in the region especially Turkey, and of the key EU member states.

(e) John Scarlett would send the Prime Minister a full intelligence update.

(f) We must not ignore the legal issues: the Attorney-General would consider legal advice with FCO/MOD legal advisers.

(I have written separately to commission this follow-up work.)

MATTHEW RYCROFT

## Appendix B
### Niger Forgeries

This letter, allegedly from Niger President Tandja Mamadou to Iraq President Saddam Hussein, has textual errors and a forged signature, done so poorly that the International Atomic Energy Agency spotted it immediately. The translation (including clumsy errors) reads:

It's my honor to refer to the agreement #3*1-NI 2000,

Regarding the supply of uranium, signed in Niamey on the 6th of July 2000 between the Government of the republic of Niger and the Government of Iraq by their respective representatives official delegates.

Above mentioned supply equivalent to 500 tons of pure uranium per year, will be delivered in two phases.

Having seen and inspected the said deal. I approve in all and each of its involved parties in regard to the powers invested in my by the Constitution of the 12th of May 1966.

Accordingly, I praise you to consider this letter as being the formal tool of approval of this agreement by the government of the Republic of Niger that becomes by this rightfully engaged.

Please accept, Mr. The President, the certainty of my highest regards.

|bUrau1

CONFIDENTIEL

URGENT

*République Du Niger*

*Fraternité - Travail - Progrès*

Niamey, le 27/07/2000.

MONSIEUR LE PRESIDENT,

J'AI L'HONNEUR DE ME REFERER A L'ACCORD N° 381-NI 2000, CONCERNANT LA FOURNITURE D'URANIUM, SIGNE A NIAMEY LE 06 JUILLET 2000 ENTRE LE GOUVERNEMENT DE LA REPUBLIQUE DU NIGER ET LE GOUVERNEMENT DE L'IRAQ PAR LEURS RESPECTIFS REPRESEN-TANTS DELEGUES OFFICIELS.

DITE FOURNITURE EQUIVALENTE A 500 TONNES D'URANIUM PUR PAR AN, SERA DELIVRE EN 2 PHASES.

AYANT VU ET EXAMINE LEDIT ACCORD, JE L'APPROUVE EN TOUTES ET CHACUNE DE SES PARTIES EN VERTU DES POUVOIRS QUI ME SONT CONFERES PAR LA CONSTITUTION DU 12 MAI 1966.

CONFIDENTIEL

URGENT

EN CONSEQUENCE, JE VOUS PRIE DE BIEN VOULOIR CONSIDERER
LA PRESENTE LETTRE COMME ETANT L'INSTRUMENT FORMEL D'PPRO-
BATION DE CET ACCORD PAR LE GOUVERNEMENT DE LA REPUBLIQUE
DU NIGER QUI SE TROUVE AINSI VALABLEMENT ENGAGE.

VEUILLEZ AGREER, MONSIEUR LE PRESIDENT, L'ASSURANCE
DE MA HAUTE CONSIDERATION.

This letter, dated October 10, 2000, is allegedly to the Niger ambassador to Rome. It is signed by one Alleli Habibou, who is described as the Niger Minister of Foreign Affairs and Cooperation. The evidence that it is a forgery is that Habibou left office in 1989.

The letter (shown on the following page) reads:

Subject: Protocol of agreement between the government of Niger and the government of Iraq relating to the supplying of uranium signed on the 5th and the 6th of July 2000 in Niamey.

I have the honor to send to you the attached, for information purposes. Copy of the protocol of agreement signed in Niamey between the Republic of Niger and the Government of Irak regarding the supplying uranium that the Niger State issued regarding the protocol cited in the subject.

TA/KA

REPUBLIQUE DU NIGER

CONSEIL MILITAIRE SUPREME

MINISTERE DES AFFAIRES ETRANGERES
ET DE LA COOPERATION

DIRECTION
DES AFFAIRES JURIDIQUES
ET CONSULAIRES

N°        MAE/C/DAJC/

№ 0 7 2 5 4

Niamey, le  10 OCT. 2000

LE MINISTERE DES AFFAIRES ETRANGERES
ET DE LA COOPERATION

à

Monsieur l'Ambassadeur du Niger/
à

ROME

OBJET: Protocole d'accord entre le Gouvernement
du Niger et le Gouvernement d'Iraq
relatif à la fourniture d'uranium
signé les 5 et 6 Juillet 2000 à Niamey.

J'ai l'honneur de vous faire tenir ci-joint, pour information, copie du Protocole d'Accord signé à Niamey entre la Republique du Niger et le Gouvernement d'Iraq concernant la founiture
d'uranium que l'Etat nigerien à émis au sujet du Protocole cité en
objet./.

P.J. : 1

## Appendix C
### The Taguba Report

In the wake of outrage over the torturing at Abu Ghraib prison in Baghdad, and after considerable delay and attempts to cover up the scandal, the Pentagon dispatched General Antonio Taguba and a team of investigators to find out what happened. General Taguba documented horrific cases of torture, as enumerated here in his report. Some of the abuses, such as the solitary confinement and the public stripping of captives, read remarkably like the instructions signed off on by Rumsfeld.

5. (S) That between October and December 2003, at the Abu Ghraib Confinement Facility (BCCF), numerous incidents of sadistic, blatant, and wanton criminal abuses were inflicted on several detainees. This systemic and illegal abuse of detainees was intentionally perpetrated by several members of the military police guard force (372nd Military Police Company, 320th Military Police Battalion, 800th MP Brigade), in Tier (section) 1-A of the Abu Ghraib Prison (BCCF). The allegations of abuse were substantiated by detailed witness statements (ANNEX 26) and the discovery of extremely graphic photographic evidence. Due to the extremely sensitive nature of these photographs and videos, the ongoing CID investigation, and the potential for the criminal prosecution of several suspects, the photographic evidence is not included in the body of my investigation. The pictures and videos are available from the Criminal Investigative Command and the CTJF-7 prosecution team. In addition to the aforementioned crimes, there were also abuses committed by members of the 325th MI Battalion, 205th MI Brigade, and Joint Interrogation and Debriefing Center (JIDC). Specifically, on 24 November 2003, SPC Luciana Spencer 205th MI Brigade, sought to degrade a detainee by having him strip and returned to cell naked. (ANNEXES 26 and 53)

6. (S) I find that the intentional abuse of detainees by military police personnel included the following acts:

a. (S) Punching, slapping, and kicking detainees; jumping on their naked feet;

b. (S) Videotaping and photographing naked male and female detainees;

c. (S) Forcibly arranging detainees in various sexually explicit positions for photographing;

d. (S) Forcing detainees to remove their clothing and keeping them naked for several days at a time;

e. (S) Forcing naked male detainees to wear women's underwear;

f. (S) Forcing groups of male detainees to masturbate themselves while being photographed and videotaped;

g. (S) Arranging naked male detainees in a pile and then jumping on them;

h. (S) Positioning a naked detainee on a MRE Box, with a sandbag on his head, and attaching wires to his fingers, toes, and penis to simulate electric torture;

i. (S) Writing "I am a Rapest" (sic) on the leg of a detainee alleged to have forcibly raped a 15-year old fellow detainee, and then photographing him naked;

j. (S) Placing a dog chain or strap around a naked detainee's neck and having a female soldier pose for a picture;

k. (S) A male MP guard having sex with a female detainee;

l. (S) Using military working dogs (without muzzles) to intimidate and frighten detainees, and in at least one case biting and severely injuring a detainee;

m. (S) Taking photographs of dead Iraqi detainees. (ANNEXES 25 and 26)

7. (U) These findings are amply supported by written confessions provided by several of the suspects, written statements provided by detainees, and witness statements. In reaching my findings, I have carefully considered the pre-existing statements of the following witnesses and suspects (ANNEX 26):

a. (U) SPC Jeremy Sivits, 372nd MP Company—Suspect

b. (U) SPC Sabrina Harman, 372nd MP Company—Suspect

c. (U) SGT Javal S. Davis, 372nd MP Company—Suspect

d. (U) PFC Lynndie R. England, 372nd MP Company—Suspect

e. (U) Adel Nakhla, Civilian Translator, Titan Corp., Assigned to the 205th MI Brigade—Suspect

f. (U) SPC Joseph M. Darby, 372nd MP Company

g. (U) SGT Neil A. Wallin, 109th Area Support Medical Battalion

h. (U) SGT Samuel Jefferson Provance, 302nd MI Battalion

i. (U) Torin S. Nelson, Contractor, Titan Corp., Assigned to the 205th MI Brigade

j. (U) CPL Matthew Scott Bolanger, 372nd MP Company

k. (U) SPC Matthew C. Wisdom, 372nd MP Company

l. (U) SSG Reuben R. Layton, Medic, 109th Medical Detachment

m. (U) SPC John V. Polak, 229th MP Company

8. (U) In addition, several detainees also described the following acts of abuse, which under the circumstances, I find credible based on the clarity of their statements and supporting evidence provided by other witnesses (ANNEX 26):

a. (U) Breaking chemical lights and pouring the phosphoric liquid on detainees;

b. (U) Threatening detainees with a charged 9mm pistol;

c. (U) Pouring cold water on naked detainees;

d. (U) Beating detainees with a broom handle and a chair;

e. (U) Threatening male detainees with rape;

f. (U) Allowing a military police guard to stitch the wound of a detainee who was injured after being slammed against the wall in his cell;

g. (U) Sodomizing a detainee with a chemical light and perhaps a broom stick.

h. (U) Using military working dogs to frighten and intimidate detainees with threats of attack, and in one instance actually biting a detainee.

9. (U) I have carefully considered the statements provided by the following detainees, which under the circumstances I find credible based on the clarity of their statements and supporting evidence provided by other witnesses:

    a. (U) Amjed Isail Waleed, Detainee # 151365

    b. (U) Hiadar Saber Abed Miktub-Aboodi, Detainee # 13077

    c. (U) Huessin Mohssein Al-Zayiadi, Detainee # 19446

    d. (U) Kasim Mehaddi Hilas, Detainee # 151108

    e. (U) Mohanded Juma Juma (sic), Detainee # 152307

    f. (U) Mustafa Jassim Mustafa, Detainee # 150542

    g. (U) Shalan Said Alsharoni, Detainee # 150422

    h. (U) Abd Alwhab Youss, Detainee # 150425

    i. (U) Asad Hamza Hanfosh, Detainee # 152529

    j. (U) Nori Samir Gunbar Al-Yasseri, Detainee # 7787

    k. (U) Thaar Salman Dawod, Detainee # 150427

    l. (U) Ameen Sa'eed Al-Sheikh, Detainee # 151362

    m. (U) Abdou Hussain Saad Faleh, Detainee # 18470 (ANNEX 26)

10. (U) I find that contrary to the provision of AR 190-8, and the findings found in MG Ryder's Report, Military Intelligence (MI) interrogators and Other US Government Agency's (OGA) interrogators actively requested that MP guards set physical and mental conditions for favorable interrogation of witnesses. Contrary to the findings of MG Ryder's Report, I find that personnel assigned to the 372nd MP Company, 800th MP Brigade were directed to change facility procedures to "set the conditions" for MI interrogations. I find no direct evidence that MP personnel actually participated in those MI interrogations. (ANNEXES 19, 21, 25, and 26).

## *Appendix D*
### *The International Committee of the Red Cross Report*

The ICRC conducted its own independent investigation of torture in Iraq, and especially at Abu Ghraib. It also enumerates interrogation techniques that are strikingly similar to what is suggested by the Secretary of Defense as appropriate techniques.

physical and psychological coercion used by the interrogators appeared to be part of the standard operating procedures by military intelligence personnel to obtain confessions and extract information. Several military intelligence officers confirmed to the ICRC that it was part of the military intelligence process to hold a person deprived of his liberty naked in a completely dark and empty call for a prolonged period to use inhumane and degrading treatment, including physical and psychological coercion, against persons deprived of their liberty to secure their cooperation.

### 3.1 Methods of Ill-treatment

25. The methods of ill-treatment most frequently alleged during interrogation included.

- Hooding, used to prevent people from seeing and to disorient them, and also to prevent them from breathing freely. One or sometimes two bags, sometimes with an elastic blindfold over the eyes which, when slipped down, further impeded proper breathing. Hooding was sometimes used in conjunction with beatings thus increasing anxiety as to when blows would come. The practice of hooding also allowed the interrogators to remain anonymous and thus to act with impunity. Hooding could last for periods from a few hours to up to two to four consecutive days, during which hoods were lifted only for drinking, eating or going to the toilets;
- Handcuffing with flexi-cuffs, which were sometimes made so tight and used for such extended periods that they caused skin lesions and long-term after-effects on the hands (nerve damage), as observed by the ICRC;
- Beatings with hard objects (including pistols and rifles), slapping, punching, kicking with knees or feet on various parts of the body (legs, sides, lower back, groin);
- Pressing the face into the ground with boots;
- Threats (of ill-treatment, reprisals against family members, imminent execution or transfer to Guantanamo):
- Being stripped naked for several days while held in solitary confinement in an empty and completely dark cell that included a latrine.
- Being held in solitary confinement combined with threats (to intern the individual indefinitely, to arrest other family members, to transfer the individual to Guantanamo), insufficient sleep, food or water deprivation, minimal access to showers (twice a week), denial of access to open air and prohibition of contacts with other persons deprived of their liberty;
- Being paraded naked outside cells in front of other persons deprived of their liberty, and guards, sometimes hooded or with women's underwear over the head;
- Acts of humiliation such as being made to stand naked against the wall of the cell with arms raised or with women's underwear over the head for prolonged periods – while being laughed at by guards, including female guards, and sometimes photographed in this position;
- Being attached repeatedly over several days, for several hours each time, with handcuffs to the bars of their cell door in humiliating (i.e. naked or in underwear) and/or uncomfortable position causing physical pain;
- Exposure while hooded to loud noise or music, prolonged exposure while hooded to the sun over several hours, including during the hottest time of the day

when temperatures could reach 50 degrees Celsius (122 degrees Fahrenheit) or higher;

• Being forced to remain for prolonged periods in stress positions such as squatting or standing with or without the arms lifted.

26. These methods of physical and psychological coercion were used by the military intelligence in a systematic way to gain confessions and extract information or other forms of cooperation from persons who had been arrested in connection with suspected security offences or deemed to have an "intelligence value".

### 3.2 Military Intelligence section, "Abu Ghraib Correctional Facility"

27. In mid-October 2003, the ICRC visited persons deprived of their liberty undergoing interrogation by military intelligence officers in Unit 1A, the "isolation section" of Abu Ghraib Correctional Facility. Most of these persons deprived of their liberty had been arrested in early October. During the visit, ICRC delegates directly witnessed and documented a variety of methods used to secure the cooperation of the persons deprived of their liberty with their interrogators. In particular they witnessed the practice of keeping persons deprived of their liberty completely naked in totally empty concrete cells and in total darkness, allegedly for several consecutive days. Upon witnessing such cases, the ICRC interrupted its visits and requested an explanation from the authorities. The military intelligence officer in charge of the interrogation explained that this practice was "part of the process". The process appeared to be a give-and-take policy whereby persons deprived of their liberty were "drip-fed" with new items (clothing, bedding, hygiene articles, lit cell, etc.) in exchange for their "cooperation". The ICRC also visited other persons deprived of their liberty held in total darkness, others in dimly lit cells who had been allowed to dress following periods during which they had been held naked. Several had been given women's underwear to wear under their jumpsuit (men's underwear was not distributed), which they felt to be humiliating.

The ICRC documented other forms of ill-treatment, usually combined with those described above, including threats, insults, verbal violence, sleep deprivation caused by the playing of loud music or constant light in cells devoid of windows, tight handcuffing with flexi-cuffs causing lesions and wounds around the wrists. Punishment included being made to walk in the corridors handcuffed and naked, or with women's underwear on the head, or being handcuffed either dressed or naked to the iron bars or the cell door. Some persons deprived of their liberty presented physical marks and psychological symptoms, which were compatible with these allegations. The ICRC medical delegate examined persons deprived of their liberty presenting signs of concentration difficulties, memory problems, verbal expression difficulties, incoherent speech, acute anxiety reactions, abnormal behaviour and suicidal tendencies. These symptoms appeared to have been caused by the methods and duration of interrogation. One person held in isolation that the ICRC examined, was unresponsive to verbal and painful stimuli. His heart rate was 120 beats per minute and his respiratory rate 18 per minute. He was diagnosed as suffering from somatoform (mental) disorder, specifically a conversion disorder, most likely due to the ill-treatment he was subjected to during interrogation.

This is the FBI memo, dated May 22, 2004, that refers to concerns expressed by an FBI agent who had been at Guantanamo Bay, Cuba. It cites a Presidential "Executive Order" by President Bush, which is said to authorize forms of "interrogation techniques" which are "beyond the bounds of standard FBI practice."

This suggests that contrary to his public statements that "America does not torture," President Bush himself was authorizing techniques that were in violation of the Geneva Conventions on Treatment of Prisoners of War.

((MSG014 RTF                                                                                    Page 3

b6 -1
b7C -1

b5 -1        [          ]      Can you let me know your thoughts on his concern for the definition of abuse? Thx
             Gary
             -----Original Message-----
             From[                    ](DL) (FBI)
             Sent  Saturday, May 22, 2004 2 08 PM
             To  BRIESE, M C (Div13) (FBI)
b6 -1        Cc  BALD, GARY M (Div13) (FBI)[                ](Div13) (FBI),[            ](Div13)
b7C -1       (FBI), HARRINGTON, T J (Div13) (FBI), BATTLE, FRANKIE (Div13) (FBI),[            ]
             (Div10) (FBI)
             Subject  BOC E-Mail, Priority, May 22, 2004,[          ]Request for Guidance regarding OGC EC,
             dated 5/19/04


             Chris  We have questions regarding the attached OGC EC

b6 -1        Since DOSC[      ]and my arrival in Iraq, we have been very careful to instruct our personnel to use
b7C -1       only standard interview techniques which we would utilize back home in our regular work  We have also
             instructed our personnel not to participate in interrogations by military personnel which might include
             techniques authorized by Executive Order but beyond the bounds of standard FBI practice  This
             instruction has been included in our in-briefs to all three rotations, periodically in staff meetings, and in
             one-on-one conversations

b6 -1        Insofar as DOSC[      ]and I are aware, no BOC employee during our three rotations witnessed the
b7C -1       abuse at Abu Gharayb that is now the subject of the ongoing investigations, nor any conduct anywhere in
             the theater that went beyond the parameters set by the applicable Executive Order  Although we have
             no reason to believe any of our personnel disobeyed our instructions and participated in interrogations
             that utilized techniques beyond the bounds of FBI practice but within the parameters of the Executive
             Order (e g , sleep deprivation, stress positions, loud music, etc ), some of our personnel were in the
             general vicinity of interrogations in which such tactics were being used, and because of their proximity to
             the sites of these interrogations, heard or saw things which would be indicative of interrogations utilizing
             the techniques authorized by the Executive Order  Examples are loud music, interrogators yelling at
             subjects, prisoners with hoods on their heads, etc

             We emphatically do not equate any of these things our personnel witnessed with the clearly unlawful and
             sickening abuse at Abu G that is come to light  The things our personnel witnessed (but did not
             participate in) were authorized by the President under his Executive Order  I can safely say that none of
             the employees during our three rotations witnessed the abuse at Abu G  The investigation into the abuse
             began before we arrived in Iraq (January 10) and the offending parties had been removed from their
             positions in the prison by then  Nonetheless, in light of OGC's EC, I wish to make clear our personnel
             have been present at various facilities when interrogation techniques made lawful by the Executive
             Order, but outside standard FBI practice, were utilized  While our personnel did not participate in these
             interrogations, they heard/saw indications that such interrogations were underway

             Our questions relate to the instruction in the EC to report abuse  The EC states that if "an FBI employee
             knows or suspects non-FBI personnel has abused or is abusing or mistreating a detainee, the FBI
             employee must report the incident  "

             This instruction begs the question of what constitutes "abuse "  We assume this does not include lawful
             interrogation techniques authorized by Executive Order  We are aware that prior to a revision in policy
             last week, an Executive Order signed by President Bush authorized the following interrogation
             techniques among others  sleep "management," use of MWDs (military working dogs), "stress positions"
             such as half squats, "environmental manipulation" such as the use of loud music, sensory deprivation
             through the use of hoods, etc  We assume the OGC instruction does not include the reporting of these
             authorized interrogation techniques, and that the use of these techniques does not constitute "abuse "

             As stated, there was a revision last week in the military's standard operating procedures based on the


                                                                                    DETAINEES-1640        1640

                                                                                                    4940

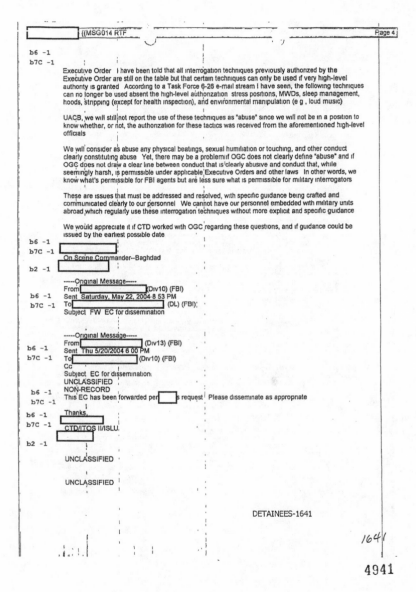

b6 -1
b7C -1

Executive Order  I have been told that all interrogation techniques previously authorized by the Executive Order are still on the table but that certain techniques can only be used if very high-level authority is granted  According to a Task Force 6-26 e-mail stream I have seen, the following techniques can no longer be used absent the high-level authorization  stress positions, MWDs, sleep management, hoods, stripping (except for health inspection), and environmental manipulation (e g , loud music)

UACB, we will still not report the use of these techniques as "abuse" since we will not be in a position to know whether, or not, the authorization for these tactics was received from the aforementioned high-level officials

We will consider as abuse any physical beatings, sexual humiliation or touching, and other conduct clearly constituting abuse  Yet, there may be a problem if OGC does not clearly define "abuse" and if OGC does not draw a clear line between conduct that is clearly abusive and conduct that, while seemingly harsh, is permissible under applicable Executive Orders and other laws  In other words, we know what's permissible for FBI agents but are less sure what is permissible for military interrogators

These are issues that must be addressed and resolved, with specific guidance being crafted and communicated clearly to our personnel  We cannot have our personnel embedded with military units abroad which regularly use these interrogation techniques without more explicit and specific guidance

We would appreciate it if CTD worked with OGC regarding these questions, and if guidance could be issued by the earliest possible date

b6 -1
b7C -1

On Scene Commander--Baghdad

b2 -1

-----Original Message-----
b6 -1    From                    (Div10) (FBI)
b7C -1   Sent  Saturday, May 22, 2004 8 53 PM
         To                    (DL) (FBI)
         Subject  FW  EC for dissemination

-----Original Message-----
b6 -1    From                    (Div13) (FBI)
b7C -1   Sent  Thu 5/20/2004 6 00 PM
         To                    (Div10) (FBI)
         Cc
         Subject  EC for dissemination
         UNCLASSIFIED
b6 -1    NON-RECORD
b7C -1   This EC has been forwarded per      s request  Please disseminate as appropriate

b6 -1    Thanks,
b7C -1

b2 -1    CTD/ITOS II/ISLU

         UNCLASSIFIED

         UNCLASSIFIED

                                              DETAINEES-1641

                                                   1641

                                              4941

## Appendix F
### The Gonzales Memo on Torture

In this draft of a legal memo from Alberto Gonzales, written on January 25, 2002, the president's then chief White House counsel not only advises President Bush that he has the authority as commander in chief to decide not to apply the Geneva Convention on Treatment of Prisoners of War (GPW) to either Al Qaeda captives or to captives in the Taliban army or government in Afghanistan. Gonzales also rather dramatically notes that the president could find himself prosecuted at some time in the future for war crimes (with a possible death penalty!) should he not accord POW status to captured fighters, but counsels that by making this determination, the president can give himself legal cover fom such action.

*DRAFT*
*1/25/2002, 3:30 p.m.*

January 25, 2002

MEMORANDUM FOR THE PRESIDENT

FROM: ALBERTO R. GONZALES

SUBJECT: DECISION RE APPLICATION OF THE GENEVA CONVENTION ON PRISONERS OF
WAR TO THE CONFLICT WITH AL QAEDA AND THE TALIBAN

Purpose

On January 18, I advised you that the Department of Justice had issued a formal legal opinion
concluding that the Geneva Convention III on the Treatment of Prisoners of War (GPW) does not apply
to the conflict with al Qaeda. I also advised you that DOJ's opinion concludes that there are reasonable
grounds for you to conclude that GPW does not apply with respect to the conflict with the Taliban. I
understand that you decided that GPW does not apply and, accordingly, that al Qaeda and Taliban
detainees are not prisoners of war under the GPW. The Secretary of State has requested that you
reconsider that decision. Specifically, he has asked that you conclude that GPW does apply to both al
Qaeda and the Taliban. I understand, however, that he would agree that al Qaeda and Taliban fighters
could be determined not to be prisoners of war (POWs) but only on a case-by-case basis following
individual hearings before a military board.

This memorandum outlines the ramifications of your decision and the Secretary's request for
reconsideration.

Legal Background

As an initial matter, I note that you have the constitutional authority to make the determination
you made on January 18 that the GPW does not apply to al Qaeda and the Taliban. (Of course, you could
nevertheless, as a matter of policy, decide to apply the principles of GPW to the conflict with al Qaeda
and the Taliban.) The Office of Legal Counsel of the Department of Justice has opined that, as a matter
of international and domestic law, GPW does not apply to the conflict with al Qaeda. OLC has further
opined that you have the authority to determine that GPW does not apply to the Taliban. As I discussed
with you, the grounds for such a determination may include:

> • A determination that Afghanistan was a failed state because the Taliban did not exercise
> full control over the territory and people, was not recognized by the international
> community, and was not capable of fulfilling its international obligations (e.g., was in
> widespread material breach of its international obligations).
> • A determination that the Taliban and its forces were, in fact, not a government, but a
> militant, terrorist-like group.

OLC's interpretation of this legal issue is definitive. The Attorney General is charged by statute
with interpreting the law for the Executive Branch. This interpretive authority extends to both domestic
and international law. He has, in turn, delegated this role to OLC. Nevertheless, you should be aware that
the Legal Adviser to the Secretary of State has expressed a different view.

Ramifications of Determination that GPW Does Not Apply

The consequences of a decision to adhere to what I understood to be your earlier determination that the CPW does not apply to the Taliban include the following:

Positive:

◊ Preserves flexibility

• As you have said, the war against terrorism is a new kind of war. It is not the traditional clash between nations adhering to the laws of war that formed the backdrop for GPW. The nature of the new war places a high premium on other factors, such as the ability to quickly obtain information from captured terrorists and their sponsors in order to avoid further atrocities against American civilians, and the need to try terrorists for war crimes such as wantonly killing civilians. In my judgment, this new paradigm renders obsolete Geneva's strict limitations on questioning of enemy prisoners and renders quaint some of its provisions requiring that captured enemy be afforded such things as commissary privileges, scrip (i.e., advances of monthly pay), athletic uniforms, and scientific instruments.
• Although some of these provisions do not apply to detainees who are not POWs, a determination that GPW does not apply to al Qaeda and the Taliban eliminates any argument regarding the need for case-by-case determinations of POW status. It also holds open options for the future conflicts in which it may be more difficult to determine whether an enemy force as a whole meets the standard for POW status.
• By concluding that GPW does not apply to al Qaeda and the Taliban, we avoid foreclosing options for the future, particularly against nonstate actors.

◊ Substantially reduces the threat of domestic criminal prosecution under the War Crimes Act (18 U.S.C. 2441).
• That statute, enacted in 1996, prohibits the commission of a "war crime" by or against a U.S. person, including U.S. officials. "War crime" for these purposes is defined to include any grave breach of GPW or any violation of common Article 3 thereof (such as "outrages against personal dignity"). Some of these provisions apply (if the GPW applies) regardless of whether the individual being detained qualifies as a POW. Punishments for violations of Section 2441 include the death penalty. A determination that the GPW is not applicable to the Taliban would mean that Section 2441 would not apply to actions taken with respect to the Taliban.
• Adhering to your determination that GPW does not apply would guard effectively against misconstruction or misapplication of Section 2441 for several reasons.

• First, some of the language of the GPW is undefined (it prohibits, for example, "outrages upon personal dignity" and "inhuman treatment"), and it is difficult to predict with confidence what actions might be deemed to constitute violations of the relevant provisions of GPW.
• Second, it is difficult to predict the needs and circumstances that could arise in the course of the war on terrorism.
• Third, it is difficult to predict the motives of prosecutors and independent counsels who may in the future decide to pursue unwarranted charges base on Section 2441. Your determination would create a reasonable basis in law that Section 2441 does not apply, which would provide a solid defense to any future prosecution.

Negative:

On the other hand, the following arguments would support reconsideration and reversal of your decision that the GPW does not apply to either al Qaeda or the Taliban:

• Since the Geneva Conventions were concluded in 1949, the United States has never denied their applicability to either U.S. or opposing forces engaged in armed conflict, despite several opportunities to do so. During the last Bush Administration, the United States stated that it "has a policy of applying the Geneva Conventions of 1949 whenever armed hostilities occur with regular foreign armed forces, even if arguments could be made that the threshold standards for the applicability of the Conventions…are not met."
• The United States could not invoke the GPW if enemy forces threatened to mistreat or mistreated U.S. or coalition forces captured during operations in Afghanistan, or if they denied Red Cross access or other POW privileges.
• The War Crimes Act could not be used against the enemy, although other criminal statutes and the customary law of war would still be available. • Our position would likely provoke widespread condemnation among our allies and in some domestic quarters, even if we make clear that we will comply with the core humanitarian principles of the treaty as a matter of policy.
• Concluding that the Geneva Convention does not apply may encourage other countries to look for technical "loopholes" in future conflicts to conclude that they are not bound by GPW either.
• Other countries may be less inclined to turn over terrorists or provide legal assistance to us if we do not recognize a legal obligation to comply with the GPW.
• A determination that GPW does not apply to al Qaeda and the Taliban could undermine U.S. military culture which emphasizes maintaining the highest standards of conduct in combat, and could introduce an element of uncertainty in the status of adversaries.

Responses to Arguments for Applying GPW to the al Qaeda and the Taliban

On balance, I believe that the arguments for reconsideration and reversal are unpersuasive.

•The argument that the U.S. has never determined that GPW did not apply is incorrect. In at least one case (Panama in 1989) the U.S. determined that GPW did not apply even though it determined for policy reasons to adhere to the convention. More importantly, as noted above, this is a new type of warfare—one not contemplated in 1949 when the GPW was framed—and requires a new approach in our actions towards captured terrorists. Indeed, as the statement quoted from the administration of President George Bush makes clear, the U.S. will apply GPW "whenever hostilities occur with regular foreign armed forces." By its terms, therefore, the policy does not apply to a conflict with terrorists, or with irregular forces, like the Taliban, who are armed militants that oppressed and terrorized the people of Afghanistan.
• In response to the argument that we should decide to apply GPW to the Taliban in order to encourage other countries to treat captured U.S. military personnel in accordance with the GPW, it should be noted that your policy of providing humane treatment to enemy detainees gives us the credibility to insist on like treatment for our soldiers. Moreover, even if GPW is not applicable, we can still bring war crimes charges against anyone who mistreats U.S. personnel. Finally, I note that our adversaries in several recent conflicts have not been deterred by GPW in their mistreatment of captured U.S. personnel, and terrorists will not follow GPW rules in any event.
• The statement that other nations would criticize the U.S. because we have determined that GPW does not apply is undoubtedly true. It is even possible that some nations would point to that determination as a basis for failing to cooperate with us on specific matters in the war against terrorism. On the other hand, some international and domestic criticism is already likely to flow from your previous decision not to treat the detainees as POWs. And we can facilitate cooperation with other nations by reassuring them that we fully support GPW where it applicable and by acknowledging that in this conflict the U.S. continues to respect other recognized standards.

• In the treatment of detainees, the U.S. will continue to be constrained by (i) its commitment to treat the detainees humanely and, to the extent appropriate and consistent with military necessity, in a manner consistent with the principles of GPW, (ii) its applicable treaty obligations, (iii) minimum standards of treatment universally recognized by the nations of the world, and (iv) applicable military regulations regarding the treatment of detainees.

• Similarly, the argument based on military culture fails to recognize that our military remain bound to apply the principles of GPW because that is what you have directed them to do.

## Appendix G
### *The Federal Indictment of I. Lewis Libby*

These pages (4 and 5) of the federal indictment of I. Lewis "Scooter" Libby, detail some of Libby's alleged efforts to ferret out information about Ambassador Joe Wilson's wife and her role as a CIA undercover operative, subsequently leaked to friendly reporters. On page 5, the document cites the Vice President's involvement in the effort, though as of press time no charges have been brought against Cheney. Page 8 of the indictment mentions the role of a White House "Official A" in the alleged conspiracy, a person widely suspected to be President Bush's political strategist and confidante Karl Rove.

4.     On or about May 29, 2003, in the White House, **LIBBY** asked an Under Secretary of State ("Under Secretary") for information concerning the unnamed ambassador's travel to Niger to investigate claims about Iraqi efforts to acquire uranium yellowcake. The Under Secretary thereafter directed the State Department's Bureau of Intelligence and Research to prepare a report concerning the ambassador and his trip. The Under Secretary provided **LIBBY** with interim oral reports in late May and early June 2003, and advised **LIBBY** that Wilson was the former ambassador who took the trip.

5.     On or about June 9, 2003, a number of classified documents from the CIA were faxed to the Office of the Vice President to the personal attention of **LIBBY** and another person in the Office of the Vice President. The faxed documents, which were marked as classified, discussed, among other things, Wilson and his trip to Niger, but did not mention Wilson by name. After receiving these documents, **LIBBY** and one or more other persons in the Office of the Vice President handwrote the names "Wilson" and "Joe Wilson" on the documents.

6.     On or about June 11 or 12, 2003, the Under Secretary of State orally advised **LIBBY** in the White House that, in sum and substance, Wilson's wife worked at the CIA and that State Department personnel were saying that Wilson's wife was involved in the planning of his trip.

7.     On or about June 11, 2003, **LIBBY** spoke with a senior officer of the CIA to ask about the origin and circumstances of Wilson's trip, and was advised by the CIA officer that Wilson's wife worked at the CIA and was believed to be responsible for sending Wilson on the trip.

8.     Prior to June 12, 2003, *Washington Post* reporter Walter Pincus contacted the Office of the Vice President in connection with a story he was writing about Wilson's trip. **LIBBY** participated in discussions in the Office of the Vice President concerning how to respond to Pincus.

4

9.    On or about June 12, 2003, **LIBBY** was advised by the Vice President of the United States that Wilson's wife worked at the Central Intelligence Agency in the Counterproliferation Division. **LIBBY** understood that the Vice President had learned this information from the CIA.

10.    On June 12, 2003, the *Washington Post* published an article by reporter Walter Pincus about Wilson's trip to Niger, which described Wilson as a retired ambassador but not by name, and reported that the CIA had sent him to Niger after an aide to the Vice President raised questions about purported Iraqi efforts to acquire uranium. Pincus's article questioned the accuracy of the "sixteen words," and stated that the retired ambassador had reported to the CIA that the uranium purchase story was false.

11.    On or about June 14, 2003, **LIBBY** met with a CIA briefer. During their conversation he expressed displeasure that CIA officials were making comments to reporters critical of the Vice President's office, and discussed with the briefer, among other things, "Joe Wilson" and his wife "Valerie Wilson," in the context of Wilson's trip to Niger.

12.    On or about June 19, 2003, an article appeared in *The New Republic* magazine online entitled *"The First Casualty: The Selling of the Iraq War."* Among other things, the article questioned the "sixteen words" and stated that following a request for information from the Vice President, the CIA had asked an unnamed ambassador to travel to Niger to investigate allegations that Iraq had sought uranium from Niger. The article included a quotation attributed to the unnamed ambassador alleging that administration officials "knew the Niger story was a flat-out lie." The article also was critical of how the administration, including the Office of the Vice President, portrayed intelligence concerning Iraqi capabilities with regard to weapons of mass destruction, and accused the administration of suppressing dissent from the intelligence agencies on this topic.

13.    Shortly after publication of the article in *The New Republic*, **LIBBY** spoke by telephone with his then Principal Deputy and discussed the article. That official asked **LIBBY** whether information about Wilson's trip could be shared with the press to rebut the allegations that the Vice President had sent Wilson. **LIBBY** responded that there would be complications at the CIA in disclosing that information publicly, and that he could not discuss the matter on a non-secure telephone line.

14.    On or about June 23, 2003, **LIBBY** met with *New York Times* reporter Judith Miller. During this meeting **LIBBY** was critical of the CIA, and disparaged what he termed "selective leaking" by the CIA concerning intelligence matters. In discussing the CIA's handling of Wilson's trip to Niger, **LIBBY** informed her that Wilson's wife might work at a bureau of the CIA.

### The July 6 "Op Ed" Article by Wilson

15.    On July 6, 2003, the *New York Times* published an Op-Ed article by Wilson entitled "What I Didn't Find in Africa." Also on July 6, 2003, the *Washington Post* published an article about Wilson's 2002 trip to Niger, which article was based in part upon an interview of Wilson. Also on July 6, Wilson appeared as a guest on the television interview show "*Meet the Press*." In his Op-Ed article and interviews in print and on television, Wilson asserted, among other things, that he had taken a trip to Niger at the request of the CIA in February 2002 to investigate allegations that Iraq had sought or obtained uranium yellowcake from Niger, and that he doubted Iraq had obtained uranium from Niger recently, for a number of reasons. Wilson stated that he believed, based on his understanding of government procedures, that the Office of the Vice President was advised of the results of his trip.

## LIBBY's Actions Following Wilson's July 6 "Op Ed" Column

16.   On or about July 7, 2003, **LIBBY** had lunch with the then White House Press Secretary and advised the Press Secretary that Wilson's wife worked at the CIA and noted that such information was not widely known.

17.   On or about the morning of July 8, 2003, **LIBBY** met with *New York Times* reporter Judith Miller. When the conversation turned to the subject of Joseph Wilson, **LIBBY** asked that the information **LIBBY** provided on the topic of Wilson be attributed to a "former Hill staffer" rather than to a "senior administration official," as had been the understanding with respect to other information that **LIBBY** provided to Miller during this meeting. **LIBBY** thereafter discussed with Miller Wilson's trip and criticized the CIA reporting concerning Wilson's trip. During this discussion, **LIBBY** advised Miller of his belief that Wilson's wife worked for the CIA.

18.   Also on or about July 8, 2003, **LIBBY** met with the Counsel to the Vice President in an anteroom outside the Vice President's Office. During their brief conversation, **LIBBY** asked the Counsel to the Vice President, in sum and substance, what paperwork there would be at the CIA if an employee's spouse undertook an overseas trip.

19.   Not earlier than June 2003, but on or before July 8, 2003, the Assistant to the Vice President for Public Affairs learned from another government official that Wilson's wife worked at the CIA, and advised **LIBBY** of this information.

20.   On or about July 10, 2003, **LIBBY** spoke to *NBC* Washington Bureau Chief Tim Russert to complain about press coverage of **LIBBY** by an *MSNBC* reporter. **LIBBY** did not discuss Wilson's wife with Russert.

7

21.     On or about July 10 or July 11, 2003, **LIBBY** spoke to a senior official in the White House ("Official A") who advised **LIBBY** of a conversation Official A had earlier that week with columnist Robert Novak in which Wilson's wife was discussed as a CIA employee involved in Wilson's trip. **LIBBY** was advised by Official A that Novak would be writing a story about Wilson's wife.

22.     On or about July 12, 2003, **LIBBY** flew with the Vice President and others to and from Norfolk, Virginia, on Air Force Two. On his return trip, **LIBBY** discussed with other officials aboard the plane what **LIBBY** should say in response to certain pending media inquiries, including questions from *Time* reporter Matthew Cooper.

23.     On or about July 12, 2003, in the afternoon, **LIBBY** spoke by telephone to Cooper, who asked whether **LIBBY** had heard that Wilson's wife was involved in sending Wilson on the trip to Niger. **LIBBY** confirmed to Cooper, without elaboration or qualification, that he had heard this information too.

24.     On or about July 12, 2003, in the late afternoon, **LIBBY** spoke by telephone with Judith Miller of the *New York Times* and discussed Wilson's wife, and that she worked at the CIA.

### The Criminal Investigation

25.     On or about September 26, 2003, the Department of Justice authorized the Federal Bureau of Investigation ("FBI") to commence a criminal investigation into the possible unauthorized disclosure of classified information regarding the disclosure of Valerie Wilson's affiliation with the CIA to various reporters in the spring of 2003.

## Appendix H
### *The Rumsfeld Memo on Torture*

In this document, signed off on by Secretary of Defense Donald Rumsfeld, interrogators at Guantanamo are told what enhanced techniques they may use to try to elicit information from captured fighters whom the President has determined are not POWs, but rather "enemy combatants." The memo notes that some friendly countries may hold that the measures, which include leaving people in solitary for as long as thirty days, using physical force, leaving people in the cold or heat, or stripping them, are violations of the Geneva Conventions—which indeed they are. It does not take much imagination to see how these instructions from the head of the Defense Department led to the torture at Guantanamo and then in Iraq.

**MEMO 27**

~~SECRET/NOFORN~~

THE SECRETARY OF DEFENSE
1000 DEFENSE PENTAGON
WASHINGTON, DC 20301-1000
APR 16 2003

MEMORANDUM FOR THE COMMANDER, US SOUTHERN COMMAND

**SUBJECT:**   Counter-Resistance Techniques in the War on Terrorism (S)

~~(S/NF)~~ (U) I have considered the report of the Working Group that I directed be established on January 15, 2003.

~~(S/NF)~~ (U) I approve the use of specified counter-resistance techniques, subject to the following:

(U) a. The techniques I authorize are those lettered A-X, set out at Tab A.

(U) b. These techniques must be used with all the safeguards described at Tab B.

~~(S)~~ (U) c. Use of these techniques is limited to interrogations of unlawful combatants held at Guantanamo Bay, Cuba.

~~(S)~~ (U) d. Prior to the use of these techniques, the Chairman of the Working Group on Detainee Interrogations in the Global War on Terrorism must brief you and your staff.

~~(S/NF)~~ (U) I reiterate that US Armed Forces shall continue to treat detainees humanely and, to the extent appropriate and consistent with military necessity, in a manner consistent with the principles of the Geneva Conventions. In addition, if you intend to use techniques B, I, O, or X, you must specifically determine that military necessity requires its use and notify me in advance.

~~(S/NF)~~ (U) If, in your view, you require additional interrogation techniques for a particular detainee, you should provide me, via the Chairman of the Joint Chiefs of Staff, a written request describing the proposed technique, recommended safeguards, and the rationale for applying it with an identified detainee.

~~(S/NF)~~ (U) Nothing in this memorandum in any way restricts your existing authority to maintain good order and discipline among detainees.

Attachments:                                    [Signed Donald Rumsfeld]
As stated

Declassified Under Authority of Executive Order 12958
By Executive Secretary, Office of the Secretary of Defense
William P. Marriott, CAPT, USN
June 18, 2004

Classified By: Secretary of Defense
Reason: 1.5(a)
Declassify On: 2 April 2013

~~SECRET/NOFORN~~

NOT RELEASABLE TO
FOREIGN NATIONALS

## TAB A

## INTERROGATION TECHNIQUES

(S/NF) (U) The use of techniques A – X is subject to the general safeguards as provided below as well as specific implementation guidelines to be provided by the appropriate authority. Specific implementation guidance with respect to techniques A – Q is provided in Army Field Manual 34–52. Further implementation guidance with respect to techniques R – X will need to be developed by the appropriate authority.

(S/NF) (U) Of the techniques set forth below, the policy aspects of certain techniques should be considered to the extent those policy aspects reflect the views of other major U.S. partner nations. Where applicable, the description of the technique is annotated to include a summary of the policy issues that should be considered before application of the technique.

A. (S/NF) (U) Direct: Asking straightforward questions.

B. (S/NF) (U) Incentive/Removal of Incentive: Providing a reward or removing a privilege, above and beyond those that are required by the Geneva Convention, from detainees. [Caution: Other nations that believe that detainees are entitled to POW protections may consider that provision and retention of religious items (e.g., the Koran) are protected under international law (see, Geneva III, Article 34). Although the provisions of the Geneva Convention are not applicable to the interrogation of unlawful combatants, consideration should be given to these views prior to application of the technique.]

C. (S/NF) (U) Emotional Love: Playing on the love a detainee has for an individual or group.

D. (S/NF) (U) Emotional Hate: Playing on the hatred a detainee has for an individual or group.

E. (S/NF) (U) Fear Up Harsh: Significantly increasing the fear level in a detainee.

F. (S/NF) (U) Fear Up Mild: Moderately increasing the fear level in a detainee.

G. (S/NF) (U) Reduced Fear: Reducing the fear level in a detainee.

H. (S/NF) (U) Pride and Ego Up: Boosting the ego of a detainee.

> Classified By:Secretary of Defense
> Reason:1.5(a)
> Declassify On:2 April 2013

I. (S/NF) (U) Pride and Ego Down: Attacking or insulting the ego of a detainee, not beyond the limits that would apply to a POW. [Caution: Article 17 of Geneva III provides, "Prisoners of war who refuse to answer may not be threatened, insulted, or exposed to any unpleasant or disadvantageous treatment of any kind." Other nations that believe that detainees are entitled to POW protections may consider this technique inconsistent with the provisions of Geneva. Although the provisions of Geneva are not applicable to the interrogation of unlawful combatants, consideration should be given to these views prior to application of the technique.]

J. (S/NF) (U) Futility: Invoking the feeling of futility of a detainee.

K. (S/NF) (U) We Know All: Convincing the detainee that the interrogator knows the answer to questions he asks the detainee.

L. (S/NF) (U) Establish Your Identity: Convincing the detainee that the interrogator has mistaken the detainee for someone else.

M. (S/NF) (U) Repetition Approach: Continuously repeating the same question to the detainee within interrogation periods of normal duration.

N. (S/NF) (U) File and Dossier: Convincing detainee that the interrogator has a damning and inaccurate file, which must be fixed.

O. (S/NF) (U) Mutt and Jeff: A team consisting of a friendly and harsh interrogator. The harsh interrogator might employ the Pride and Ego Down technique. [Caution: Other nations that believe that POW protections apply to detainees may view this technique as inconsistent with Geneva III, Article 13 which provides that POWs must be protected against acts of intimidation. Although the provisions of Geneva are not applicable to the interrogation of unlawful combatants, consideration should be given to these views prior to application of the technique.]

P. (S/NF) (U) Rapid Fire: Questioning in rapid succession without allowing detainee to answer.

Q. (S/NF) (U) Silence: Staring at the detainee to encourage discomfort.

R. (S/NF) (U) Change of Scenery Up: Removing the detainee from the standard interrogation setting (generally to a location more pleasant, but no worse).

S. (S/NF) (U) Change of Scenery Down: Removing the detainee from the standard interrogation setting and placing him in a setting that may be less comfortable; would not constitute a substantial change in environmental quality.

T. (S/NF) (U) Dietary Manipulation: Changing the diet of a detainee; no intended deprivation of food or water; no adverse medical or cultural effect and without intent to deprive subject of food or water, e.g., hot rations to MREs.

U. (S/NF) (U) Environmental Manipulation: Altering the environment to create moderate discomfort (e.g., adjusting temperature or introducing an unpleasant smell). Conditions would not be such that they would injure the detainee. Detainee would be accompanied by interrogator at all times. [Caution: Based on court cases in other countries, some nations may view application of this technique in certain circumstances to be inhumane. Consideration of these views should be given prior to use of this technique.]

V. (S/NF) (U) Sleep Adjustment: Adjusting the sleeping times of the detainee (e.g., reversing sleep cycles from night to day.) This technique is NOT sleep deprivation.

W. (S/NF) (U) False Flag: Convincing the detainee that individuals from a country other than the United States are interrogating him.

X. (S/NF) (U) Isolation: Isolating the detainee from other detainees while still complying with basic standards of treatment. [Caution: The use of isolation as an interrogation technique requires detailed implementation instructions, including specific guidelines regarding the length of isolation, medical and psychological review, and approval for extensions of the length of isolation by the appropriate level in the chain of command. This technique is not known to have been generally used for interrogation purposes for longer than 30 days. Those nations that believe detainees are subject to POW protections may view use of this technique as inconsistent with the requirements of Geneva III, Article 13 which provides that POWs must be protected against acts of intimidation; Article 14 which provides that POWs are entitled to respect for their person; Article 34 which prohibits coercion and Article 126 which ensures access and basic standards of treatment. Although the provisions of Geneva are not applicable to the interrogation of unlawful combatants, consideration should be given to these views prior to application of the technique.]

* * * * * * * * * * * * *

# ACKNOWLEDGMENTS

* * * * * * * * * * * * *

We knew that researching and writing a book of this kind in just four months was a daunting task. It would not have even been possible without the help of many people.

First of all, we'd like to thank our publisher, Tom Dunne, whose idea this project was in the first place, both for his political acumen in seeing earlier than most that this issue would grow into a major subject of political discourse, and for his invitation to us to be the authors.

Second, our thanks to historians Ellen Schrecker and Marvin Gettleman and their agent Ron Goldfarb for steering Tom to us.

Third, we'd like to thank our editor, Sean Desmond, who has managed the seemingly oxymoronic challenge of being encouraging, patient, and demanding all at the same time—three critical qualities when writers are confronting such a deadline.

We are grateful to many sources who responded readily to requests on short notice for interviews, among them former Senators George McGovern, Lowell Weicker, and Bob Graham.

We also want to acknowledge the supportive role played by the president and his administration, who almost every week have provided us with shocking new material for the book, with priceless publicity and, as the polls show, with an ever-growing army of angry citizens anxious to rid Washington of the whole gang.

We want especially to thank our spouses, Joyce Lindorff and Craig Acorn, both busy professionals themselves, for supporting us during the course of this uniquely intense and stressful project, and for their always incisive (if occasionally painful) editorial critiques.

Friends, colleagues at the Center for Constitutional Rights, legal experts, political activists, and others too numerous to mention have offered crucial advice, suggestions, and encouragement along the way. We thank them all, but hasten to add that any errors, shortcomings, or omissions are wholly our own responsibility.

**A NOTE** on quotations. Except in the case of Founding Fathers long deceased, quotations that are not footnoted were from interviews conducted by the authors specifically for this book.

# NOTES

## ONE  *Why Impeachment?*

1. House Judiciary Articles of Impeachment, 1974.
2. Thomas M. DeFrank, "Bush Whacked Rove on CIA Leak," New York *Daily News,* October 19, 2005.
3. Ralph Nader and Kevin Zeese, "The 'I' Word," *Boston Globe,* May 31, 2005.
4. Bob Graham with Jeff Nussbaum, *Intelligence Matters: The CIA, the FBI, Saudi Arabia, and the Failure of America's War on Terror* (New York: Random House, 2004), 232.

## TWO  *An Agenda of Deceit and a Case of Overreaching*

1. Wayne Madsen, "Questionable Ties: Tracking bin Laden's Money Flow Leads Back to Midland, Texas," *In These Times,* November 12, 2001.
2. Steven R. Reed, "President Bush's Son on a Roll/Important Decisions Ahead for George W.," *Houston Chronicle,* July 2, 1989.
3. Dave Lindorff, "Keeping Dissent Invisible," salon.com, October 16, 2003.
4. Dave Lindorff, "When Bush Came to My Neighborhood: Close Encounters of the Worst Kind," counterpunch.org, February 14, 2005.
5. John Dean, *Worse than Watergate* (New York: Little Brown & Co., 2004), 56.
6. Ibid.
7. Ruth Rosen, "The Day Ashcroft Censored Freedom of Information," *The San Francisco Chronicle,* January 7, 2002.
8. Dick Cheney, "Covert Operations: Who's in Charge?" *The Wall Street Journal,* May 3, 1988, A30.

9. "Iran Contra Affair: The Final Report—Excerpts: Majority, Minority Views of Committees," *Los Angeles Times,* November 19, 1987, 16.

10. Dean, 136.

11. Thomas Donnelly, et al., "Rebuilding America's Defenses," Project for a New American Century, September 2000.

12. Ibid., ii.

13. "Americans Down on the Economy," CBS News, September 5, 2001.

14. Ibid.

15. John King, "Bush Vacation Agenda," CNN, August 6, 2001.

16. Donnelly, 51.

17. "O'Neill: Bush planned Iraq invasion before 9/11," CNN, January 14, 2004.

18. William Rivers Pitt, "The Project for a New American Century," truthout.org, February 25, 2003.

## THREE  *The Origins of Impeachment*

1. Raoul Berger, *Impeachment: The Constitutional Problems* (Cambridge, Mass.: Harvard University Press, 1974), 4.

2. Ibid., 5.

3. Ibid., 1 (quoting Sir W. S. Holdsworth, *A History of English Law* 383 [London, England, 3d ed., 1922]).

4. Berger, *Impeachment,* 1.

5. Zechariah Chafee, *Three Human Rights in the Constitution* (Lawrence, Kan: University of Kansas Press, 1956), 98–140.

6. Berger, *Impeachment,* 67.

7. Berger, *Impeachment,* 67–69.

8. *See* Michael J. Gerhardt, "The Lessons of Impeachment History," 67 *George Washington Law Review* (March 1999), 603, 609–10 (delineating scholars and their works).

9. Ibid.

10. Berger, *Impeachment,* 61.

11. Arthur Bestor, "Impeachment," 49 *Washington Law Review* 255, 264 (1973).

12. Berger, *Impeachment,* 263–64.

13. See Stephen B. Presser, "Testimony of Stephen B. Presser, Professor of Legal History, Northwestern University School of Law, Before the House Ju-

diciary Committee, Subcommittee on the Constitution, Hearing on the Background and History of Impeachment," (November 9, 1998), available at http://jurist.law.pitt.edu/presser.htm (last visited on January 23, 2006).

14. Clinton Rossiter, ed., *The Federalist Papers* (New York: Penguin Putnam, 2003). *The Federalist* No. 64, at 380 (emphasis added).

15. Michael J. Gerhardt, *The Federal Impeachment Process: A Constitutional and Historical Analysis* (London: University of Chicago Press, 1996).

16. Ibid., 104.

17. *The Federalist* No. 65, at 396.

18. James Madison, Constitutional Convention, July 20, 1787.

19. See Michael J. Gerhardt, "The Lessons of Impeachment History," 67 *Geo. Wash. L. Rev.* at 609 (quoting from *The Works of James Wilson*).

20. Joseph Story, *Commentaries on the Constitution of the United States* (Durham: Carolina Academic Press, 1987), § 385, 272–73.

21. See Michael J. Gerhardt, "The Lessons of Impeachment History," 67 *George Washington Law Review* at 611–12.

22. Story, *Commentaries,* § 405, 288.

23. U.S. Constitution, Article III, Section 3.

24. See Michael J. Gerhardt, "The Lessons of Impeachment History," 67 *George Washington Law Review* at 606–07.

25. Ibid.

26. Ibid.

27. Ibid., 604.

28. See Laurence H. Tribe, "Testimony of Laurence H. Tribe, Tyler Professor of Constitutional Law, Harvard Law School, Before the House Judiciary Committee, Subcommittee on the Constitution, Hearing on the Background and History of Impeachment," (November 9, 1998), available at http://jurist.law.pitt.edu/tribe.htm (last visited on January 31, 2006).

29. Gerhardt, "The Lessons of Impeachment History," 613.

30. Ibid.

31. Ibid., 615.

32. Ibid., 617.

33. Ibid., 617.

34. House Committee on the Judiciary, 93rd Cong., 2d Sess., *Constitutional Grounds for Presidential Impeachment* 26 (Comm. Print 1974).

35. Ibid.

36. Ibid.

37. Ibid.

38. 116 Cong. Rec. 11,913 (daily ed. April 15, 1973) (statement of Rep. Ford).

39. Gerhardt, *The Federal Impeachment Process* at 103 and n.2.

40. Berger, *Impeachment*, 103.

41. See Laurence H. Tribe, "Testimony of Laurence H. Tribe, Tyler Professor of Constitutional Law, Harvard Law School, Before the House Judiciary Committee, Subcommittee on the Constitution, Hearing on the Background and History of Impeachment," (November 9, 1998), available at http://jurist.law.pitt.edu/tribe.htm (last visited on January 31, 2006).

42. Berger, *Impeachment*, 69 (quoting Justice Story).

### FOUR    *Impeachment, Trial, and Removal*

1. U.S. Constitution article I, section 2, column 5.

2. U.S. Constitution article I, section. 3, column 6.

3. U.S. Constitution article I, section 3, column 7.

4. Ruth Marcus, "Trial Guide: Frequently Asked Questions," *The Washington Post* (January 16, 1999).

5. Ibid.

6. Vikram David Amar, "Book Review: The Truth, the Whole Truth, and Nothing but the Truth about 'High Crimes and Misdemeanors' and the Constitution's Impeachment Process," 16 *Constitutional Commentary* (Summer 1999), 403, 414.

7. Ibid., 412, n.9.

8. Amar, "Book Review," 412, n.9 (quoting from *The Federalist* No. 65 [Hamilton] in Clinton Rossiter, ed., *The Federalist Papers*, 396, 398 [Mentor, 1961]).

9. Amar, "Book Review," 411–12.

10. Amar, "Book Review," 413.

11. Ann Coulter, *High Crimes and Misdemeanors: The Case Against Bill Clinton* (Washington, D.C.: Regnery Publishing, Inc., 1998), 18–19.

12. See U.S. Constitution article I, section 2, column 5; U.S. Constitution article I, section 3, column 6.

13. Amar, "Book Review," 410–11.

14. See Paul v. Davis, 424 U.S. 693, 713–14 (1976). *See also* Amar, "Book Review," 416.

15. William H. Rehnquist, *Grand Inquests* (New York: William Morrow and Co., 1992), 150.
16. Ibid., 204.
17. Ibid., 208.
18. Ibid., 217.
19. Ibid., 218.
20. Ibid., 227.
21. Ibid., 231.
22. Ibid., 234–35.
23. Ibid., 269.
24. Ibid., 272.
25. Ibid., 273.
26. Jonathan Elliott, ed., *Debates in the Several States Conventions on the Adoption of the Federal Constitution*, Vol. 4 (Philadelphia: J. B. Lippincott, 1936) (James Iredell addressing the North Carolina Convention), 113.
27. Arthur M. Schlesinger, Jr., "Reflections on Impeachment," 67 *George Washington Law Review*, 693, 694 (March, 1999).
28. See House Committee on the Judiciary, "Impeachment of Richard M. Nixon, President of the United States," H.R. Rep. No. 93-1305 (1974) (hereinafter referred to as "Rodino Report") at 223.
29. Charles E. Black, *Impeachment: A Handbook* (New Haven: Yale University Press, 1974), 39.
30. See Rodino Report, 346–47 (setting for the dissenting views to the rejection of the tax evasion charges against Nixon).
31. U.S. Constitution article II, section 3.
32. U.S. Constitution article II, section 4.
33. See, *e.g.*, Arthur M. Schlesinger, Jr., 693, 694.
34. Ibid.
35. "Reagan Tries to Silence Reports of Iran Arms Deal," *The Los Angeles Times* (November 6, 1986), A1.
36. "Transcript of Remarks by Reagan about Iran," *The New York Times* (November 14, 1986), A8.
37. See Walsh, "Iran/Contra Report, Concluding Observations, Part XI" (August 4, 1993), available at http://www.fas.org/irp/offdocs/walsh/part_xi.htm (last visited February 2, 2006).
38. Ibid.
39. Ibid.

40. Ibid.
41. See Iran-Contra Investigation Report, S. Rep. No. 100-216, 100th Cong., (1987), 20–22.
42. See Online News Hour, "A Historical Look at the Impeachment Trial of President William Clinton," (February 15, 1999), available at http://www.pbs.org/newshour/bb/congress/jan-june99/historians_2-15.html (last visited on February 6, 2006).
43. See Susan Low Bloch, "Testimony of Susan Low Bloch, Professor of Constitutional Law, Georgetown University Law Center, Before the House Judiciary Committee, Subcommittee on the Constitution, Hearing on the Background and History of Impeachment," (November 9, 1998), available at http://jurist.law.pitt.edu/bloch1.htm (last visited on January 23, 2006).

**FIVE** *Deadly Lies and an Illegal War*

1. Tom Regan, "When Contemplating War, Beware Babies in Incubators," *Christian Science Monitor,* September 6, 2002.
2. Richard Clarke, *Against All Enemies*, New York: Simon & Schuster, 32.
3. Mike Wallace interview, "Woodward Shares War Secrets," *60 Minutes*, CBS, April 18, 2004.
4. Tommy Franks, *American Soldier* (New York: Regan Books, 2004), 341.
5. Bob Graham with Jeff Nussbaum, *Intelligence Matters,* (New York: Random House, 2004), 230.
6. "Downing Street Memo," *The Sunday Times* (U.K.), May 1, 2005.
7. Franks, 341.
8. Richard Norton-Taylor, "Bush Told Blair We're Going to War, Memo Reveals," *The Guardian* (U.K.), February 2, 2006.
9. Julian Coman, "Fury over Pentagon cell that briefed White House on Iraq's 'imaginary' al-Qaeda links." *The Telegraph* (U.K.), July 11, 2004.
10. Barton Gellman and Walter Pincus, "Depiction of Threat Outgrew Supporting Evidence," *The Washington Post*, August 10, 2003.
11. Matthew Miller, "Commentary: Bush Administration's Marketing of the Possible War Against Iraq," National Public Radio, September 2, 2002.
12. Presidential address, October 7, 2002.
13. From Senator Russell Feingold (D-WI), Senate speech, October 11, 2002.

14. State of the Union address to Congress, January 28, 2003.
15. George W. Bush, "Letter to the Speaker of the House and the President of the Senate," March 18, 2003.
16. Dean, 148.
17. Rep. John Conyers, House Resolution, 365.
18. House Judiciary Committee Democratic Staff, *The Constitution in Crisis: The Downing Street Minutes and Deception, Manipulation, Torture, Retribution, and Coverups in the Iraq War*, December 20, 2005.

## SIX  *Dark Questions About a Dark Day*

1. "Quickvote," CNN, November 10, 2004.
2. James Ridgeway, *The 5 Unanswered Questions About 9/11* (New York: Seven Stories Press, 2005), 9.
3. "U.S. Had 'Steady Stream' of Pre-9/11 Warnings," Online NewsHour, pbs.org/newshour, September 18, 2002.
4. Presidential Briefing Transcript: "Bin Laden Determined to Strike in United States," CNN, August 16, 2004.
5. Brendon McGinty, "CIA Warned About Major Attack on U.S.," *The Sunday Mail* (U.K.), September 16, 2001. According to *The Sunday Mail*, quoting sources in Mossad, the Israeli intelligence agency warned the CIA, but the CIA has reportedly denied this. The same article says that the embassy warning was confirmed.
6. James Ridgeway, "How Much Did the Administration Know?" counterpunch.org, January 3, 2006.
7. Richard A. Clarke, 235.
8. Graham, 230.
9. Clarke, 282.
10. Graham, 216.
11. The editors, "Secrets and Lies," *The New Republic,* July 26, 2004.
12. John Solomon, "FBI Agent Warned Last July That Middle Easterners Training at U.S. Flight Schools," Associated Press, May 3, 2002.
13. Dean, 118.
14. Ridgeway, *The 5 Unanswered Questions About 9/11,* 12.
15. James Rosen, "What Did the US Military Know Before 9/11?" *The Minneapolis Star Tribune,* November 26, 2005.

16. "Conversations with Kathleen Dunn," Wisconsin Public Radio, December 4, 2005.

### SEVEN  *Taking Liberties*

1. Jamie Wilson, "Torture Claims 'Forced U.S. to Cut Terror Charges,' " *The Guardian* (U.K.), November 25, 2005.
2. *The Federalist*, No. 84.
3. *The Federalist*, No. 47.
4. Doug Thompson, "Bush on the Constitution: It's Just a Goddamned Piece of Paper," *Capital Hill Blue,* December 9, 2005.
5. David Cole, "Bush's Illegal Spying," salon.com, December 20, 2005.
6. John Dean, "George W. Bush as the New Richard M. Nixon: Both Wiretapped Illegally, and Impeachably," findlaw.com, December 30, 2005.
7. Barton Gellmon, "Daschle: Congress Denied Bush War Powers in U.S.," *The Washington Post*, December 23, 2005.
8. Eric Lichtblau and Scott Shane, "Basis for Spying in U.S. is Doubted," *The New York Times,* January 7, 2006.
9. Dan Eggen, "Congressional Agency Questions Legality of Wiretaps," *The Washington Post,* January 19, 2006.
10. Authorization for the Use of Military Force, passed by Congress on September 18, 2001.
11. Laurence Tribe, Letter to Rep. John Conyers (D-Michigan), January 6, 2006.
12. Charlie Savage, "Some Conservatives Break with Bush," *The Boston Globe,* February 5, 2006.
13. Ibid.
14. See Bush April 20, 2004, speech in Buffalo, New York, White House Web site, http://www.whitehouse.gov/news/releases/2004/04/20040420-2.html
15. Senate Speeches of Robert Byrd, http://byrd.senate.gov/speeches/2005_december/law_for_all.htm, December 19, 2005.
16. Eric Lichtblau and James Risen, "Justice Deputy Resisted Parts of Spy Program," *The New York Times,* January 1, 2006.
17. James Ridgeway, "The Bush Family Coup," *The Village Voice,* December 30, 2005.

18.  Russell Tice, "National Security Agency Whistleblower Warns Domestic Spying Program Is Sign the U.S. Is Decaying Into a 'Police State,'" *Democracy Now!*, WBAI/Pacifica Radio, January 3, 2006.

19.  Editorial, *Deseret Morning News,* December 20, 2005.

20.  *Diane Rehm Show,* National Public Radio, December 19, 2005.

21.  Charles Babington and Dan Eggen, "Gonzales Seeks to Clarify Testimony on Spying," *The Washington Post,* March 1, 2006.

22.  Ibid.

23.  Ibid.

24.  04 CV 1809 (JG)(JA), Ehab Elmaghraby and Javaid Iqbal v. John Ashcroft et al. Federal Lawsuit.

25.  Glenn Fine, "Issues Report on Treatment of Aliens Held on Immigration Charges in Connection with the Investigation of the September 11 Terrorist Attacks," U.S. Department of Justice, June 2003.

26.  David Cole, *Enemy Aliens* (New York: The New Press, 2003), p. 4.

## EIGHT   *Vengeance and Betrayal*

1.  Carlo Bonini and Giuseppi d'Avanzo, "Berlusconi Behind Fake Yellow Cake Documents," *La Repubblica,* Oct. 24, 2005.

2.  Samuel Loewenberg, "Niger forgeries: The Italian connection: Did Italian spooks collude with American neocons to trump up evidence for war?" Salon, November 9, 2005. Carlo Bonini and Giuseppe D'Avanzo, "La missione del direttore del Sismi negli States per accreditare l'acquisto di materiale nucleare da parte di Saddam 'Pollari andò alla Casa Bianca per offrire la sua verità sull'Iraq,' Il dossier sull'uranio dal Niger non coinvolgeva la Cia," *La Repubblica,* October 25, 2005. James Moore, "Fitzgerald's Historic Opportunity," tompaine.com, October 21, 2005.

3.  Ibid.

4.  Larisa Alexandrovna, "American who advised Pentagon says he wrote for magazine that found forged Niger documents," rawstory.com, January 17, 2006.

5.  Carlo Bonini and Giuseppe D'Avanzo, "La missione del direttore del Sismi negli States per accreditare l'acquisto di materiale nucleare da parte di Saddam 'Pollari andò alla Casa Bianca per offrire la sua verità sull'Iraq,' Il dossier sull'uranio dal Niger non coinvolgeva la Cia."

6.  Seymour Hersh, "The Stovepipe," *The New Yorker,* October 27, 2003.

7.  Barton Gellman and Walter Pincus, "Depiction of Threat Outgrew Supporting Evidence," *The Washington Post,* August 10, 2003.

8.  President George Bush, 2003. State of the Union address.

9.  Joseph C. Wilson, IV, "What I Didn't Find in Africa," *The New York Times,* July 6, 2003.

10. *United States of America v. I. Lewis Libby a/k/a/ "Scooter" Libby,* Indictment, Case number. 05-394 (RBW).

11. Michael Isikoff, "Matt Cooper's Source: What Karl Rove told *Time* magazine's reporter," *Newsweek,* July 18, 2005.

12. Murray Waas, "Cheney 'Authorized' Libby to Leak Classified Information," *National Journal,* February 9, 2006.

13. Jason Leopold, "Details Emerge in Latest Plame Emails," truthout.org, March 1, 2006.

14. Rob Christiansen, Barbara Barrett, Jane Stancill, and Dan Kane, "Bush Can Settle CIA Leak Riddle, Novak Says," *Raleigh News-Observer,* December 14, 2005.

15. "Bush Consults Lawyer in CIA Leak Case," Associated Press, June 2, 2004.

16. John Dean, "The Serious Implications of President Bush's Hiring a Personal Outside Counsel for the Valerie Plame Investigation," findlaw.com, June 4, 2004.

17. Thomas M. DeFrank, "Bush Whacked Rove on CIA Leak," *Daily News,* October 19, 2005.

18. Statement of Rep. John Conyers, Oct. 29, 2005.

## NINE  *Breaking Things: Bush's Way of War*

1.  Third Geneva Convention Relating to the Treatment of Prisoners of War.

2.  Leila Zerrougui, et. al., "Situation of Detainees at Guantanamo Bay," UN Commission on Human Rights, February 15, 2006.

3.  "Guantanamo and Beyond: The Continuing Pursuit of Unchecked Executive Power," Amnesty International, May 13, 2005.

4.  Mark Denbeaux, et al., "Report on Guantanamo Detainees: A Profile of 517 Detainees through Analysis of Department of Defense Data," Seton Hall University Law School, February 2006, 2.

5. Dick Cheney with Tim Russert, *Meet the Press,* NBC, September 16, 2001.

6. Elizabeth Holtzman, "The Impeachment of George W. Bush," *The Nation,* January 30, 2006.

7. USD Justice Department, "Gonzales memo," factcheck.org, http://www.factcheck.org/article365.html.

8. Ibid.

9. Tom Golden, "Senior Lawyer at Pentagon Broke Ranks on Detainees," *The New York Times,* February 20, 2006.

10. Taguba Report, U.S. Department of Defense, March 2004.

11. Seymour Hersh, *Chain of Command: The Road from 9/11 to Abu Ghraib* (New York: Harper Perennial, 2004), 4.

12. This story first appeared in an article I wrote for *The Nation* magazine, titled "Chertoff and Torture," and published on February 15, 2005—Dave Lindorff.

13. Kareem Fahim, "The Invisible Men: Canadian Inquiry May Reveal CIA Secrets on Outsourcing Torture," *The Village Voice,* March 30, 2004.

14. Petition in *Masri v. Tenet,* U.S. Federal District Court.

15. "Guantanamo detainees say Muslims sold for bounties," Associated Press, June 1, 2005.

16. Forward to "Guantanamo," *Amnesty International Report,* May 2005.

17. Tim Golden and Eric Schmitt, "U.S. Quietly Expands Afghan Prison," *The New York Times,* February 26, 2006.

18. William Fisher, "Son of Gitmo," truthout.org, March 2, 2006.

19. Geneva Convention Relates to the Treatment of Prisoners of War, August 12, 1949.

20. Charter of the Nuremberg Tribunal, 1950, Principle 6a.

**TEN** *Abuse of Power, Criminal Negligence, and Other Crimes*

1. "Transition of Power," CNN, December 18, 2000.

2. Charlie Savage, "Bush Could Bypass New Torture Ban," *The Boston Globe,* January 4, 2006.

3. Elizabeth de la Vega, "The President Does Not Know Best," alternet.org, January 19, 2006.

4. Holtzman, *The Nation.*

5. Office of the Governor, State of Louisiana.

6. Jim Bradshaw, "Forecasters Fear Levees Won't Hold Katrina," *Lafayette Daily Advertiser,* August 28, 2005.

7. Tamara Lush, "For Forecasting Chief, No Joy in Being Right," *St. Petersburg Times,* August 30, 2005.

8. National Weather Service report, August 29, 2005.

9. Keith O'Brien and Bryan Bender, "Chronology of Errors, How a Disaster Spread," *The Boston Globe,* September 11, 2005.

10. White House Web site, http://www.whitehouse.gov/news/releases/2005/08/20050829-5.html

11. White House Web site, http://www.whitehouse.gov/news/releases/2005/08/images/20050829-5_p082905pm-0125-515h.html.

12. Evan Thomas, "How Bush Blew It," *Newsweek*, September 19, 2005.

13. "Waiting for a Leader," *The New York Times*, August 31, 2005.

14. Thomas, *Newsweek*.

15. "Official: Astrodome Can't Take Any More Refugees," Fox News, September 2, 2005.

16. Adam Nagourney, and Anne E. Kornblutt, "White House Enacts a Plan to Ease Political Damage," *The New York Times*, September 5, 2005.

17. Margaret Ebrahim and John Solomon, "Tape: Bush, Chertoff Warned Before Katrina," Associated Press, March 1, 2006.

18. Ibid.

19. Holtzman, *The Nation.*

20. Eric Schmitt, "Pentagon Contradicts General on Iraq Occupation Force's Size," *The New York Times*, February 28, 2003.

21. Ann Scott Tyson, "Body Armor Gaps Are Shown to Endanger Troops," *The Washington Post,* January 7, 2006.

22. Holtzman, *The Nation.*

23. "White House Guts Global Warming Study," CBS News, June 19, 2003.

24. Andrew Revkin, "Climate Expert Says NASA Tried to Silence Him," *The New York Times*, January 29, 2005.

25. Michael McCarthy, "Environment in Crisis," *The Independent* (U.K.), January 16, 2006.

26. Mark Townsend, and Paul Harris, "Now the Pentagon Tells Bush: Climate Change Will Destroy Us," *The Observer* (U.K.), February 22, 2004.

27. R. Jeffrey Smith and Susan Schmidt, "Bush Official Arrested in Corruption Probe," *The Washington Post*, September 20, 2005.

28. Sheryl Fred, "Postwar Profits," *Capital Eye,* March 12, 2003.

29. James Glanz, "Iraq Rebuilding Badly Hobbled, US Report Finds," *The New York Times,* January 24, 2006.

## ELEVEN    *Impeaching Other Bush Administration Officials*

1. "Wilkerson Points Finger at Cheney on Torture," Associated Press, November 4, 2005.

2. Rupert Cornwell, "Cheney 'Created Climate for U.S. War Crimes,' " *The Independent* (U.K.), November 30, 2005.

3. *United States of America v. I. Lewis Libby.*

4. Jane Mayer, "Contract Sport: What Did the Vice President Do for Halliburton?" *The New Yorker,* February 23, 2004.

5. "Cheney May Still Have Halliburton Ties," CNN, September 25, 2003.

6. "Cheney's Halliburton Ties Remain," CBS, September 26, 2003.

7. Randeep Ramesh, "The Two Faces of Rumsfeld," *The Guardian* (U.K.), May 9, 2003.

8. Judy Mathew, and Eugene Tang, "Rumsfeld Was in Group Financing Chinese Anti-Spying Software," Bloomberg News, August 24, 2001.

9. "Col. Janis Karpinski, the Former Head of Abu Ghraib, Admits She Broke the Geneva Conventions But Says the Blame 'Goes All the Way to The Top,' " *Democracy Now!,* WBAI/Pacifica, October 25, 2005.

10. Faye Bowers, "Lawsuit lays blame for torture at the top," *Christian Science Monitor,* March 2, 2005.

11. Hersh, *Chain of Command,* 65.

12. Eric Schmitt, "Iraq-Bound Troops Confront Rumsfeld Over Lack of Armor," *The New York Times,* December 8, 2004.

13. "Feinstein demands Rumsfeld explain UCSC spying," *Santa Cruz Sentinel,* January 13, 2006.

14. Michael Isikoff, "The Other Big Brother," *Newsweek,* January 30, 2006.

15. Lisa Myers, Douglas Pasternak, Rich Gardella, and the NBC Investigative Unit, "Is the Pentagon spying on Americans? Secret database obtained by NBC News tracks 'suspicious' domestic groups," NBC, December 13, 2005.

16. Francis Boyle, "The National Campaign to Impeach George W. Bush," *Dissident Voice,* June 14, 2005.

17. Sigfrido Ranucci, and Maurizio Torrealta, producers, *The Hidden Massacre,* RAI-TV (Italy).
18. "The Pentagon Used White Phosphorus in Iraq," Associated Press, November 15, 2005.
19. Instruction Manual, U.S. Army Command and General Staff School (CGSC), Fort Leavenworth, Kansas.
20. Dave Lindorff, "Troops to Bush: Get us out of here!" counterpunch.org, March 2, 2006.
21. "Top Bush Officials Push Case Against Saddam," CNN, September 8, 2002.
22. James Moore, "How Chalabi and the White House held the front page," *The Guardian* (U.K.), May 29, 2004.
23. Sidney, Blumenthal, "Condi's Trail of Lies," salon.com, December 8, 2005.
24. Robert Bryce, "Prosecutor says Bush 'directly deceived' him to avoid jury duty," salon.com, November 5, 2000.
25. Alan Berlow, "The Texas Clemency Memos," *The Atlantic Monthly,* July/August 2003.
26. Alberto R. Gonzales, "Memorandum for the President: Decision Re Application of the Geneva Convention on Prisoners of War to the Conflict with Al Qaeda and the Taliban," January 25, 2002.
27. Alberto Gonzales, "Legal Authorities Supporting the Activities of the National Security Agency Described by the President," U.S. Department of Justice, January 19, 2006.
28. *Youngstown Sheet & Tube Co. v. Sawyer,* 343 U.S. 579, 637 (1952) (Jackson, J., concurring).
29. Ibid.
30. Gonzales, "Legal Authorities."
31. "Spies, Lies and Wiretaps," *The New York Times,* January 29, 2006.
32. Carol D. Leonnig, "Feingold says attorney general misled Senators in hearings," *The Washington Post,* January 30, 200.

★ ★ ★ ★ ★ ★ ★ ★ ★ ★ ★ ★ ★ ★

# SELECT BIBLIOGRAPHY

★ ★ ★ ★ ★ ★ ★ ★ ★ ★ ★ ★ ★ ★

## *Impeachment Politics*

Bonifaz, John. *Warrior-King: The Case for Impeaching George W. Bush.* New York: Nation Books, 2003.

Boyle, Francis A. *Destroying World Order: US Imperialism in the Middle East Before and After September 11.* Atlanta: Clarity Press, 2004.

Clarke, Richard A. *Against All Enemies: Inside America's War on Terror.* New York: Simon & Schuster, 2004.

Cole, David. *Enemy Aliens: Double Standards and Constitutional Freedoms in the War on Terrorism.* New York: The New Press, 2003.

Dean, John W. *Worse Than Watergate: The Secret Presidency of George W. Bush.* New York: Little Brown, 2004.

Graham, Bob, with Jeff Nussbaum. *Intelligence Matters: The CIA, the FBI, Saudi Arabia and the Failure of America's War on Terror.* New York: Random House, 2004.

Hersh, Seymour. *Chain of Command: The Road from 9/11 to Abu Ghraib.* New York: Harper Perennial, 2005.

Mann, James. *Rise of the Vulcans: The History of Bush's War Cabinet.* New York: Viking, 2004.

Palast, Greg. *The Best Democracy Money Can Buy.* London: Pluto Press, 2002.

Phillips, Kevin. *American Dynasty: Aristocracy, Fortune and the Politics of Deceit in the House of Bush.* New York: Viking, 2004.

Ridgeway, James. *The 5 Unanswered Questions About 9/11: What the 9/11 Commission Report Failed to Tell Us.* New York: Seven Stories Press, 2005.

Risen, James. *State of War: The Secret History of the CIA and the Bush Administration.* New York: Simon & Schuster, 2006.

## Impeachment Law and History

Berger, Raoul. *Impeachment: The Constitutional Problem.* Cambridge, Mass.: Harvard Universitiy Press, 1974.

Black, Charles. *Impeachment: A Handbook.* New Haven: Yale University Press 1974.

Bushnell, Eleanore. *Crimes, Follies and Misfortunes: The Federal Impeachment Trials.* Champaign: University of Illinois Press 1992.

Gerhardt, Michael. *The Federal Impeachment Process: A Constitutional and Historical Analysis.* London: University of Chicago Press 1996.

Hoffer, Peter, and N. E. H. Hull. *Impeachment in America, 1635 to 1805.*: Yale University Press, 1984.

Labovitz, John R. *Presidential Impeachment.* New Haven: Yale University Press, 1978.

Les Benedict, Michael. *The Impeachment and Trial of Andrew Johnson.* New York: WW Norton & Co., 1973.

Rehnquist, William H. *Grand Inquests.* New York: William Morrow & Co, 1992.

Smith, Gene. *High Crimes and Misdemeanors: The Impeachment and Trial of Andrew Johnson.* New York: William Morrow, 1977.

White, Theodore H. *Breach of Faith: The Fall of Richard Nixon.* New York: Scribner, 1975.

# INDEX